THE MINDFUL SCHOOL

HOW TO TEACH BALANCED READING AND WRITING

Bonnie Burns

PEARSON
SkyLight

Glenview, Illinois

To all those I love who have been so patient.
—B.B.

The Mindful School: How to Teach Balanced Reading and Writing

Published by SkyLight Professional Development
1900 E. Lake Ave., Glenview, IL 60025
800-348-4474 or 847-657-7450
Fax 847-486-3183
info@pearsonpd.com
http://www.pearsonpd.com

LCCN 98-61814
ISBN 1-57517-149-X

2406-V
Item Number 1720

ZYXWVUTSRQPONMLKJIHGFE
06 05 04 03   15 14 13 12 11 10 9 8 7 6 5

Contents

SkyLight Training and Publishing Inc.

Introduction

Throughout the 1990s, reading teachers, especially primary reading teachers, have felt as though they were adrift on a storm-tossed sea, heaved from one all-purpose program for teaching reading to another. They're ready to get off the ship and find a calm harbor where experts not only concur with each other but tout findings that validate the teachers' experiences and judgments about how children actually learn. The time has come to end the animosity, to seek common ground, and to blend and coordinate practices that result in a balanced approach to teaching reading.

The last decade has been one of the most contentious in education as the whole-language versus phonics war has continued unabated. Whole-language proponents advocate that beginning readers start with whole pieces of children's literature and indirect instruction, while the phonics proponents prefer that readers start with simplified literature in order to learn sound-symbol relationships through direct instruction. The traditionalist, phonics camp considers the whole-language approach haphazard, and the whole-language camp regards the phonics approach as sterile (Willis, 1995).

The controversy spread well beyond the schoolhouse door after it was widely reported in the general media. A small sampling of mainstream magazine articles reveals the combative tone: *The Wall Street Journal* reported on "The Reading and Writing Wars" (November 22, 1996) and *U.S. News & World Reports* declared that "The Reading Wars Continue" (October 27, 1997). Even *Modern Maturity* (January-February, 1998), the magazine of the American Association of Retired People, published "In-dict-ment," an interview with Lynne Cheney, cohost of CNN's *Crossfire Sunday,* who sided with the phonics camp.

Entire states declared whole-language practices the culprit responsible for low reading scores and mandated reversals in policy and practice. California had been considered in the vanguard in moving toward the whole-language philosophy, but when the state's 1994 reading scores on the National Assessment of Educational Progress (NAEP) tied with Louisiana's as the lowest in the country, it passed mandates requiring schools to teach explicit phonics and spelling, to use skill-based basals emphasizing phonics instruction, and to provide staff development in a phonics curriculum (Flippo, 1997; Willis, 1995). The diverse population of California's schools, poverty, limited spending for schools, and crowded classrooms were not noted as contributing factors to these low reading scores. Back to phonics movements were also initiated in North Carolina, Ohio, Texas, Illinois, Maryland, and Massachusetts. "Overall, switching philosophies and taking extreme positions, whether right or left, have become the panaceas of school reform in the U.S." (Flippo, 1997, p. 302). Contributing to the hostile climate were the educators and researchers who published thousands of articles and books not only proclaiming superiority for their preferred approach but calling other positions ineffective.

Unfortunately, these rancorous debates over reading programs have eroded public confidence as well as teacher morale. Classroom teachers who have been mandated to use a specific approach to teach reading have taken to subterfuge. Some post guards at the copier room door so they can duplicate unsanctioned materials. Others keep unauthorized texts hidden in the back of a cupboard. The cloak-and-dagger atmosphere is downright silly!

Children have different backgrounds, different abilities and levels of achievement, different styles of learning, different motivations, and even different languages. Humans exhibit intelligence in a variety of ways. They have multiple intelligences and vary in their responses according to the context. A single standardized approach to teaching reading will inevitably lead to the failure of some students. No single methodology or philosophy can be the solution to teaching reading to all children.

Finding Common Ground

"Enough is now known about reading that the destructive and often rancorous debates about how best to teach it can and should be put to rest" (Diamond and Mandel, 1998, p. 1). Finding common ground is not just a matter of compromise. It is a matter of acknowledging validated research, recognizing commonalities, using various solutions for specific problems, rediscovering venerable strategies with a new twist, and establishing a balanced approach.

Reading experts have known for years that single, end-of-the-spectrum philosophies are not workable solutions, and recent reports support this. In 1998, Timothy Shanahan reviewed twelve research studies that have influenced reading instruction. Included in Shanahan's reviews was the "U.S. Cooperative First-Grade Studies" (Bond and Dykstra, 1967), in which data had been compiled from twenty-seven individual studies of differing approaches to beginning reading, such as phonics, linguistic readers, basals, initial teaching alphabet, individualized reading, language experience approaches, and various grouping schemes. Shanahan reports, "These studies found that none of the instructional methods were superior to the others for students at either high or low levels of readiness." But, a big "however" is attached to his conclusion: "[These studies] did find that some combinations of methods (such as including phonics and writing with other approaches) were associated with more learning" (Shanahan, 1998, p. 51).

Despite the continuing deluge of comparative studies, no study has successfully challenged these early findings. Steven Stahl, in a recent meta-analysis of comparative reading studies, found no differences in student achievement between whole language and traditional instruction. Are we then supposed to believe that any one approach in isolation is as good as any other? Jeffrey Founts, coauthor of *Research on Educational Innovations,* offers some insight into this question. He found it very difficult to attribute effects to isolated practices in research studies because, "Very few teachers are either all whole language or all direct instruction" (Willis, 1995). Combining methods may frustrate researchers such as Stahl and Founts, but it validates the practices of caring classroom teachers as well as the findings of the "U.S. Cooperative First-Grade Studies."

Classroom teachers are seeking solutions that span philosophies but are not just a patchwork of incompatible practices. They want to know what is crucial and what works in various circumstances. They want children to know how to take apart a strategy, learn how it works, and then put it back together in the context of reading for understanding. They want each part of the reading curriculum to build on and strengthen the others. Classroom practitioners are not accepting the all or nothing methodologies but instead are looking for a feasible and compatible blend of practices—a balanced approach to teaching reading.

The reading wars are coming to an end.

About *How to Teach Balanced Reading and Writing*

Each chapter in this book is organized in the same manner. It starts with the underpinnings of how students actually learn to read and write. Activities that teach a skill or strategy follow. Beginning teachers often ask for just the activities—what to do with their classes on Monday. However, without knowing why it works and when it works, they aren't able to successfully adapt activities for their classes. It takes knowledge of both underlying principles and actual activities for a teacher to make the right lesson plans for her class.

The recommendedations in each chapter are developed around a balanced philosophy so that all students have an opportunity to learn successfully based on their different needs and learning styles. This is especially important since the classroom teacher is now faced with teaching inclusion and second-language learners in addition to the regular range of abilities and interests found in the average classroom. The balanced approach in this book includes a whole-part-whole approach to teaching reading and writing, which means the child learns the whole concept first—what the skill is and how it is used in the reading-writing process. Next the skill is directly and explicitly taught so that it can be mastered, and then the skill is applied in the context of whole text. Balance is also achieved by integrating the language arts and balancing teacher and student leadership.

The first part of the book is about teaching primary reading, writing, and spelling. Learning how to understand the concept of reading, how to recognize words, and how to learn sound representations present the early reader with significantly different tasks than the more experienced reader. Thus, developing phonemic awareness, teaching phonics and word recognition, and teaching emergent comprehension and writing strategies are the main features of this part of the book. The developmental nature of spelling is also explained so that teachers can better identify and proscribe activities based on the needs of their students.

The next section deals with more experienced readers in fourth through twelfth grades. It includes strategies for teaching with literature for the whole class, for small groups, and for individual students. The underlying principles and methods for teaching comprehension follow the literature chapter and include activities for prereading, during reading, and after reading.

Specific strategies for teaching vocabulary and teaching students how to read and learn from content and textbooks make up the next section. It is followed by strategies to teach both personal and structured writing. The book concludes with a chapter on assessment to help teachers make informed decisions about what to teach and to show how children can demonstrate their abilities through a variety of means.

Choose the sections that are needed for your classroom, but read chapter 1 first to see how both theories and activities can be successfully intertwined. Learning to read is a long and complicated process, but there are proven strategies that can make the entire process more coordinated and effective in your classroom.

Balanced Reading and Writing

Reading maketh a full man.

—Francis Bacon

Reading is a complex process that involves recognizing written symbolic representations of speech, coordinating the words into thoughts, matching the thoughts to a previous bank of knowledge, and constructing meaning. The basic process takes several years to learn, and the more advanced aspects of reading, such as critical thinking and the synthesis of ideas, take several years more. Potential readers also come from a multiplicity of backgrounds and with divergent levels of knowledge, verbal skills, and reasoning abilities. How could there be a single method of instruction that would make every child a successful reader?

Nonetheless, in the field of reading, "magic" methodologies continue to be proposed. Though each method may contain worthwhile elements when applied to particular situations, many new ideas tend to be adopted wholesale. The information then filters down to classroom teachers in the form of mandates, one-day workshops, or in teaching materials that arrive without explanation or training. Many teachers have only a single undergraduate course in teaching reading and, thus, lack the background for interpreting new trends. Essential parts of the theory get lost, and some flashy component becomes all that is left. These flashy leftovers may become popular, but they are usually not rich enough in philosophical content to accomplish the complex task of teaching reading or complete enough to meet the variety of student needs.

> A balanced position provides a comfortable place for experienced reading teachers who have enhanced their instruction by thoughtfully adopting and adapting new ideas appropriate for their students.

Looking for a balanced approach in instructional methods may be a reaction to unworkable single methodologies. Yet when found, a balanced position provides a comfortable place for experienced reading teachers who have enhanced their instruction by thoughtfully adopting and adapting new ideas appropriate for their students.

Surveys of practicing teachers find the majority using eclectic or balanced approaches (Baumann et al., 1998; Worthy and Hoffman, 1997; Pressley and Rankin as cited in Metsala, 1997). In a survey conducted by J. Baumann of more than 1,200 pre-kindergarten through fifth-grade teachers, 89% said they used a balanced approach, blending phonics and skills instruction with holistic principles and practices. They also allocated classroom time in a balanced way, spending moderate amounts of time for reading strategy instruction and moderate amounts of time for more holistic activities such as reading aloud to students, independent reading, responding to literature, and writing. Eighty-three percent also balanced instructional materials using a combination of basal reading programs and children's trade books.

Yet, teachers are still left wondering about the blend of activities they are using. Is there a better sequence or a more powerful combination? Is it an eclectic, tossed salad approach when it should be a melting pot?

> It is not just the presence of a variety of activities that makes a program of reading instruction effective or ineffective. It is the way in which its pieces are fitted together to complement and support one another, always with full consideration of the needs and progress of the young readers with whom it will be used (Adams, 1990, p. 122).

Balanced instruction is more than an eclectic approach. It resolves the whole language/direct instruction dilemma by thoughtfully integrating practices. Balanced reading and balanced writing use a whole-part-whole approach, integrate the language arts, and blend teacher and student leadership. The components do support one another and are flexible enough to be adjusted to meet the needs of a variety of students.

This chapter summarizes the whole-part-whole approach, includes a brief discussion on integrating the language arts, and covers the importance of blending teacher and student leadership. In doing so, we hope to introduce you to the benefits of balanced reading and writing.

> **Balanced reading and writing use a whole-part-whole approach, integrate the language arts, and blend teacher and student leadership.**

Solving the Whole-Part Dilemma Through Balance

Proponents of explicit instruction and whole language often speak in extremes, especially about the other's approach, but both share the same long-term objectives. Their goals are to develop in children the desire to read, and for them to take pleasure in and to read a variety of materials with deep understanding. The debate as to whether reading instruction should proceed from discrete skills toward a whole or start with the whole has created a dilemma for teachers, especially first-grade teachers, over choosing the best approach.

One solution is to use a whole-part-whole approach, which combines both methods of instruction. The whole-part-whole approach is truly representative of the way people learn. For example, in understanding something, both students and adults need to see the big picture first. Then, they proceed to the question, "So exactly how does this thing work?", as they deconstruct the big picture into parts. Finally, they are able to successfully assemble the parts in their entirety. When the whole concept is understood, the details make sense and are relevant; they can be applied in specific ways within the overall concept.

The big picture in reading, that is, the first "whole," involves the idea that print represents spoken language and is used to communicate meaningful thoughts in books, magazines, signs, letters, notes, newspapers, advertisements, and computer screens. In a balanced reading approach, literacy skills are developed, practiced, and reinforced with these types of reading matter. In reading instruction, these materials are called authentic texts, that is, any materials that people actually read rather than materials that were invented just to teach reading. Does that mean that the only materials that should be used to teach reading are materials that weren't written for reading instruction? Well, students do need to learn that reading is a real-life activity, used by adults and children for functional purposes, and that completing worksheets isn't the primary goal of reading. If children only see practice materials, they may not understand this idea. Children should learn to read with interesting content that is long enough to get them involved so they understand that reading serves a useful, real purpose. Authentic texts serve this purpose admirably, though a basal story can also be interesting, connected text. The idea is to teach reading with engaging materials.

The "parts" are all the ways that the symbols in print represent words in speech, how the author transmits thoughts, and how the reader incorporates those thoughts into his own knowledge. For most children, these inner workings of literacy do not develop naturally or simply through exposure to print. Most three- and many four-year-olds think the story is told through the pictures (Strommen and Mates, 1997). These parts, which are skills and strategies, are learned through explicit instruction and coaching. When the parts are taught in relation to authentic texts, their usefulness and relevancy are understood.

The final "whole" is using the newly acquired skills to reread the same material with increased comprehension or using the skills with other materials for initial increased comprehension. Children need considerable time to practice and consolidate the skills they have learned so part of balanced reading is to provide students with a rich variety of texts and sufficient time to unify the skills and strategies so they can be used purposefully and selectively. Reading gains depend on the amount of time

Completing worksheets isn't the primary goal of reading.

students spend reading in school (Allington, as cited in Anderson et al., 1985). The more children read, the easier it becomes.

Yet, beneath the fury of debate between explicit versus whole-language instruction, experts with opposing points of view—when read in the original—tend to agree that both the whole and the parts need to be included in reading instruction. For example, in 1960, Helen Robinson, one of the coauthors of Scott Foresman's Dick and Jane, wrote the following, which advocates both skills and application:

> Neither is competence in reading acquired in a short time or by learning specific aspects of reading in isolation. Phonics is of little value unless it is a tool used consistently in recognizing words. Word perception is not an isolated skill, but a tool in securing meaning. On the other hand, thoughtful reaction to, and assimilation of, what is read cannot be effective without accurate word perception and acquisition of correct meanings (p. 239).

And, according to Ellen McIntyre in *Balanced Instruction: Strategies and Skills in Whole Language* (1996, p. 12), "Inclusion of strategy and skill instruction in whole language teaching may necessarily involve extensive, systematic, explicit instruction, particularly for children for whom the language of school is not part of their culture."

These two experts, separated by more than a third of a century, do not really sound very different, but the philosophies they represent have not easily translated into popular practice. As McIntyre contends, "Those who write about whole language often use ambiguous language that says little about what teachers actually do" (p. 10). For example, phrases such as "celebrating literacy in a community of learners" have never been of any help for what I am going to do on Monday. On the other hand, while the philosophy behind traditional basals proposed that reading competence was not acquired by learning specific aspects in isolation, the skills lessons never seemed to match the stories.

Although whole-language and traditional reading philosophies have been represented as opposing beliefs, both approaches have always recognized the need for including whole concepts and specific skills. When thoroughly investigated, these approaches aren't as different as they seem on the surface or in popular practice. Neither approach has ever excluded key features of the other method. Balanced reading is about putting into practice the complete philosophy of reading instruction that has always been there.

Both whole-language and traditional reading philosophies have always recognized the need for including whole concepts and specific skills.

Whole-Part-Whole in Beginning Reading

First, beginning readers need to grasp the whole picture about reading. They need to understand that print is written speech, that books generally use more formal language patterns than conversation, that print is read left to right and top to bottom, that the power of a good story and useful information can be conveyed through print, and that reading is an enjoyable and practical skill that can be learned. Immersing children in rich language by reading aloud, by showing how print matches words, by modeling expert reading, and by thinking aloud all give emergent readers the idea of how and why one reads.

The parts are the multiplicity of skills and strategies that beginning readers must use to obtain meaning from the text: segmenting sounds, understanding that letters have a reasonably consistent correspondence to the sounds, blending, and identifying words. They must learn this system so well that words can be identified at a glance, with automaticity, so they can think about the meaning. They must match the words and thoughts to things they already know, make sure what they have read fits into English sentence patterns, and make sure it makes sense. This is complicated and requires explicit instruction. To help readers connect these skills to the concept of reading, many of these skills are taught through authentic texts. Sometimes the instruction is about just one of these aspects to make sure the child really knows how the system works and what is expected of him as a reader.

Then the skills need to be applied to whole text once again. Without conscious attention to transfer and significant practice, the skills are left dangling without an apparent purpose.

> To help readers connect these skills to the concept of reading, many of these skills are taught through authentic text.

Whole-Part-Whole Instruction for Upper Grade Students

As students become more experienced readers in the third through twelfth grades, they achieve competency in word attack skills and concentrate more on comprehension skills. Most, but not all upper grade readers, understand the first whole—that reading is an interactive and useful process. Some still need to learn this basic idea. But all upper grade readers need to learn the specific strategies of comprehension and how to apply those skills in authentic texts. In the upper grades, whole-part-whole instruction often means teaching reading skills and strategies from stories, novels, or informational texts so there is an immediate opportunity to apply the skills.

The same principle applies in writing. The main purpose of writing is to communicate, and students need opportunities to write stories, letters, reports, and responses to reading. They also need direct instruction in the conventions of composition and English. What better place to learn and apply them than in their own writing. For example, a great time to learn about quotation marks and attendant punctuation is after the student has written the first draft of a story that uses dialogue. Teach when the kids have a need to know and an opportunity to apply.

Explicit Instruction

The parts in whole-part-whole instruction—that is, specific reading skills and strategies—need to be taught through explicit instruction. Knowledge of how the reader is supposed to interact with text doesn't just happen naturally. It happens even less with children who do not come from a background of literacy or who do not see the purpose of becoming fluent in the language arts. Developing fluency in speech may be natural because everyone, toddler to octogenarian, has a need to communicate, but there is nothing natural in learning the symbolic code of sound-symbol relationships or that expository text has a different organizational pattern than narrative text. Seeing a lot of it doesn't necessarily mean that a child is going to "get it" by himself. The idea that children will learn to read as naturally as they learn to speak is so strongly contested that Keith Stanovich states, "The idea that learning to read is just like learning to speak is accepted by no responsible linguist, psychologist, or cognitive scientist in the research community" (as cited in Lyon, 1998, p. 17).

Children require instruction to learn how to read. Explicit instruction, also known as direct or systematic instruction, entails letting children know what is being taught, why it is being taught, how they can connect this information to other things they already know, how the procedure works, and how it can be used in the future. Extensive research indicates that clearly defined objectives and teacher-directed instruction are characteristics of effective reading programs. Systematic instruction does not preclude on-the-spot coaching or teaching, and it does not encourage mindless, rote learning. At its best, it teaches strategies that help "make reading and writing more doable and, hence, less frustrating" (Pressley, 1996, p. 282).

> Knowledge of how the reader is supposed to interact with text doesn't just happen naturally.

Explicit instruction uses direct explanations and teacher modeling. With direct instruction, the teacher explains how to select and use a reading strategy and models how the strategy is applied in actual reading situations. It can be as simple as telling the child that *ch* sounds /ch/. Or, the teacher may say something like, "In order to make an inference, the reader must use knowledge she already possesses plus information given by the author. In order to figure out how Julie felt, I combined . . . ." The children's attention is focused on a single reading strategy so they can learn how the strategy works. "Direct instruction is based on providing enough sustained, focused practice to enable learners to use strategies effectively" (Spiegel, 1992, p. 41). It is followed by guided practice as students try out their interpretations while the teacher monitors and provides feedback.

Explicit instruction is especially important for struggling readers because it provides additional support and instruction before failure overwhelms the student.

Most children need systematic instruction in word identification and comprehension skills, and "some students require extremely systematic, explicit instruction" (Pressley, 1996). Explicit instruction is especially important for struggling readers because it provides additional support and instruction before failure overwhelms the student. Inclusion students and students who struggle with English as a second language often find it difficult to infer a process or generalize a rule from a broad discussion. They often benefit the most from direct instruction. Teaching with a whole-part-whole approach requires teaching skills and strategies explicitly within authentic contexts. This requires considerable knowledge on the part of the teacher. Without the predetermined curriculum and materials that a basal series provided, the teacher must be knowledgeable enough to orchestrate the wide range of experiences needed to become a successful reader and writer. This is not just reading and writing stories and then talking about them, which produces readers with very vague strategies and gaps in their knowledge. Using authentic texts may be beyond what a beginning teacher can manage, but it gives the experienced teacher great leeway in using her professional judgment to match instruction to the needs of the class. Teachers may wish to start by developing just one unit based on a novel or a set of coordinated primary trade books accompanied by a limited group of strategies that can be taught through these books.

To begin, the teacher needs to understand the entire reading process and how its components function in a coordinated manner. The reading process includes the developmental stages of decoding and recognizing words, then developing comprehension strategies, attaining fluency, acquiring vocabulary, learning how expository text differs from narrative text, and incorporating higher-order thinking skills into reading. The teacher must also possess a broad knowledge of children's literature. The teacher must understand the reading process well enough to be able to explain and model it and re-explain and remodel in themes and variations. Hopefully, the ideas and strategies presented in this book will help to broaden the reader's repertoire.

In addition, when integrating authentic text and explicit instruction, the teacher needs to have an overall instructional plan that considers both the developmental level of the children and the scope of strategies that children are going to need to become successful readers. She needs to ensure that a wide range of reading strategies are learned, not just the ones that seem to surface naturally from the literature that has been chosen. Most text selections can be used for a variety of purposes, but some are much more suitable for learning cause and effect, comparison and contrast, visualization of a scene, predicting, or especially for inferring and interpreting. Teaching skills through literature or other authentic texts may mean choosing a particular piece because the author requires that certain strategies be used to fully comprehend the text.

> **Teaching skills through literature may mean choosing a particular piece because the author requires that certain strategies be used to fully comprehend the text.**

Similarly, in the primary grades, a teacher may choose a whole language reader to accelerate language development, a controlled-vocabulary reader to minimize frustration with word identification, a phonetic reader to provide decoding practice (Richardson, as cited in Worthy and Hoffman, 1997), or a particular story to emphasize a certain set of rhyming or word family words.

Explicit instruction within a literature curriculum may not have a set sequence as the sequence may be altered by the needs of the children and the content of the literature. Therefore, basing skills instruction on literature requires being a good record keeper, that is, keeping track of what has been taught and reviewed and what still needs to be learned.

Integrating the Language Arts

In addition to using a whole-part-whole approach, balanced literacy instruction includes integrating all the components of the language arts— listening and speaking, phonemic awareness, sound-symbol relationships, spelling, writing, vocabulary, comprehension, and reading to and with students.

When skills are centered around authentic text, most often literature, instruction is naturally integrated. The components feel less disjointed to both the teacher and the learners. Writing in particular is no longer an add-on when the children are writing about what they read. Teachers who have been teaching thematic units have known this for years.

In teaching integrated literacy in a primary classroom, a teacher may read a story aloud as the children listen and make predictions. They then discuss the story together, talking about unfamiliar vocabulary words. An aspect of word recognition is taught and practiced based on the words in the story. Depending on the maturity of the readers, it may be matching sounds, initial letter sounds, word families, blends, or word endings. The story is reread with partners or in shared reading with the support of the teacher for practice and fluency. The teacher may explain sequencing, and the children place sentence strips in order to reassemble the story. The students may write about the story or about personal experiences connected to the topic. As they write, knowledge of decoding influences their spelling and figuring out how to spell influences their decoding. Irregularly spelled words or word family words in their writing can be checked against the word wall or added to their spelling lists. Children then orally retell the story to ensure they comprehend the meaning.

In teaching integrated literacy in an intermediate classroom, the teacher may use guided reading as children are asked to read for a purpose and then discuss both the content and strategies they used to comprehend the selection. The teacher may model a strategy in which she connected prior knowledge to the selection, and then asks students to try the strategy on the next section. Vocabulary words from the selection are discussed, predicted by context, or sorted. Students respond to the story in writing by retelling from another character's perspective or connecting the theme to personal experiences. Unusual or complex sentence structure from the story may be used as a model to develop other similar sentences. The first draft may be examined for logical paragraph structure. Students read independently or in small groups and discuss the content. They make oral presentations about related topics as their classmates listen and ask questions.

An area that has been neglected by both publishers and many classroom teachers is reading and writing nonfiction. A balanced program definitely includes nonfiction reading whether done within the language arts program or through using content area textbooks or trade books. The style of

> **An area that has been neglected by many classroom teachers is reading and writing nonfiction.**

writing used in nonfiction books—expository text—differs significantly from narrative text in organization patterns, in concept and vocabulary loads, in the use of visual aids, such as charts and graphs, and even in sentence complexity. Developing literacy with expositional text takes considerable teacher support and direct instruction so that children will eventually be able to learn the content independently.

Integrating all of the language arts—reading, writing, speaking, and listening—places considerable responsibility on the teacher because integrated preprepared materials are not always available. Although publishers are moving in this direction, a teacher often finds herself with a literature anthology, a spelling book, an English book, a variety of trade books, and perhaps a separate vocabulary or phonics program, each from a different publisher and each bearing no relation to the other. It often takes considerable time to coordinate materials or develop lessons that are complimentary. Perhaps nowhere is it more challenging to integrate successfully than in first grade with a systematic phonics program and an unsystematic collection of little books and trade books.

> Integrating all of the language arts places considerable responsibility on the teacher.

However, the benefits of integrated instruction are numerous. Children see how all the aspects of literacy are coordinated. They discover that what is learned in one area can be used in another. The student doesn't have to start each activity with new background introductions, and interest is already established. It is also more time efficient, and time is always a precious commodity.

Balancing Student and Teacher Leadership

One aspect of balanced instruction that is definitely different from traditional instruction is that classroom leadership is more varied. In traditional instruction, the teacher is the focus of instruction, and the content and sequence are determined by the teacher or by the publisher of the basal series. This is not entirely bad. Teachers and publishers have a broader perspective than a six-year-old for making informed decisions about the reading process, and they understand the scope of abilities that a mature reader is going to need to possess. It may also be a fallacy to describe decisions made by the teacher as being teacher centered since the content of the lesson is based upon the needs of the students.

In lessons directed by the teacher, things tend to move along more briskly in a clear direction with a defined purpose. The role of the teacher as planner, guide, and instructor is an important one.

Some whole language proponents prefer that the curriculum exclusively follow the needs and interests of children. Watson (as cited in Spiegel, 1992, p. 42) advises, "Nothing is set into classroom motion until it is validated by learners' interest and motivated by their needs." Students' interests and needs are important, but it is tricky to develop lessons when there are twenty-five sets of interests and a wide range of needs and abilities. To add to the mix, some learners are reasonably content to stay within their comfort zones or narrow interests.

Decision-making needs to be balanced between students' needs and interests and the broader, long-range perspective of the teacher. However, it is possible to meet many individual needs and preferences within the setting of a classroom. Humans seek the basic needs of power, freedom, fun, and belonging, according to William Glasser (1986). Power, as Glasser uses it, means control over one's own destiny as well as the power of knowledge. In the classroom, power and freedom translate to children having choices of topics, activities, or reading materials based on individual or small-group preferences. Interest and choice are powerful factors in motivation. These choices are made within parameters set by the teacher. Classrooms that allow for choice also have a more positive climate. Fun translates to participating in intriguing activities and using interesting materials. Being an accepted member of the class provides the feeling of belonging.

In a balanced program, many teachers use a blend of activities and materials. They include activities and materials chosen by the teacher for direct instruction, materials and activities chosen by the students for interest, and materials and activities that are chosen by consensus of the teacher and the class that provide choice and interest and but also meet curriculum goals. Sometimes the teacher directs a lesson, sometimes groups work together in literature circles with novels or stories they have chosen, and sometimes students pursue their own interests in a readers' workshop or a writers' workshop. Not only is there more variety in classroom leadership, there is greater choice in what materials are being read. The new balance takes greater advantage of the social aspects of learning; that is, sometimes understandings are reached through discussion rather than instruction. Skills learned through socially and academically sup-

> The new balance takes greater advantage of the social aspects of learning; that is, sometimes understandings are reached through discussion rather than instruction.

SkyLight Training and Publishing Inc.

ported situations, such as guided practice and cooperative learning, can later be replicated independently. The ratio of teacher-directed, shared, and student-directed activities can be easily adjusted depending on the needs and independence of the class.

A balanced blend of activities can be used at all grade levels. When the teacher is directing the class, she may be reading aloud, or specifically explaining sound-symbol relationships, or modeling a comprehension strategy. The teacher also instructs students in models of learning, such as how to work independently with materials in a learning center or how to work cooperatively with students in a small group. Students and the teacher share responsibility when the students join the teacher in shared reading as they choral read and discuss a story together. In guided reading, students read silently but interpret the story with the teacher and with each other. They discuss how they used strategies to comprehend the meaning, or they relay what they did when something went wrong with the meaning, what they cued in on, and how they corrected it. Students also read in pairs to obtain both academic and social support. Before the children become truly independent, the teacher scaffolds instruction by activating prior knowledge, giving reminders of organizational patterns, coaching students with critical vocabulary, or asking students to predict. Students have choices about how to respond to the text. They receive feedback during ample practice time. Finally students are able to read independently from materials of their own choosing without help from the teacher.

Students and the teacher share responsibility when the students join the teacher in shared reading as they choral read and discuss a story together.

The same pattern of fostering ever-greater independence also occurs in writing. Primary students see modeled writing when they construct a language experience story with the teacher. They begin to share in the writing as they add the words and work out the sounds and letters on a chart. As organizational patterns, genre, and content become more prominent, the teacher presents criteria, models effective writing, and shares samples with the class. Some writing is developed together during guided practice. The students work in peer editing groups to develop ideas and discuss and evaluate the work. The class discusses benchmarks and criteria as they assess the effectiveness of their writing. Also, students write on their own from the very beginning.

Another aspect that ameliorates this debate about who determines the curriculum is that reading and writing progress in developmental stages. No matter who picked the lesson or content—publisher, teacher, or child—the activity is usually developmentally appropriate for the needs of the students and is a topic of general interest. When it isn't, the teacher knows immediately by the sea of glazed faces or unengaged learners and makes a quick adjustment. The criticism about a lockstep curriculum, the publisher's or district's prescribed curriculum that must be followed according to a specified timetable, usually isn't applicable in an experienced or even an inexperienced teacher's classroom because the feedback from the students is so immediate and apparent. Anything inappropriate is changed immediately.

Balanced reading and writing solves the whole-part dilemma by using a whole-part-whole approach, integrates the language arts, and blends teacher and student leadership. It requires skillful and knowledgeable teaching and a great degree of creativity and ingenuity especially when the materials that are available were not specifically designed to meet these purposes. The rewards, however, are substantial when children understand the relevancy of reading and writing in general and explicitly understand how the processes work. They are able to build relationships among the components—reading, writing, listening, and speaking—because each is used to compliment and reinforce the others. Children are also able to participate in the process with some degree of choice and control while still benefiting from guidance and instruction from the teacher. Balanced reading and writing is a very strong model for instruction in literacy.

Balanced reading and writing requires skillful and knowledgeable teaching and a great degree of creativity and ingenuity.

Developing Phonemic Awareness and Teaching Phonics

Good readers decode rapidly and automatically.

—MARILYN ADAMS

"**L**earning to read is made much easier when children have acquired three prerequisite understandings about print: print carries messages, printed words are composed of letters, and letters correspond to the sounds in spoken words" (Lapp and Flood, 1997, p. 698).

Is there a preliminary level of understanding that helps children reach those first three prerequisites? Yes, there is. To help children reach the three prerequisites, they need to understand that words can be divided into individual sounds, the smallest unit of sound being a *phoneme*. *Phonemic awareness* is the ability to notice, to think about, and to manipulate the individual sounds in words (Torgesen, 1998). Children need to be consciously aware of this concept to successfully link sounds to letters, and sound-letter correspondence is the basis of teaching phonics. *Phonics* includes the consistent sound-letter correspondences and the patterns of multiple sounds for certain letters, such as *c* in *caught* or *city* or *ou* in *doubt* or *cough*. It also includes learning multiple spelling patterns for the same sound such as /e/in *meat, mete,* or *meet.* The study of phonics enables readers to identify unfamiliar words on their own. While phonics is the most common name for this reading strategy, it is also referred to as sound-symbol relationship, word attack, the graphophonemic cueing system, letter-sound correspondence, word identification, decoding, and the orthographic processing system (although this term has more to do with spelling patterns). Some terms are a bit broader than others, but they all have to do with how letters and spelling patterns represent speech sounds. If children do not develop phonemic awareness, they will have a very difficult time learning phonics and will be limited in the independent identification of new words.

> Phonemic awareness is the ability to notice, to think about, and to manipulate the individual sounds in words.

Developing Phonemic Awareness

A major difference between children who score well on phonemic awareness tests and those who do not is the ability to understand the directions (Calfee, as cited in Adams, 1990). Those who do not score well are able to hear the phonemes, but they do not understand the concepts behind the tasks, which involve assembling and disassembling the sounds within a word. They are not yet aware of the concept that words are composed of sounds. Steven A. Stahl (1992) relates a story about a young child who was asked to say *coat* but without the *c.* She answered, "Jacket." She had not yet learned that words could be thought of as a composite of individual sounds; thus, something less than a coat must be a jacket.

That words are composed of individual sounds is a difficult concept for many young children because they have previously only considered words as whole, meaning-carrying units. *Dog* is the furry creature that licks your face, not a composite of the sounds /d/ /o/ /g/. For most preschoolers, phonemic awareness is not acquired naturally because they have had no need to divide words into component sounds; they have been concentrating on the meaning in spoken language. It is only when they start playing with words, often through exposure to rhyming words in nursery rhymes and patterned rhyming books, that they begin to think about the sounds of words—their similarities, their differences, and their combinations.

For a new reader, hearing the individual sounds is not easy. When a word is analyzed using a spectrograph, the sounds blend into one another and are not identifiable in isolation without distortion. Several sounds— /b/, /p/, /d/, and /t/— are almost impossible to produce without adding a vowel sound. Thus, identifying sounds in isolation is an abstraction, something that does not happen in actuality in the way we conceptualize it in print. When children can repeat a word with all of the sounds intact, they have auditory discrimination, but being able to separate and combine sounds consciously is a different skill than auditory discrimination.

Identifying sounds in isolation is an abstraction, something that does not happen in actuality in the way we conceptualize it in print.

Alphabetic languages have one symbol for each elementary speech sound or phoneme. Although English is an alphabetic language, it is not a language of one to one correspondences. However, the correspondences are close enough to be able to make generalizations. Learning to read alphabetic systems requires the ability to analyze words into phonemes (Lundberg, Frost, and Petersen, 1988). Visual memory of words is not as important in learning words as once thought. If children do not understand that words are composed of individual sounds, it is very difficult for them to benefit from phonics instruction or to grasp the alphabetic principle, which is that certain alphabetic symbols consistently represent certain sounds. If a reader does not make the sound-letter connection, that is understand the alphabetic principle, then reading becomes a memory intensive act with each word being memorized by its visual characteristics. This method is sufficient for perhaps learning the first dozen or so words, and it was once the basis of the look-say method. However, it is not sufficient for learning to read the 6,000 words that most first graders have in their speaking vocabulary.

Although some children acquire phonemic awareness without direct instruction through exposure to print and initial word play, many do not.

Those children who have a slow start in reading are often those who lack phonemic awareness. Black and Hispanic children of low socioeconomic status are more likely than Anglo children of low socioeconomic status to have poor phonemic awareness of school English. This may be attributed to greater differences between home and school language as well as to cultural differences involving the time spent with word play and exposure to print (Juel, 1988).

Many studies show that success in beginning reading is significantly related to phonemic awareness that develops gradually and reciprocally with reading instruction. The greater the phonemic awareness of a beginning reader, the more fully he or she will be able to process (get into memory) the letter-sound properties of individual printed words. Phonemic awareness is a better predictor of early reading success than IQ or socioeconomic status (Ball and Blachman, 1991). The importance of phonemic awareness is summarized by P. L. Griffith, J. P. Klesius, and J. D. Kromrey (as cited in Castle, Riach, and Nicholson, 1994, p. 356). "The method of reading instruction in the first year of school is not as important to literacy acquisition as are beginning-of-the-year levels of phonemic awareness."

> **Phonemic awareness develops gradually and reciprocally with reading instruction.**

There are several components of phonemic awareness in addition to other associated skills that come under the broader term *phonological awareness*. Rhyming and the ability to separate syllables are part of the phonological awareness, whereas phonemic awareness is limited to consciously manipulating individual sounds.

The following components, whether phonemic or phonological, are important in developing phonemic awareness to facilitate beginning reading.

Rhyming

Rhyming belongs under the classification of phonological awareness rather than phonemic awareness because a unit of sound is processed rather than a single phoneme. Many sound awareness activities start with rhyming because the ending part of the word—the rime—is a more psychologically cohesive unit, more similar to a syllable than a phoneme. (There are two parts to a word; the beginning sound is called the *onset*, and the vowel and ending consonants are called the *rime*.) Rhyming becomes important in learning to read. Children who cannot rhyme cannot match ending rimes, so they will not be able to understand the relationships among words in word families. They will have a hard time learning new words by analogy to a known word in the family. An example of making an analogy to a known word in a given family would be "if this is *time,* then that is *dime.*"

Alphabet Knowledge

Knowing the letters of the alphabet is a strong predictor of successful first-grade reading. Knowing letter names is not truly a part of phonemic awareness, but it gets very cumbersome to discuss beginning reading concepts without referring to alphabet letter names.

Children who know the names of the letters have spent some time learning about print. If the letters can be named rapidly and accurately, the children have spent considerable time learning about print. They have one concept under their belts that gives them an advantage in beginning reading. The names of many letters are also closely related to their sounds, which is helpful in decoding and in developmental spelling. Many phonemic awareness programs also teach the alphabet.

> The names of many letters are also closely related to their sounds, which is helpful in decoding and in developmental spelling.

Differentiating or Odd One Out

In odd-one-out tasks, children are orally given two or three words that have the same beginning sound and one that has a different beginning sound. For example, which word doesn't start the same: *man, moon, saw, mom*? This task is easier than many of the other phonemic skills because it requires only comparison and contrast; therefore, it is a task suitable for prereaders. There is a strong correlation between students who can identify the odd one out and reading acquisition (Lundberg et al., 1988).

Phoneme Identity

Identifying individual phonemes, the smallest units of sound that roughly correspond with individual letters, is not a skill that comes easily, but it can be taught. If children can conceptualize and identify individual sounds, they will be able to match them to alphabet letters later. Some studies found that teaching phoneme identity seemed to lead to better reading skills than teaching segmenting and blending (Byrne and Fielding-Barnsley, 1993; Murray, as cited in Stahl, 1997).

Phonemes can be identified in testing by matching initial sounds to pictures. Which of the pictured objects, *shoe, lock, heart,* starts the same as *lamp*? A lamp is also pictured, and all items are named by the teacher.

Both beginning and ending sounds can be matched to the key word, and practice items are often compound words such as *football* and *footpath* to ensure that children understand the phrase "starts the same as."

Partial Segmentation

Partial segmentation means that children can partially disassemble the sounds in a word, most often the first sound from the remainder of the word. Learning to isolate the initial sound is the phonemic skill most related to beginning reading because the initial consonant is the first clue used to identify unknown words. Unless a child has a basic awareness that the sounds in words can be segmented, he won't be able to understand a question as simple as, "What is the first sound in *ball*?"

One form of segmentation is known as onset and rime. In *wink*, /w/ is the onset and /*ink*/ is the rime. Separating the onset and rime is often the first word analysis skill that young children can execute, and it can be accomplished by many preschoolers. It is more complex than syllabic awareness, but only slightly.

Full Segmentation

Full segmentation is the ability to break apart an entire word into its component sounds. For example, the word *sat* is composed of /s/ /a/ /t/. Game is /g/ /ā/ /m/. Sight is /s/ /ī/ /t/. There are often more letters than sounds in words. The ability to fully segment words is strongly related to reading and spelling. In an important study, half of the six-year-olds who were unable to fully segment words scored in the lowest third of a test of reading achievement, and none was in the top third (Liberman, Shankweiler, Liberman, Fowler, and Fischer, as cited in Adams, 1990).

Segmentation is often tested by tapping. *Sat, game* and *sight* have three sounds so there are three taps. Being able to count the number of phonemes in a word was the best predictor of pseudoword reading in a study by Maggie Bruck and Rebecca Treiman (1992). Apparently the children who could count all the sounds had discovered the alphabetic principle (that each letter has a sound) when deciphering decodable pseudowords, which are nonsense words that can only be pronounced by decoding.

Another method for testing full segmentation is to move a marker or chip for each sound in a word. This method for testing brings up a point regarding the age appropriateness of certain phonemic awareness tasks.

In a study by I. Y. Liberman (as cited in Adams, 1990), none of the four-year-olds and only 17% of the five-year-olds were successful at this task. However, the task was completed successfully by 70% of six-year-olds. Thus, several phonemic awareness tasks may not be beneficial for kindergarten children or for those who have not yet begun to read.

One of the most interesting findings regarding phonemic awareness is that certain aspects, such as full segmentation, develop as a result of learning to read as children begin to decode. It is not a prerequisite for the early stages of learning to read. Therefore, it is not necessary to delay reading instruction until all aspects of phonemic awareness have been mastered.

Age is a consideration for certain phonemic awareness tasks. Some may not be beneficial for those who have not yet begun to read.

Blending

Blending is the opposite of segmentation. Children are presented with separate sounds, /f/ /a/ /n/, and are asked to blend the sounds together into a word. Blending is easier than segmenting.

Sound Deletion

Sound deletion involves removing a sound from a word and then pronouncing the remaining sounds. When children are asked to delete sounds, they are usually asked to remove the first or last sound from a word. Say *hill*. Say *hill* without the /h/. Say *pink* without the /k/. Some sound deletions are harder than others. It is especially difficult to delete one sound from a consonant cluster such as /bl/. Deleting the ending clusters *-nt* or *-mp* is also very difficult, because they do not seem to be a cohesive unit. The phonograms *-amp* or *-ent* hold together better as units so it is easier to delete an entire phonogram.

Sound deletion is a strong predictor of reading achievement but has been found to be beyond the ability of children before the end of first grade (Adams, 1990). Byrne and Fielding-Barnsley (1993) found a relationship between success at sound deletion and spelling in first grade. Deletion may be another result of learning to read rather than a requirement.

Sound Substitution

Sound substitution requires both segmenting and blending. An example of a sound substitution task is to ask the student to say *side*. Then, take off the /s/. Add /r/. What word is it? The ability to delete, transpose, or add phonemes to a syllable continues to develop at least through high school (Adams, 1991).

When Should Phonemic Awareness Be Taught?

Phonemic awareness is a skill that can be taught, but should it be taught prior to reading instruction or simultaneously with reading instruction? The answer seems to be yes and yes. "Some aspects of phonemic awareness may lead and some may follow the acquisition of alphabetic reading and spelling" (Byrne and Fielding-Barnsley, 1993, p. 110).

Preschoolers and beginning kindergarten students can learn some phonemic concepts well before reading instruction begins. In Denmark, children who received phonemic awareness training prior to any reading instruction progressed significantly in phonemic awareness, though the training did not have any influence on letter acquisition or language comprehension (Lundberg et al., 1988). But, it did make learning to read easier. Teaching phonemic awareness prior to reading instruction facilitates subsequent reading acquisition in several ways. When the kindergarten children in the Danish study learned to read in first grade, they were more able to analyze initial sounds, segment phonemes, and spell than a group of comparable kindergartners who had not received training. These abilities facilitate word recognition, and rapid, automatic word recognition facilitates comprehension.

The children's phonemic background enabled them to learn and use sound-letter correspondences to a greater extent. They did better in reading pseudowords. Students who can identify pseudowords can also identify unknown, phonetically regular real words independently.

Phonemic awareness also facilitates early spelling acquisition. Children who understand sound-symbol relationships spell better than those who rely on visual memory (Byrne and Fielding-Barnsley, 1993).

Coordinating Phonemic Awareness with Reading Instruction

While totally auditory training of phonemic awareness may provide subsequent benefits, teaming phonemic awareness with letter identification is more powerful. There is no clear answer from the research about

Teaching phonemic awareness prior to reading instruction facilitates subsequent reading acquisition in several ways.

when letters and sound-symbol correspondence should be added to phonemic awareness but as soon as possible seems reasonable. As letters are learned, they can be incorporated into phonemic awareness activities as the visual aspect is very helpful for many students. (Have you ever tried to learn a foreign language without seeing it written down?) Both knowledge of letter names and phonemic awareness are good predictors of early reading success, and knowing both is better than knowing one or the other. "Functional knowledge of the alphabetic principle depends equally on the knowledge of letters and on explicit awareness of phonemes because it depends integrally on the association between them" (Adams, 1991, p. 304).

Children who become aware of phonemes and learn letter names have labels and concepts for what the teacher is talking about when reading instruction begins. Each word will not be a new and unique entity, unrelated to anything ever seen before. They realize there is a system for reading, and it is composed of familiar parts—sounds, letters, and words.

Byrne and Fielding-Barnsley (as cited in Castle et al., 1994) found, "Phonological awareness was more successful when combined with letter-sound correspondence training." It is not until students have a clear idea of letter-sound relationships that they are able to perform all the phonemic tasks, especially segmentation. When phonemic awareness training has included a component of explicit instruction in sound-symbol associations, consistently positive effects on reading have been reported (Ball and Blachman, 1991).

Phonemic training becomes more powerful when other emergent literacy activities are also part of instruction, such as the shared reading of big books in which the teacher re-examines the text with students to analyze words. To borrow Stahl's analogy on phonics (1992), children can learn phonemic awareness skills in isolation, but without connecting them to letters and texts, they don't understand what they're good for.

Although the very first words that most children learn to read are learned holistically by sight, it is only when a beginning reader understands phonemes, letters, and their fairly consistent relationships that he will be able to understand several interrelated concepts and thus be able to independently identify new words. These concepts are:

1. Words are made up of individual sounds.
2. Words are made up of individual letters.

> **Children can learn phonemic awareness skills in isolation, but they don't understand what it's good for if they don't connect it to letters and text.**

3. Letters can be reliably matched to sounds that can be blended to-gether to identify words for reading.

4. Word sounds can be segmented and reliably matched to letters for spelling.

5. The sequence of the letters represents the sound sequence.

6. Changing the letter changes the sound and makes a new word.

7. Changing the sound changes the letter and makes a new word.

As adults, we know it is not that simple because English is not a language of one-to-one correspondences. Patterns, irregular words, and multiple letter-sound and sound-letter correspondences must also be learned. But, if beginning readers learn the alphabetic principle, they will make an excellent start with the complexities of English.

To reverse the line of thought, teaching basic sound-symbol relationships and alphabet names without phonemic awareness is not sufficient either. Neither provides awareness of nor practice with segmenting or blending. Although many phonics programs get to that stage, having phonemic skills first seems to make it easier to make the connection.

Before anyone gets carried away with the wonders of phonemic aware-ness, consider Keith Stanovich's reminder. Phonological awareness may be a necessary but not sufficient condition for the acquisition of reading (1986). Reading still has to be taught, and having phonemic concepts doesn't alleviate the need for multiple exposures to and practice with sound-letter correspondences and word identification strategies as well as extensive experiences with print in reading and writing. Without these other aspects of emergent literacy, it is not likely that phonemic aware-ness training and sound-symbol relationships will generalize to actual reading and spelling skills (Foorman et al., 1998).

This brings us back to the whole-part-whole principle of balanced read-ing. Children need to understand the broader concept of reading (the whole) so they know why they are learning discrete skills (the parts). They also need the opportunity to apply what they have learned (the whole). Readers are more successful when the teacher integrates the instruction.

Knowledge of letter names and phonemic awareness are both good predictors of early reading success.

At-Risk Readers

Two of the reasons young children may be at risk in reading acquisition are their lack of exposure to print and their lack of opportunity to play with language. Phonemic awareness training provides language play, while read-alouds and shared reading provide the experience with print. Barbara Foorman et al. (1998) found that at-risk emergent readers benefited from phonemic awareness training combined with direct instruction in the alphabetic principle and literature activities. At-risk readers improved in word-reading skills at a significantly faster rate when provided with direct instruction as compared to a group that was indirectly instructed in the alphabetic principle only through exposure to literature. Also, the number of children who made no demonstrable growth whatsoever was much lower in the direct instruction group.

By the end of the year, the direct instruction group of at-risk readers scored in the 43rd percentile in decoding and the 45th percentile in comprehension whereas the literature group scored in the 29th and 35th percentiles, respectively. The literature group did have more positive attitudes toward reading, and it may be that their positive attitudes could sustain motivation to improve their reading skills and read extensively in future years despite initial difficulties. However, Connie Juel's and Keith Stanovich's studies cited below do not seem to offer encouragement that this will happen.

Intensive support of primary children may prevent reading difficulties. F. R. Vellutino (as cited in Foorman et al., 1998) tutored poor first-grade readers in first-grade letter identification, phoneme awareness, word-reading skills, and practice in connected text. The majority of these students became average readers. A balanced approach of phonemic awareness, direct instruction in sound-symbol relationships, and reading in connected text seems to hold particular promise for at-risk readers as well as average readers.

Readers are also at risk if they fail to "catch on" early. Failure in beginning reading has a snowball effect. Stanovich (1986) calls it the "Matthew Effect," which is a variation on the old maxim that the rich get richer, and the poor get poorer. Readers who experience early success read more so they become even more successful. Children who have had difficulties in learning to read tend to be exposed to less text.

> **A balanced approach of phonemic awareness, direct instruction in sound-symbol relationships, and reading in connected text seems to hold particular promise for at-risk readers.**

Due to their slower start, less advanced readers get less practice with reading. They are often asked to read materials that are too difficult, they have difficulty with decoding, and they are less motivated to read than their successful peers. Lack of exposure and practice delays the development of automaticity and speed at the word-recognition level. Readers who must spend their time decoding have less cognitive energy for comprehension. "Thus, reading for meaning is hindered, unrewarding reading experiences multiply, and practice is avoided or merely tolerated without real cognitive involvement" (Stanovich, 1986, p. 364). Because uninvolved readers read less, they miss out on vocabulary, language development, and content knowledge. These readers do not catch up.

Juel (1988) in a four-year study of fifty-four children found an 88% probability that children who were poor readers at the end of first grade would remain poor readers by the end of fourth grade. The probability that an average reader in first grade would become a poor reader in fourth grade was 12%. The Matthew Effect holds true.

The children who became poor readers entered first grade with little phonemic awareness and did not reach the ceiling of the phonemic awareness test until the end of third grade, which the good readers had nearly reached by the end of first grade. Nine of the poor readers, who had little or no phonemic awareness upon entering school, could read no pseudowords at the end of first grade despite a year of phonics instruction.

By the end of fourth grade, the poor readers had not reached the level of decoding achieved by the good readers at the beginning of second grade, which prevented them from reading as much text as the good readers both in school and out of school. Juel estimates that by the end of fourth grade, good readers had read 178,000 words of running text in their basals, but the poor readers had read only 80,000. And, the gap between the groups in out-of-school reading widened each year.

In response to attitude questionnaires, 40% of the poor readers said they would rather clean their rooms than read, and one stated, "I'd rather clean the mold around the bathtub than read." Interestingly, 70% of both groups said they would rather watch television or play with their friends than read. (Don't underestimate the competition!)

It is critical to get first graders off to a good start. Phonemic awareness training and abundant experience with print may be the keys.

> Connie Juel found an 88% probability that children who were poor readers at the end of first grade would remain poor readers by the end of fourth grade.

Classroom Activities for Learning Phonemic Awareness

To begin teaching phonemic awareness, Marilyn Adams, Barbara Foorman, Ingvar Lundberg, and Terri Beeler (1998) suggest starting with environmental sounds; then move on to word and sentence awareness, rhyming, segmenting syllables, and breaking onsets from rimes. They suggest working with all of these activities before even starting with phonemes.

Stahl (1997) recommends that teachers start with a small set of sounds, possibly teaching them one at a time. The consonant sounds that are continuant, or can be stretched, such as / m, s, n, f, z, v /, can be worked with more easily than stop-consonant sounds, / t, d, b, k /, which are hard to manipulate. He also recommends using the alphabet letters and their corresponding sounds as part of phonemic awareness instruction. Again, phonemic awareness is more easily learned in conjunction with sounds and letters. The combination also has a stronger effect on reading acquisition.

> To begin teaching phonemic awareness, start with environmental sounds.

Getting Started

Environmental sounds are those sounds from common, everyday activities that can be found in a young reader's surroundings. One activity using environmental sounds includes having children listen to a familiar sound with their eyes closed or their backs to the teacher. Sounds could include cutting paper with scissors, turning on a computer, sharpening a pencil, writing on the board, pouring water from a glass, crumpling paper, or snapping fingers. Next, the teachers asks the children to identify two sounds in sequence. A good book to accompany these early activities is *The Listening Walk* (Showers, 1961).

Because words are easier to identify than phonemes, it is better to begin **listening activities at the whole-word level.** The teacher can read familiar nursery rhymes that are mixed up. As children hear the error, they raise their hands and explain what is wrong (Adams et al., 1998).

Song a sing of sixpence	reversed words
Baa baa purple sheep	substituted word
Humpty Dumpty wall on a sat	swapped word order - ungrammatical

Jack fell down and crown his broke	swapped word order - ungrammatical
One, two, shuckle my boo	swapped initial consonants
One, two, buckle my shoe Five, six, pick up sticks	switched order of events

Rhyming

Reading aloud to children is very important in helping children acquire concepts about reading. Teaching **nursery rhymes** and reading **rhyming books** provides a vehicle for learning about rhymes. Fewer children these days seem as familiar with the classic nursery rhymes as past generations so it may take longer for your students to learn them, but they will be as delighted with them as children have been in the past. Contemporary rhyming books such as *Fire! Fire! Said Mrs. McGuire* (Martin, 1996) and *Jesse Bear, What Will You Wear?* (Carlstrom, 1986) are also filled with delightful rhymes. After reading a couplet, the teacher can stop to ask the children which words rhymed. Or, just before the second rhyme in a couplet, the teacher can ask the students what the rhyming word will be.

The following provides an example of a **rhyming poem**:

> Two little feet go tap, tap, tap
> Two little hands go clap, clap, clap
> A quiet little leap up from my chair
> Two little arms reach up in the air.
> Two little feet go jump, jump, jump
> Two little fists go thump, thump, thump.
> One little body goes round, round, round,
> And one little child sits quietly down.
> —Adams et al., 1998

First, the teacher reads the poem for the children emphasizing the rhythm and rhyme. Then the poem is reread line by line as the students repeat in unison. Many repetitions are necessary. Variations on this exercise include: reciting the poem in whispers but saying the rhyming words in a loud voice; reciting the poem in a loud tone but whispering the rhyme; asking different groups of children to say different lines; having each child in a circle recite one line each; having each child in a circle recite one word each.

Because words are easier to identify than phonemes, begin listening activities at the whole-word level.

In the **rhyming game** called Did You Ever See?, the teacher thinks of a rhyming situation, and the students fill in the last word.

Did you ever see a boy playing with a ___? (toy)

Did you ever see a mouse that lived in a ___? (house)

Did you ever see a shoe held together with ___?(glue)

Did you ever see a bear with brown shaggy ___?(hair)

Did you ever see a chair floating in the ___?(air)

Differentiating or Odd One Out

To learn the concept of which word in a series is different, the teacher may start with words that rhyme: *rake, make, pen, take*. Many children already know this activity from a *Sesame Street* game called "One of these isn't like the other ones."

To play odd one out, ask students which word begins with a different sound: *turtle, nut, toaster, tent,* etc. This can be done with a four square of pictures that very closely resembles the *Sesame Street* segment. Oddity tasks are easier than segmentation or blending because they require only comparison and contrast so they are excellent initial activities for the study of sounds.

Phoneme Identity

Phoneme identity tasks teach children to identify and match sounds. For example, the /s/ heard at the beginning of *sand* and *sister* is the same sound. It is also the same as the /s/ at the end of *miss*.

At the most basic level, the question to ask is, "Is there /w/ in *watch*?" "Is there /s/ in *tooth*?" An alphabetical word list from an old teacher's manual or a picture dictionary are useful to have, because it is not as easy to think of words with the same sound without a prompt as you might think. For children who are just learning to segment sounds, it may be less confusing for the teacher to ask, "Is there /w/ in *watch*?" rather than "Is there a /w/ in *watch*?" Beginners sometimes think the word "a" is part of the sound.

Slightly more advanced questions require **matching**. The teacher can ask children if the beginning sound of a word is the same or different than another word(s). Does *ring* begin the same as *river* and *race*? Does *pen* begin the same as *cup* and *can*? Identifying location in a word is still more

> Oddity tasks are easier than segmentation or blending because they require only comparison and contrast.

complex. Does *lamp* have /l/ at the beginning or end? Does *fall* have /l/ at the beginning or end?

In the phoneme identity activity known as **concentration**, children lay out five pairs of picture cards face down that have matching initial sounds. Two at a time are turned over. If they match in initial sound, the child keeps the cards. If they don't match, they are turned face down again. The child must say, "These are *sun* and *sock*. They both start with /s/." More advanced students can play concentration with final sounds.

Alliterative phrases and tongue twisters draw children's attention to matching initial letters as in Silly Sally snores. Hallie Kay Yopp has identified a whole list of read-aloud books that are excellent for developing phonological awareness. The list can be found in *The Reading Teacher* (1995 pp. 538–543).

Sound matching provides another phoneme identity activity. The following words are sung to the tune of "Jimmy Cracked Corn and I Don't Care" (Yopp, 1992).

Who has a /d/ word to share with us?   *Dog* is a word that starts with /d/
Who has a /d/ word to share with us?   *Dog* is a word that starts with /d/
Who has a /d/ word to share with us?   *Dog* is a word that starts with /d/
It must start with the /d/ sound.   *Dog* starts with the /d/ sound.

The teacher will tire of this long before the children will.

In **What Was on the Tray?**, several objects that start with the same sound are placed on a tray. Ask children to remember them and remove the tray from sight. The students can draw the items and then name them. Having students use a patterned sentence such as "This is a *key* and it starts with /k/", helps them to make an explicit connection. Paying close attention to items on a tray, or letters in a word, is a skill worth encouraging.

To make **alphabet book pages**, write an alphabet letter on a large sheet of drawing paper. Children draw pictures or cut out magazine pictures of objects starting with that sound. This is tricky with /c/, /g/, and the vowels. Later, pictures can be labeled—if anyone can still figure out what the drawing represents. Selected pages can be assembled into a class alphabet book.

Phoneme identity tasks teach children to identify and match sounds.

Partial Segmentation

Partial segmentation, also called phoneme isolation, often begins with segmenting sentences into words, and then words into syllables before segmenting words into sounds.

In **syllable segmenting**, children clap the syllables in their own names and in the names of other items in the room. A game using this idea is called "King's/Queen's Successor." The children circle the teacher, who is wearing a crown, and she issues an order, which is an action. She repeats the word rhythmically, accentuating the syllables: *march - ing, march - ing, march - ing*. The children perform the action in rhythm. A child is chosen as the royal successor who will give the next order (Lundberg et al., 1988).

Tapping out the syllables is also a way to teach partial segmentation. Two cubes can be placed on a table. As the teacher says a two syllable word, she taps the two cubes and asks the student to repeat the word and say the first or last syllable. Three syllable words can be done next by adding the word *middle* to the instructions. If the teacher is sitting across from the student, be sure the cubes are arranged from the student's left to right.

When children progress to **segmenting phonemes**, initial consonants are easiest to segment, then final consonants, and finally medial sounds. Vowels are even harder, and young children are resistant to the idea that blends such as /pl/ are two sounds. Segmentation of consonant blends develops relatively late. Partial segmentation corresponds to initial stages of learning sound-symbol relationships whereas accuracy in word identification requires full segmentation abilities.

> Initial consonants are easiest to segment, then final consonants, and finally medial sounds.

To teach students how to **separate the sounds**, ask children to "tell," for example, the beginning sound in *zipper*. Ending sounds can also be separated. An easy way to start is with two different sets of picture cards. Each set should start with the same single consonant: *nail, nut, nest, net, nurse*. Have a child pick a card and draw out the initial sound /nnnnest/. Have the children repeat and notice how their tongues and lips are placed. After both sets of cards are completed they can be mixed up and sorted by initial sound.

Troll at the Bridge is a charming game to teach partial segmentation. A troll puppet says, "Only children whose names start with /d/ may cross the bridge." Of course, the troll eventually says all the beginning sounds of the names of the children in the class. More advanced students can play the game with ending or middle sounds (Stahl, 1997). For a variation, ask students to line up for a specials class by giving the initial sounds of their first names.

Riddles can be used to teach partial segmentation. The teacher asks riddles (questions) in which all the answers must start with a certain sound. On what do you put a stamp? *Mail.* What does a boy grow up to be? *Man.* With what do you light a fire? *Match.* What do you take when you're sick? *Medicine.* What animal is chased by a cat? *Mouse.* What's between the beginning and the end? *Middle.*

In an activity known as **every student responds**, students are given the same four to six picture cards, each with a different beginning and ending sound, which are placed face up on their desks. The teacher asks, "Which one begins with /t/?" Each child must hold up the appropriate picture. For one more round, the teacher can ask the class, "What begins the same as *tiger*?" For more advanced students, ask for the ending sounds. As children learn sound-symbol relationships, the teacher can ask, "Which one begins with *t*?" The children all hold up their cards and one can be called upon to respond, "*Toe* begins with *t*. It sounds /t/.

For those teachers who have no qualms about singing before the class, try **singing the beginning sounds** for a set of words. For example, to the tune of "Old MacDonald," sing the following verse (Yopp, 1992). This can also be adapted to final sounds.

> What's the sound that starts these words:
> Turtle, time, and teeth? [Wait for a response.]
> /T/ is the sound that starts these words:
> Turtle, time, and teeth.
> With a /t/ /t/ here and a /t/ /t/ there,
> Here a /t/, there a /t/, everywhere a /t/ /t/.
> /T/ is the sound that starts these words:
> Turtle, time, and teeth.

In **partial segmentation bingo**, students have nine square or sixteen square bingo cards with pictures of objects beginning with different sounds. The teacher says a sound, /r/, and if the students have a picture beginning with that sound, they use a marker to cover it. Sometimes old

Troll at the Bridge is a charming game to teach partial segmentation, and there are several variations of the game.

phonics books can be cut and pasted together to make bingo cards. Since each card must be different, it is a daunting task to assemble the cards. However, once made and laminated, they can be used over and over for various tasks. Another idea is to have several sets of loose identical pictures and the children can place them in blank divided squares, but with loose pictures and loose markers, the whole thing gets a little wiggly.

Once the children learn sound-letter relationships, they can write their own letters on a bingo card and the teacher can "call" words that start with the sounds of the letters.

Full Segmentation

A simple activity to teach full segmentation involves **stretching words**. The teacher simply asks the child, "Say *sun* so that I can hear all the sounds." /Sssuuunnn/.

In **say it and move it**, children identify individual phonemes by moving markers. Provide the students with sheets of paper with sets of empty squares, one square for one phoneme words, two squares for two phoneme words, and three squares for three phoneme words. A picture card is placed above the squares, and a word is said by the instructor. The child repeats the word once, and as he repeats it the second time, he moves markers from the bottom of the paper into the empty squares, one marker and square for each sound. The child repeats the word again. This is a variation of Elkonin Boxes. Plastic letters or letter cards replace the markers in later stages.

An interesting intermediate technique was developed by Eileen Ball and Benita Blachman (1991). They suggest that as children learn their first sound-letter correspondence, use a letter tile for that letter and allow the other markers to remain blank. Begin with no more than two marked letter tiles in a lesson. Heavy duty laminated cardboard or white boards survive all this sliding and moving better than ordinary paper.

After any of the above activities, children can be asked to **count the sounds**, or tap out the number of sounds.

As children learn sound-letter correspondence, **invented spelling** is a natural follow-up to stretching words since one must stretch out a word in order to spell it. Invented spelling also facilitates segmentation skills.

Activities to teach full segmentation include stretching words, say it and move it, counting the sounds, and invented spelling.

Blending

The most difficult part about teaching the blending of individual phonemes is saying them in segmented form because vowel sounds tend to be added to certain consonants when trying to say them in isolation. Teachers often start with blending together compound words, then syllables and next onsets and rimes. What word is /g/ /ate/? /t/ /ub/? /b/ /est/? The rimes are stronger psychologically and the idea of blending can still be accessed.

Begin with a simple blending exercise known as **echo and blend**. To blend sounds, the teacher says a sequence of sounds, such as /l/ /e/ /g/, and the students echo the sequence, blend the sounds, and then say the whole word.

Troll Talk brightens up blending exercises. The teacher tells the students a story about a troll who likes to give presents, but the child must first guess what the present is. When the teacher (as the troll) segments the name of the presents, such as /b-oo-k/, /tr-u-k/, the student must blend the sounds together. For beginners, the consonant blends, such as /tr/, can be preblended, but for more experienced students, segment the consonant blends (Adams et al., 1998).

Teachers can also teach blending using **words in context**. Use a book that is being read in class: Omit a word, segment it, and ask the children to blend it back together. The words should not be ones that could be guessed from context.

Sound Deletion and Sound Substitution

Simple sound deletion works as follows: "Say *moon*. Now say it without the /m/. Say *coat*. Now say it without the /t/."

Pig Latin is another deletion task. It is of course more complicated because the deleted sound must be added to the end of the word. It is such fun that most children will work to learn the system. Trying to decode someone else's word in Pig Latin is a great sound manipulation task also. An interesting note to Pig Latin is that both consonant digraphs, /ch/, and consonant blends, /pl/ stick together as in *ickenchay* and *aceplay*. It's never *lacepay*. Their psychological stickiness as units explains why it is difficult for children to split blends apart.

Like Pig Latin, **sound substitution** is complicated because it requires both deletion and blending. The directions are "Say *boat*. Take off the /b/.

The most difficult part about teaching the blending of individual phonemes is saying them in segmented form.

Add /c/. What is the new word? "Once students get the idea, the directions can be shortened to "Say *fat*. Change the /f/ to /b/." It seems much easier to do this with written words than trying to do it orally. Since deletion and substitution are two of the most difficult phonemic skills (Vandervelden and Siegel, 1995), it may be better to try this task after students have a grounding in sound-symbol relationships.

In written form, give children a limited number of letter cards or tiles. Every child should have the same letters. Start by saying a three-letter word such as *sit*. The children move the appropriate letters into a working space on their desks. The teacher should write the word on the board so each child can check if he is right. Then remove the /s/ and replace it with /b/. Have the children say the word *bit*. Various other words can be formed by changing the beginning or ending letter. The really advanced students can change the vowels.

A very basic substitution activity is to change the words in the chorus of familiar songs. "Fe-Fi-Fiddly -i-o" in "Someone's in the Kitchen with Dinah" can become "Ze-Zi-Ziddly-i-o;" "Ee-igh, ee-igh, oh!" in "Old MacDonald" can become "See-sigh, see-sigh, soh," and "Happy Birthday" can become "Bappy Birthday bo bou" (Yopp, 1992).

Alphabet Knowledge

Children should be able to recognize both uppercase and lowercase letters in a variety of print fonts and manuscript writing. Speed in letter recognition is important because it indicates that the letters are thoroughly learned and can be discriminated at a glance.

In the activity called **limited choice**, the teacher uses a card containing five or six letters and then asks the child to point to the *S*. It is not as daunting as a choice of twenty-six letters.

Alphabet war is similar to the card game war. It is played in pairs with an alphabet strip on the desk. Each child has a pile of letter cards. They each take a card from the pile, and whoever has the card closer to *A* wins both cards. They must say, "___ is closer to *A* than ___ so I win."

In **alphabet pattern**, the teacher says the alphabet with a repeating pattern of voice tone while pointing to an alphabet strip.

AB (loud) CD (soft) EF (loud) GH (soft) IJ (loud) KL (soft) ...

A (low) BC (high) D (low) EF (high) G (low) HI (high) J (low) KL (high) . . .

> Speed in letter recognition is important because it indicates that the letters are thoroughly learned and can be discriminated at a glance.

Alphabet books help students see the letters and hear words with the sounds. Reading alphabet books to preschoolers also helps to develop phonemic awareness. The alphabet book *The Z Was Zapped* (1987) combines the letters of the alphabet with Van Allsburg's intriguing pictures.

Assessment Tools for Phonemic Awareness

Many teachers are screening their kindergarten and first-grade students for phonemic awareness. The extra help that can be targeted for these students in the primary grades often means the difference between a successful primary student and one who faces frustration with learning to read, write, and spell.

If children have begun developing sound-symbol relationships, invented spelling can be used as an informal assessment of phonemic awareness. As young children improve in their ability to segment and identify sounds within a word, they spell more accurately. For example, *S, SP, SAP, STAP* for *stamp* all represent increasingly more complex levels of spelling, and thus higher levels of phonemic awareness (Morris, 1992).

There are a variety of formal assessment tools available to test phonemic and phonological awareness. A partial, annotated list follows:

1. Adams, Foorman, Lundberg, and Beeler Assessment Test in *Phonemic Awareness in Young Children* (Baltimore: Brooks Publishing, 1998). This test can be given to groups of six kindergarten children or up to fifteen first graders. It includes rhyming, counting syllables, matching initial sounds, counting phonemes, comparing word lengths, and representing phonemes with letters.

2. Lindamood Auditory Conceptualization Test (Patricia Lindamood and Charles Lindamood. Itasca, Illinois: Riverside, 1979). This individually administered test can be used with all ages.

3. The Phonological Awareness Test (Carolyn Robertson and Wanda Salter. 3100 4th Avenue, East Moline, Illinois: LinguiSystems, 1995). It contains subsections on rhyming, segmentation, isolation, deletions, substitution, blending, graphemes, and decoding. It is administered individually.

4. Test of Auditory Analysis Skills (TAAS) in *Helping Children Overcome Learning Difficulties* (Joseph Rosner. Walker & Company, 1979). This is a brief individually administered test. It is a very short deletion test with a scale that converts to grade level.

5. Test of Phonological Awareness (Joseph Torgesen and Brian Bryant. Austin, Texas: Pro-Ed.) This test can be used in small groups or individually. It is nationally standardized.

6. Yopp-Singer Test of Phoneme Segmentation. It is printed in its entirety in the September 1995 issue of *The Reading Teacher*.

As teachers become aware of phonemic awareness and provide instruction and activities to ensure that primary students learn the skills that underlie emergent literacy, the success rate of young readers will improve. There is a high probability that this will also mean more successful readers through all the grades.

Teaching Phonics and Word Recognition

How large a role does phonics play in beginning reading, in mature reading? Does it need to be taught explicitly and systematically or can it be taught as the need arises? Can phonics be taught best in isolation or in context? Should phonics be taught sounds to words or words to sounds? Can meaning and interest be maintained while teaching phonics? Where does phonics fit in a balanced reading program? These are questions vital to primary teachers and to many teachers in intermediate grades who are working with poor readers, and these are issues considered in this chapter.

The squitly tourmarands vashornly blained the cloughts in the wroked knanflede. You probably didn't have much trouble "reading" the previous sentence. It is fairly straightforward to someone who has broken the code. *Cloughts* may be /cl-ow-t-s/ or /cl-aw-t-s/, but it can't be /cleets/ or /clats/. *Wroked* may be /rok-ed/, /rokd/ or /rokt/ but not much else, and the other words are simple to pronounce once the system is known. The best thing about understanding the phonetic patterns of English is that words that are visually unfamiliar can still be pronounced. Of course, this doesn't address knowing the meaning or being able to comprehend the message, but comprehension will certainly be hindered if the words cannot be identified.

> Studies of readers as they proceed through the phases of word learning suggest that the more functional knowledge students have about the alphabetic system and how words are structured systematically to represent speech, the more fluent and automatic they become as readers. Research indicates that students having difficulty learning to read are the ones who understand the least about the alphabetic system (Gaskins et al., 1997, pp. 172–173).

"...the more functional knowledge students have about the alphabetic system and how words are structured systematically to represent speech, the more fluent and automatic they become as readers" (Gaskins et al., 1997).

The Phonics Debate Isn't New

Eventually all the components of reading blend together into a seamless act, but where to start? Should beginning reading start with sounds and letters or whole words and meaning? In Colonial times, beginning reading started with the alphabet often using key words and phrases such as, "A in Adam's fall, we sinned all." Children learned the letters, some syllables, and then learned to read text from memorized passages from the Bible and patriotic essays.

In 1836 the first McGuffey Readers were introduced that included a series of five books of graduated difficulty. It was the first time vocabulary was controlled. Word families were taught such as *play, pray, bray* and *gray*. Articulation and correct pronunciation were stressed. Over a period of fifty years, 122 million McGuffey Readers were published (Kismaric and Heiferman, 1996).

By the middle of the 1800s Horace Mann was pleading for children to learn whole meaningful words first and for teachers to stop the drill of isolated letter-sound correspondence. (Sound familiar?)

The figures of Dick and Jane first appeared in the 1930 Elson Basic Reader preprimer. These readers used sight words first, which were to be recognized holistically and featured stories with a simplistic, highly controlled vocabulary. Dick, Jane, Sally, Spot, and Puff became part of Scott Foresman's New Basic Reading Program. "By the 1950s, 80 percent of the first-graders in the United States who were learning to read were growing up with Dick and Jane" (Kismaric and Heiferman, 1996, p. 21).

During the 1950s, prompted by Rudolph Flesch's book, *Why Johnny Can't Read*, which strongly advocated a phonics approach, educators began to reexamine what advantages phonics instruction might offer. Flesch provided the motivation. "There is a connection between phonics and democracy—a fundamental connection. Equal opportunity for all is one of the inalienable rights, and the word method interferes with that right" (Flesch as cited in Adams, 1991, p. 24).

It was time for a serious look into beginning reading methods and strategies. The U.S. Office of Education Cooperative Research Program in First-Grade Reading Instruction was a compilation of twenty-seven individual studies of various approaches to beginning reading reported by Bond and Dykstra in 1967. The studies were coordinated with common research questions, pretests, and outcome measures.

Over a period of fifty years, 122 million McGuffey Readers were published.

According to Bond and Dykstra's analyses, the approaches that, one way or another, included systematic phonic instruction consistently exceeded the straight basal programs in word recognition achievement scores. The approaches that included both systematic phonics and considerable emphasis on connected reading and meaning surpassed the basal-alone approaches on virtually all outcome measures. (The exceptions were in the speed and accuracy of oral reading for which there were no significant differences between approaches.) In addition, the data indicated that exercise in writing was a positive component of beginning reading instruction (Adams, 1991, p. 42).

No approach proved to be superior for students with higher or lower degrees of readiness. School, community, and teacher characteristics did not predict success, but certain student characteristics were strong predictors of end-of-the-year achievement. The best predictor was the student's ability to recognize and name uppercase and lowercase letters. This ability accounted for 25 to 36% of the variation despite the instructional approach. The next best predictors were the students' scores on an auditory phoneme discrimination task and a general intelligence test. Another important finding was that there were pupils who learned to read with thorough success and others who experienced difficulty within every instructional method studied.

Jeanne Chall confirmed the findings of the First Grade Studies in *Learning to Read: The Great Debate* published in 1967. Although the students taught by the look-say (sight word) method had an early advantage in rate and comprehension, students who were taught phonics caught up and surpassed the sight word group in rate, comprehension, and vocabulary by the end of second grade. The phonics group initially excelled in word recognition, especially in untaught words, and maintained their advantage. In addition, Chall found that systematic instruction in phonics, as compared to teaching sound-letter correspondence as the need arose, resulted in significantly better word recognition, better spelling, better vocabulary, and better reading comprehension at least through the third grade (Adams, 1991).

In a study supported by the U.S. Department of Education Cooperative Agreement with the Reading Research and Education Center at the University of Illinois, Marilyn Jager Adams concluded:

> [D]eep and thorough knowledge of letters, spelling patterns, and words, as well as the phonological translations of all three, are of inescapable importance to both skillful reading and its acquisition. By extension, instruction designed to develop students' sensitivity to

. . . approaches that . . . included systemic phonic instruction consistently exceeded the straight basal programs in word recognition achievement scores.

spellings and their relations to pronunciations should be of paramount importance in the development of skillful reading. This is, of course, precisely the goal of good phonics instruction (Adams, 1990, p. 117).

In the summer of 1998, a panel convened by the National Research Council recommended in a 344-page report on preventing reading difficulties in young children that "getting started in alphabetic reading depends critically on mapping the letters and spellings of words onto the speech units that they represent" (Snow, Burns, and Griffin, 1998, p. 7). The belief of the council is that words are recognized primarily by their letter-sound relationships. Context is a tool to monitor word recognition but is not a substitute for information provided by the letters in a word.

So the question does not seem to be is phonics necessary. Yes it is. Phonics is one of the major cueing systems in reading, which includes graphophonemic cues (phonics), context clues including semantic cues (does it fit with meaning of the text), and syntactic cues (does it fit into expected sentence structure), and sight words. Phonics is the principal way readers identify unknown words.

> The belief of the National Research Council is that words are recognized primarily by their letter-sound relationships.

How Does Word Recognition Develop?

Readers identify words through a combination of individual letter-sound correspondences, by analogy and patterns, by sight, and by context. Good readers use all of these strategies, switching from one to another as the need arises.

Students progress through distinctive stages of word recognition which are closely aligned to the stages of spelling. Children first learn some words by visual features such as the *M* in the arches of the McDonalds logo. However, when *McDonalds* is written in regular type, children at this stage are unable to recognize the word. This form of "reading" is memory intensive because there is no systematic link of spelling to pronunciation. As children move into reading, they shift from visual cues to phonetic cues (Ehri and Wilce, 1985).

Sound-Letter Correspondence

As children learn the alphabet and some sound-letter correspondences, they tend to select one or two salient letter-sound cues to identify a word. However, too many words are too similar for this strategy to be very effective for long. Students who notice only a few letters, who are unable to blend the sounds together to form recognizable words, or who guess from the context will not have a reliable or efficient enough system for rapid decoding (Gaskins, et al., 1997).

In the complete alphabetic stage, readers analyze all the letters in a word as a sequence of letters symbolizing the spoken sounds of words. Mature readers process virtually every letter of every word as they read, whether the word is isolated or in context (McConkie and Zola, as cited in Adams, 1990). Their eyes leap from word to word taking in about three letters to the left of center and six to the right.

Good readers also habitually translate spellings to sounds as they read (Barron, as cited in Adams, 1990). They silently pronounce the words (reading aloud in one's head) even though the word is instantly recognized. This is very useful for those words that are less frequently seen and end up being processed auditorily. The sounds remain in memory longer than visual images (Aaronson and Scarborough, as cited in Adams, 1990), and even expert readers resort to subvocalization with very difficult texts. If it sounds familiar, the meaning is accessed, and the word is known.

> **Good readers habitually translate spelling to sounds as they read.**

Patterns

However, successful decoding is not really done letter by letter. It is not so much individual letters that represent sounds but patterns of letters that represent units of sound. You probably pronounced *cloughts* in the "squitly tourmarands" sentence to rhyme with *bought* or *bough*. The last syllable in tourmarands probably sounded like *bands* and *sands*. *Blained* rhymed with *rained*. These nonsense words followed familiar patterns of letters.

Words are more often identified by pattern and analogy than by recalling rules for combinations of sounds. The patterns are learned first through analysis of the sounds and then by practice until the patterns become so well known, it seems as if the words are processed as a whole—as a sight word. Learning common letter patterns helps readers syllabicate. For example, the letters *dn* are not a common sequence so good readers know those letters will define a syllable boundary as in *midnight*.

Sight Words: The Stage of Automatic Decoding

Sight word reading is the principal way that familiar words are read (Gaskins et al., 1997), but this is not the same as learning words by their shape, or by some idiosyncratic characteristic, or even as a whole as in a

Chinese logogram. Words become sight words only when they have been thoroughly analyzed phonetically and when the written letters are bonded with their spoken identities through repeated practice. A scant 109 words account for 50% of what is encountered in children's textbooks (Carroll, Davies, and Richman as cited in Adams, 1990). They are encountered so frequently that once learned, they are accessed at a glance. As children read more and more text, even the less frequently encountered words become sight words.

It was once thought that children learned to read words by memorizing them as a whole—as "sight words"—but this is untrue. Beginning readers use letter-sound clues more effectively than visual clues, even if their knowledge is incomplete (Ehri and Wilce, 1985). As their phonetic knowledge increases, words can be more thoroughly analyzed and practiced until the entire unit can be dependably recognized and discriminated at a glance. "Whereas learning is essentially phonetic, recognition is essentially visual" (Ehri and Wilce, 1985, p. 176). Thus the word recognition sequence is visual, phonetic, and then visual again.

Students need substantial practice for words to be stored in memory and retrieved with ease. Reading connected text provides that practice.

Using the Context for Word Recognition

Fluent readers use context, both sentence level cues and meaning cues, to predict words and to confirm words more than to identify words. Context is never sufficient as a sole strategy to reliably identify unknown words. The kinds of words that can be predicted from context tend to be short, common words that children already know. The longer and less common words that carry the meaning of the passage are less likely to be predicted from context (Bruck and Treiman, 1992). Good readers also use context to decide on the meaning of a word with multiple definitions: The princess went to the ball versus Harry hit the ball.

When analyzing the mistakes of beginning and struggling readers, many of the errors are contextually appropriate. Struggling readers rely heavily on context only because their decoding skills are not sufficiently developed to provide enough phonetic clues (Stanovich, 1986).

A helpful exercise points out how context can help limit the choices for word identification. The teacher writes several sentences on the board

> **Words become sight words only when they have been thoroughly analyzed phonetically.**

and covers one word in each sentence with sticky notes. Children read the sentence and guess several words that would make sense in context. The guesses are written on the board, and then the first letter of the mystery word is uncovered. Guesses that did not start with that letter are erased. The remainder of the word is uncovered, and the word is confirmed (Cunningham et al., 1998).

Teachers who are aware of the stages of word recognition are more diagnostic than those who are not and can teach children word-identification strategies that are appropriate to their needs. Through learning sound-letter correspondences, learning common spelling patterns, developing sight words, and using context, children can learn automatic and efficient word recognition. Students need to become fluent with these strategies to be able to concentrate on meaning, which is never automatic and never without active attention and thought.

Fitting Phonics into a Balanced Reading Program

Teaching phonics first is like teaching batting to a child who has never seen a baseball game. He can learn to do it but can't figure out what it's good for (Stahl, 1992). Children first need to understand the "whole" concept of reading—that the black squiggles say something and say the same thing consistently, and that ideas and information can be transmitted through words that are interpreted by the reader. Early meaningful encounters with print include being read to, identifying logos, learning letter names, playing with magnetic letters, learning to write letters, and having dictated words written down by an adult. While many children come to school with these experiences, others encounter print for the first time in kindergarten when their teachers read books aloud. Or, they first encounter print by having their words written down on a language experience chart. When children understand the concept of reading, know the letters of the alphabet, and can segment and blend sounds, they usually make good progress in learning to read. Many reading programs blend these elements into early reading instruction.

The "parts" in the whole-parts-whole balance are the skills and strategies of reading, and they require explicit instruction to be thoroughly learned. Phonics is no exception. There is nothing natural about how sounds are represented in print. There is nothing intrinsic in the symbol *h* that gives

> **Teaching phonics first is like teaching batting to a child who has never seen a baseball game. He can learn to do it but can't figure out what it's good for.**

it an /h/ sound. In Spanish, *h* is silent and the /h/ sound is represented by the letter *j*. It is only through common convention that we have assigned certain speech sounds to certain symbols. Making these generalizations is not something easily picked up by five- and six-year-olds, even with repeated exposure to print.

"Classroom research shows that on the average, children who are taught phonics get off to a better start in learning to read than children who are not taught phonics" (Anderson et al., 1985). This is true through approximately the third grade and is especially apparent on tests of word identification. After word recognition skills have been attained, comprehension is better predicted by verbal fluency factors, prior knowledge, personal motivation, and reasoning ability.

A nationally commissioned report, *Becoming a Nation of Readers*, sums up the place of phonics. "The picture that emerges from the research is that phonics facilitates word identification and that fast, accurate word identification is a necessary but not sufficient condition for comprehension" (1985, pp. 37-38). What makes the condition sufficient is extended practice with real connected text, the last "whole" in whole-part-whole instruction. "The best way to get children to refine and extend their knowledge of letter-sound correspondences is through repeated opportunities to read" (Anderson et al., 1985, p. 38) Not only do children need to see that baseball game, they need to practice their batting in a game.

Thus, real text and phonics can and should be combined. Using literature and being immersed in print prior to and simultaneously with instruction in phonics is a hallmark of a balanced reading program. Beginning reading programs that use both phonics and connected reading make good sense.

This is never easy because the pace of phonics instruction, which seems excruciatingly slow, lags behind the word identification challenges of the readers (Adams, 1990). Thorough learning of phonics generalizations requires time until it is overlearned and thus automatic, but reading cannot be postponed. This is what makes first-grade reading so challenging and why it feels so haphazard. Many teachers spiral or repeat phonics lessons in a variety of settings because children are at varying instructional levels. In the same lesson, some are learning phonemic awareness, some are learning sound-letter correspondences, and some are learning to read the words used as examples. Everything eventually evens out, and

There is nothing natural about how sounds are represented in print.

children acquire the phonemic generalizations to meet word identification demands.

Stahl (1992) recommends an integrated reading program with at least half of the time devoted to reading connected text—stories, poems, plays, and trade books—with 25% or less of the time spent on phonics instruction. Cunningham (1998) recommends the four block approach—guided reading, self-selected reading, writing, and working with words—with each receiving about one fourth of the time allotted for reading class. These two recommendations are equivalent.

The biggest question is what is the most efficient way to teach phonics. Most of the debate centers around whether phonics should be taught directly or indirectly, not whether decoding is an important skill in beginning reading. Direct teaching refers to the explicit and systematic instruction of the sound-letter correspondences and of spelling patterns using decontextualized, direct instructional strategies. Indirect teaching occurs during shared or guided reading, or during writing experiences as the need occurs. A combined approach uses explicit instruction but draws the content for the lesson from literature. In reality, few classrooms use only one method exclusively, and the goal of any method is to apply what is learned to real reading.

Most of the debate centers around whether phonics should be taught directly or indirectly, not whether decoding is an important skill.

Direct Teaching

Direct teaching needs to be clear and explicit. This is not easy, especially at the very beginning, because whatever word part is taught, there will be some other part of the word that hasn't been learned. Nonetheless, most phonics programs start with consonants that have consistent sound-letter relationships and sounds that can be drawn out in isolation such as those for *f, m,* or *s.* The sounds for *l, n r, v,* and *z* are also dependable (Adams, 1991). The sounds for *b, d, p,* and *t* are difficult to make without adding a vowel sound so they usually come later. The letters *c* and *g* usually are studied much later because their sounds depend on adjacent letters. The idea is to establish the alphabetic principle, which is when certain letters are seen, they can be expected to consistently produce a specific sound.

Most programs start with two- or three-letter decodable words. Although English vowels have multiple sounds, they must be included, or there would be no words to study. Long vowels say their own names, which is an advantage, but they are not found in one consistent pattern. They can be found in at least three common patterns (represented as cvce, cvvc, and cv). Short vowels are more consistent but harder to learn. Phonics programs usually pick a limited number of short or long vowels and start there.

A common sequence for teaching phonics is listed below, but it is never as fixed or as sequential as the list suggests. It is, however, a developmental sequence, and it is helpful for the beginning teacher to know the categories and general order. Most phonics instruction should be completed by the end of second grade (Anderson et al., 1985).

1. Consonants in initial, final, and medial positions

2. Consonant digraphs: *ch, ph, sh, th, wh, -ck, -ng, -nk*

3. Short vowels

4. Long vowels, usually starting with words that end in silent *e*

5. Consonant clusters: *bl, gl, cl, fl, pl, sl, br, cr, dr, fr, gr, pr, tr, sc, sk, sm, sn, sp, squ, st, sw, nd, dw, tw, qu, scr, spl, spr, str, thr* (not necessarily in this order)

6. Vowel combinations: *ai, ea, oa, ee,* the *r*-controlled vowels, *aw, ou, oi, oo, oy, ow*

I met a very young primary teacher and asked her how she taught phonics. She said it was too difficult to keep track of the odd order in which the sounds were presented in the phonics program, so she just started in alphabetical order, with *a, b, c,* etc. She did not realize that she was starting instruction with mostly inconsistent letter-sound relationships that make it difficult for children to form generalizations. Vowels, such as *a,* are much harder to hear and identify and have short and long sounds as well as vowel combinations. The letter *c* represents the /k/ or /s/ sound so only *b* was consistent for the students of this young teacher. An experienced phonics teacher sequences instruction so that easy and dependable letter-sound correspondences are learned first and children come to understand there is a correspondence between letters and sounds.

Teaching the rules of phonics to children is problematic. Countless problems in instruction are generated by the complex language of rules and explanations. Try explaining to a six-year-old that phonics is the translation of letter sequences into their phonological correspondences. Although the explanations of many first-grade teachers may not be very satisfactory to a professor of linguistics, most teachers know how to simplify explanations. Some programs try to avoid confusion between letter sounds and letter names, and it does seem best to learn one or the other first. After that, say the letter, say the sound, use words that have the sound, and then relate the correspondence to words in print. This way the child is able to interrelate all of the parts (Stahl, 1992).

Most teachers have also learned that it works better to illustrate and practice rules than to tell and memorize them.

> . . . children cannot become skillful decoders by memorizing generalizations or rules . . . . Rules are useful only as far as they pertain to experience. Rules are intended to capture the patterns of spelling. But productive use of those patterns depends on relevant experience, not on rote memorization (Adams, 1990, p. 83).

The research on phonics rules says that almost all the rules apply between 40 and 85% of the time, and even those rules that are useful are not memorized but generalized. Rosso and Emans (as cited in May, 1998) gave students a list of fourteen words, each exemplifying a different phonetic rule. The children could identify an average of 75% of the words but could explain the rule for their correct pronunciation only 15% of the time. Generalizing rules through practice is more productive than memorizing phonics rules.

Most teachers have learned that it works better to illustrate and practice rules than to tell and memorize them.

Synthetic Teaching of Phonics: Sounds to Words

The synthetic method starts with letters and sounds in isolation, which are then blended into words. A sample lesson might be taught this way. The teacher writes *sh* on the board and tells the children that those letters stand for the /sh/ sound. Each child produces the sound. Then the teacher reviews other sounds from the targeted words: /p/, /l/, /t/, /i/, /e/, and /ee/. The children write *sh* on their papers. The teacher writes the letters-sounds to be blended on the board: sh-i-p, sh-e-ll, sh-u-t, sh-ee-p, and the children sound them out slowly and then blend them together more rapidly. After the teacher writes a whole word, the children write it on their papers, proceeding word by word through the process. The words can be used in sentences, other *sh* words can be brainstormed, or the children may do a word search finding *sh* words in other sources. This lesson is adapted from Frank May (1998). The synthetic method is explicit because the children are told the sound-letter correspondence and do not have to discover it by themselves.

To **blend sounds**, students can use alphabet tiles or letter cards placed a few inches apart from each other. To teach *met*, the letters *m e t* are separated and pushed together as the students say /mmm/ /eee/ /ttt/. The process is repeated several times, each time a little faster, until the word is pronounced normally. "Research indicates that teachers who spend more than average amounts of time on blending produce larger than average gains on first- and second-grade reading achievement tests" (Anderson et al., 1985, p. 39).

Word play is enjoyed by children and can help to strengthen sound-letter relationships. Jump rope rhymes offer many possibilities. *M, my name is Molly. My brother's name is Mike. We eat mustard,* and we live in *Moscow.* The geography part is a lesson in itself. Tongue twisters also emphasize initial sounds, as does the game is I Spy. "I spy with my little eye something beginning with *d*." Other children must then guess what has been spotted in the room that begins with the letter *d*. In addition, spoonerisms (i.e. beanut putter) are useful, as is teaching the students Pig Latin as a form of initial sound substitution.

> Word play is enjoyed by children and can help strengthen sound-letter relationships.

Sentences can then be devised, and patterns can also be pointed out in shared or guided reading. The object at this stage is to learn letter-sound correspondences and that this has application in connected reading.

During practice activities, teachers can use letter cards, magnetic or plastic letters, key words, key pictures, matching, sorting, games, charts, and writing. Children enjoy using individual lap chalk boards or dry erase boards for participating in practice activities.

Analytic Teaching of Phonics: Words to Sounds

The analytic method starts with words rather than isolated sounds. Some approaches use the words in context from the beginning, and some do not. The teacher selects a sound that the children are to learn and presents sentences with words containing the sound. The dominant mode is auditory as children listen for similar sounds in whole words. This sample lesson is adapted from May (1998).

Can Kate *please* come out to *play*?

The *plastic plane* was red.

The *plump* dog *plopped* down on his bed.

The teacher reads the sentences aloud and has the students echo read them. Next she reads the underlined words and has the children repeat them. She asks which sounds are the same in the words and which letters are the same so as to establish the sound-letter correspondence. The teacher can ask the students to produce the sound that /pl/ makes and think of other words that begin with /pl/. The children return to the sentences and choral read them followed by individual reading. The students then do a word search, looking through books to find and write other examples of /pl/ words. This lesson focused on just one particular sound. The following strategy analyzes all the sounds in a word.

Another analytic technique is **fully analyzing words**. It includes "stretching out the pronunciations of words to analyze constituent sounds in the words, analyzing the visual forms of words, talking about matches between sounds and letters (and grouping letters into chunks where necessary), noting similarities to sounds and letters in other words already learned, and remembering how to spell the words" (Gaskins et al., 1997, p. 319).

> **When students are guided with teacher modeling and support, they soon learn to replicate the process by themselves.**

C A N	W I L L	L O O K	S N A I L	S M A S H	P H O N E
c a n	w i l	l <u>oo</u> k	s n ā l	s m a <u>sh</u>	f ō n

The teaching of fully analyzed words can be done by modeling the process in a "talk-to-yourself chart" (Gaskins et al., 1997). When students are guided through the following process with teacher modeling and support, they soon learn to replicate the process by themselves.

1. The word is _____.

2. Stretch the word.   I hear ____ sounds.

3. I see ___ letters because _____.

4. The spelling pattern is _____.

5. This is what I know about the vowel. _____

6. Another word on the word wall like _____ is _____. They are alike because _____.

It sounds like this. The word is *red*, /rrr/, /eee/, /ddd/. I hear three sounds and see three letters so every letter has a sound. There is a vowel between two consonants. The vowel will sound /e/ because it's like *let*. They both have two consonants with a vowel in the middle so they both sound /e/. *Red* is like *not*. They both have three sounds and three letters.

As children learn to fully analyze a word, relating all the sounds to the letters, they begin to see the one-to-one correspondences and to see which sounds require two letters. *Back* has three sounds but four letters. *Head* has three sounds but four letters. They notice the consistencies as they compare words and also notice which words are irregular and how they are different from expected patterns.

It is only when words are fully analyzed phonetically that they will become true sight words. Sight words can be called upon as key words when new words with similar patterns are encountered. Without thorough analysis of all the letters in the word, children do not seem to recognize similar patterns and are unable to take advantage of word families. Students also need to consciously know that this information about analyzed key words is truly useful for reading and writing. If I know *stop*, then I can read *drop*.

> **It is only when words are fully analyzed phonetically that they will become true sight words.**

Partners can use the talk-to-yourself chart to work on new words. Comparing old and new words to words on the word wall (see below) reinforces the patterns.

The spelling part of fully analyzed words is done through **Elkonin boxes**, as in Figure 2.1. This activity also reinforces phonemic segmentation and sound-letter relationships. Students have worksheets that contain groups of boxes, each containing the same number of empty boxes as there are sounds. For *back*, there would be three boxes, *b-a-ck*. As the teacher stretches the sounds in the target word, the students write the letters. Clues are given about how many letters it takes to make a particular sound. For example, to make /k/ at the end of a word, two letters are needed (Gaskins et al., 1997).

Word walls are a display of high-frequency or key words listed above or below an alphabet chart. These words are thoroughly analyzed and can be used as key words for word families, or they are words that do not follow regular patterns, such as *have*. They can be easily seen and used for comparison to new words or for spelling. Usually no more than five words are added each week. With word walls, "Students practice new and old words daily by looking at them, saying them, clapping or snapping the letters, writing the words on paper, and self-correcting the words with the teacher" (Cunningham, Hall, and Defee, 1998).

When **making words**, children are given a set of six, seven, or eight letters that will eventually be combined into a big word, or a secret word.

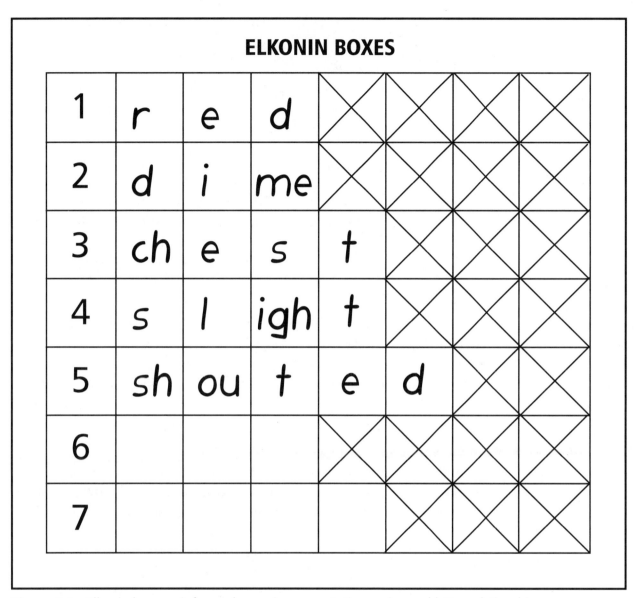

ELKONIN BOXES

1	r	e	d					
2	d	i	me					
3	ch	e	s	t				
4	s	l	igh	t				
5	sh	ou	t	e	d			
6								
7								

Figure 2.1 Elkonin boxes reinforce phonemic segmentation and sound-letter relationships.

The students start by making two-letter words and continue with three-, four-, five-letter words, and so on. "Making Words is an active, hands-on, manipulative activity in which children discover letter-sound relationships and learn how to look for patterns in words. They also learn that changing just one letter or even just the sequence of the letters changes the whole word" (Cunningham and Hall, 1994, p. 1). The vowels are a different color so children learn that they must include a vowel in every word.

be	sea	ball	balls	labels	baseball
as	all	bell	bells		
		sell	bales		
		seal	label		
		sale			
		bale			
		base			

After making a set of words from the given letters, vowel substitution practice can occur, sounds can be matched, or words can be sorted into patterns. This activity can be done individually or guided by the teacher with groups. Every child should have a set of letters to manipulate.

In **Ready-Set-Show** (Gaskins et al., 1997), students prepare four key-word cards that are copied from the board. These words are analyzed and placed face up on each student's desk. The teacher pronounces a word and the students stretch and analyze the sounds they hear. They then compare what they heard with their key words. When the teacher says, "Ready, set, show," each student holds up his card that contains the word with the same sound(s), which can be beginning or ending sounds, vowel matches, or pattern matches depending on the maturity of the students. The steps are repeated for approximately twelve words, providing students with practice in phonemic segmentation and sound-letter matching. An advantage to this technique is that every student is involved with each sound match.

Another helpful activity is called **What's in My Head?** In this game, the teacher gives clues about a certain word, and students attempt to guess the word from the clues. They can posit a guess after any clue. "The word begins with the same letter as the word _____. My word has ___ sounds. It has ____ letters. The vowel makes the same sound as you hear in _____. The spelling pattern is _____." Finally, a context sentence is given with the targeted word missing (Gaskins et al., 1997).

Phonograms, Word Families, and Analogies

Learning the sounds of common spelling patterns (-*ime, -ate, -uck*), alternate spellings for the same sounds (-*eat, -eet*), and alternate sounds for the same letter combinations (*fought, though*) is the second stage in phonics instruction. These patterns should be taught after students have a grounding in single sound-letter correspondences (Ehri and Robbins, 1992).

An excellent method for teaching patterns is through word families. Word families are also called phonograms or onsets and rimes. In the word *bank, b* is the onset and *-ank* is the rime. *Bank* is part of the word family *tank, sank, drank, rank, thank, blank, prank, flank,* and *spank.* The strategy of identifying new words by comparison to a known word in the family is called word recognition by analogy. Key words are often posted on a word wall so that new words in the family can be compared and decoded or spelled by rhyme and analogy.

Rimes are easy to learn, but unless all the sounds of the rime have been thoroughly analyzed, the rime may not have staying power in memory, and similar patterns will not easily be recognized by beginning readers (Gaskins et al., 1997; Bruck and Treiman, 1992).

Letter-sound correspondences in rimes are more dependable than sounding out words letter-by-letter, especially vowel sounds. The combination *ea* has multiple sounds but is regular in all rimes except *-ead, -eaf,* and *-ear.* "Of the 286 phonograms that appear in primary grade texts, 95% of them were pronounced the same in every word in which they appeared" (Stahl, 1992, p. 623).

R. E. Wylie and D. D. Durrell (as cited in May, 1998) found that only 37 rimes were necessary to generate 500 words frequently used by children and that it was easier for children to identify rimes or word families than it was for them to learn individual vowel sounds because patterns are easier to learn than rules. That list of 37 rimes and another longer list of less common rimes can be found in the spelling chapter. Wylie and Durrell found other interesting characteristics about learning word families.

1. The long vowel families (*-ail, -ine, -oke*) are as easy to learn as the short vowel families (*-ap, -og, -et*).

2. Double vowel words (vowel digraphs *-eal, -eed, -ail*) are as easy to learn as long vowel words with a silent *e* (*-ame, -ive, -ope*).

3. The odd vowel combinations (*-ou, -ar, -all, -aw*) are a little harder to learn than regular long and short vowel families but not so much harder that they should be postponed. [These sounds are also harder because there are multiple pronunciations for the same word, as in *route, roof,* or *root.*]

4. Those word families that end with a single consonant (*-ap, -it*) are easier to learn than the word families that end with consonant blends (*-ump, -ank*).

An excellent method for teaching spelling patterns is through word families.

Of course, many of the most common words do not follow the patterns: *go, so*, and *to, do; gave, save, brave* and *have*; and *maid, paid*, and *said*. Those words need to be taught as sight words or as infrequent patterns. Still, patterns are common enough that children benefit from learning word families when decoding both single syllable and multiple syllable words.

In **rhyming word sorts**, several words from three or four word families are listed in random order on the top of a worksheet or pocket chart. Key words are already in place at the tops of columns. Children must sort the words according to their spelling patterns. The words are pronounced by the analogy strategy. "If this is (the key word at the top of the list), then this is (the word to which the teacher points)" (Gaskins et al., 1997).

Any phonogram found in a story can be the starting point for word-family **sliding pockets**. A sleeve can be made from construction paper or a manila folder that is open at both the top and bottom. The word family rime (-*ink*) is written on the outside next to a hole that has been cut in the sleeve, which will reveal the different onsets. A piece of paper can be fit inside the sleeve with the onsets *p, m, dr, l, r, st, s, th*, and *w* written in a column. They can be pronounced, written, spelled, and used in context.

Children love **word games with rhymes**. Find a copy of the 1960s song "The Name Game," or use hink pinks. An example of a hink pink is: What is a chubby kitty called? A fat cat.

Books of poems and **pattern books** that are filled with rhymes provide vivid oral language and enjoyable stories. The book *Pickles Have Pimples and Other Silly Statements* (Barrett, 1986) is filled with couplets like this: Ice creams have cones, skeletons have bones.

A delightful learning activity can be based on Brown's *Good Night Moon* (1947). The story tells of several characters saying good night and follows a pattern of rhymes. L. M. Morrow and D. H. Tracey (1997) cite a classroom adaptation of the book. An excerpt follows.

> There were three big crickets, sitting on tickets
> And two big frogs, sitting on logs.
> There were three gold fish, swimming in a dish
> And a bowl full of jello, and a bird that said "hello"...
> Good night crickets, good night tickets;
> Good night frogs, sitting on logs.

Common words that do not follow patterns need to be taught as sight words or as infrequent patterns.

Many other patterned or rhyming books can be used to teach word families or as models for writing with phonograms.

Vowels

Vowels are always a problem. They are harder to discriminate and remember than consonants yet no word study can be done without them. Key words and phonograms seem to be easier to remember than the vowel rules, which work only fairly well. Still, there are some patterns that are worthwhile to learn because words do frequently follow these patterns. Children who have had experience with phonograms are much more likely to be able to generalize and apply the vowel rules.

1. cvc or cvcc. The vowel is usually short (*top, sink*).

2. cvce. The vowel is usually long (*face*).

3. cvvc. The first vowel "does the talking" or is long (*mail*).

4. cv. The vowel sound is usually long (*he, no*).

5. Sometimes *y* and *w* act as vowels.

6. The sound of the vowel can be controlled by *r, l,* and *w* (*are, call, few*).

The difficult vowel combinations are *oi, ou, oo, oy, ow, ei, ie,* and the infamous *ough* as in *bough, though, through, hiccough,* and *cough*. These vowel combinations are best taught after other generalizations are established and are easiest to teach as phonograms. Cheryl Harding (1998), a speech and language pathologist, advises that teachers should not fear working with vowels in isolation, especially with children who are having a difficult time discriminating the sounds. Key words work well and she uses *Ed* for short *e* because the usual *elephant* and *egg* cause problems. The *l* makes it difficult to isolate the short sound of *e* and some children say *egg* with a long *a* sound.

More advanced primary students can do **vowel sorts**. Fifteen to twenty words encountered in reading that contain the same vowel can be gathered and sorted by the vowel sound. It usually turns out that there are two to three categories and an exception or two. This can be done with cards and a pocket chart or with pencil and paper. The good thing about sorting with sturdy cards is that the words can be resorted by parts of speech (a simplified version), syllables, or other word patterns.

Vowels are always a problem.

May (1998) recommends matching patterns across vowels so that *face, nice,* and *bone* are grouped together. (Words with *e* or *u* are uncommon in a silent *e* pattern.) Gaskins et al. (1997) recommend word play where the vowel is changed but the other letters must remain the same, such as *treat* to *trout.*

Syllables

Teaching children two rules of syllabication is sufficient: (1) Divide between consonants; and, (2) each syllable must have a vowel. Teaching eleven rules of syllabication and then matching words to the appropriate rule will produce little in the way of results. It is familiarity with spelling patterns that allows good readers to syllabicate unknown words, not learning a number of rules.

The time honored advice of looking for the small words within the big word works reasonably well but not as well as looking for phonograms, which hold together better as units. Finding the little words often leaves leftover letters. A wonderful way to play with syllables is the book *Marms in the Marmalade* (Morley, 1984). It is just filled with such sentences as: "Is a DENTist covered with DENTS? Does a CARpenter look like a CAR?"

Indirect or Informal Teaching of Phonics

There is considerable debate over what teaching phonics informally through literature means. Does it mean that sound-letter relationships are taught incidentally as the need arises, or does it mean that the content of explicit lessons is taken from literature (the combined approach)? Gay Fawcett, director of curriculum and instruction for the Summit County Ohio Education Service Center (as cited in Willis, 1995) states that whole language teachers do not teach phonics skills in a carefully sequenced hierarchy. Instead they allow the teaching of skills to emerge naturally from activities in which the class is engaged. Likewise, Dorothy Strickland, professor of reading at Rutgers University (as cited in Willis, 1995), believes when the reading process is repeated on a daily basis with a variety of texts, children begin to form generalizations about written language and internalize the rules.

However, the idea of incidental phonics teaching is a little wiggly and haphazard for many teachers, especially beginning teachers. Many teachers are unsure of exactly what to do to help those generalizations form. They are not sure when and how often to stop to analyze a word.

> It is familiarity with spelling patterns that allows good readers to syllabicate unknown words, not learning a number of rules.

Other experts disagree that sufficient phonics generalizations can be developed indirectly. Jeanne Chall (as cited in Willis, 1995), professor emerita of Harvard's Graduate School of Education and author of *Learning to Read: The Great Debate*, says that teachers must ensure that their pupils understand the phonetic system. Doing it solely in the context of literature with an entire class is merely incidental and inadequate. Linda Diamond and Sheila Mandel (1998) believe the indirect approach lacks precision, order, and clarity. Steven Stahl, professor of reading at the University of Georgia, "expresses skepticism that a whole language teacher can teach skills when the need arises in context, seizing the teachable moment" (Willis, 1995, p. 4).

Keeping track of what has "come up," how much repetition has occurred, and who knows what, is a formidable task of record keeping. There are also some sounds that are easier to learn than others, and if /tch/ happens to occur in early reading, it may not be the easiest place to start. Incidental phonics may be sufficient for children who have had wide exposure to print, understand intuitively the alphabetic principle, can segment sounds, and have a solid foundation in language. For those children without a substantial background, explicit instruction is better.

Some philosophies are a reaction to isolated, boring phonics worksheets that dominated primary reading in past decades, but phonics need not be isolated, boring, or precede connected text. In fact, phonics must be applied to text to be meaningful and to obtain sufficient practice.

Writing and Invented Spelling

Using writing and invented or developmental spelling as vehicles to focus students' attention on sound-symbol relationships is almost as uncontroversial as using incidental methods to teach phonics is controversial. The beneficial relationship between reading and writing has been understood for a long time. The comparative first-grade studies of the 1960s found that when writing was included as a component of beginning reading programs, the program had a high degree of success. Despite the strong relationship, including writing as a coordinated part of beginning reading has fallen in and out of favor. In current use, Cunningham's four block strategy includes writing as one-fourth of the total beginning reading program.

"Writing is a principal vehicle for developing word analysis skills" (Adams, 1991, p. 420). As students work to determine the written repre-

> **The beneficial relationship between reading and writing has been understood for a long time.**

sentation of a word, they are compelled to actively look for letter-sound correspondences.

Both writing words with standard spelling as part of formal practice and writing with invented spelling as a part of informal practice help children become more aware of letter-sound correspondences and patterns. As teachers give feedback to developing writers, the students approximate the standard spelling to a greater degree and solidify sound-symbol relationships.

The Combined Approach

Words that arise from meaningful contexts are more memorable.

L. M. Morrow and D. H. Tracey (1997) have used the term Combined Approach, which signifies that there is a sequential plan for explicit teaching of phonics, but the materials for teaching come from literature. They cite a lesson in which a teacher planned to focus on the consonant *p*. She read *The Pet Show* (Keats, 1972), *Peter Rabbit* (Potter, 1903), *Petunia* (Duvoisin, 1950), and *Katy No-Pockets* (Payne, 1972). In teaching the latter book, the teacher wore a pocket apron full of cards with words on them beginning with *p*, such as *pig, puppy, peacock*, and *panda*. The children sounded out the animal names, and the teacher wrote them on a chart. They wrote the letter *p* on a worksheet with pictures of the animals they had named. Then they found other *p* words to list on their worksheets and place in the pockets of the apron.

Diane Lapp and James Flood (1997, p. 699) also advocate contextualized instruction. "When phonics is taught devoid of books, children are asked to postpone their excitement for literacy . . . . Attitude and enthusiasm matter." Words that arise from meaningful contexts are more memorable (Moustafa, 1998).

Predictable books containing rhymes, such as Dr. Seuss books, are a natural source for decoding new words in families. The story is always read and discussed first. Selected word study follows when the story is reread. The rhyming words are listed on cards and placed in a pocket chart, and spelling and sounds are compared. Care needs to be taken, however, to use words that match in spelling and sound, such as *say, today,* and *away,* especially when children are first learning the pattern. *Sheets* and *seats* can also be noted, but one card can be dramatically torn and discarded because it does not match the spelling pattern of the day. P. M. Cunningham, D. P. Hall, and M. Defee (1998) recommend that children brainstorm other words that have the same pattern (*play, lay*), so that generalization and transfer of the pattern occur.

Phonics instruction that includes context, sentences, and whole text is not only more interesting, but children's identification of words improves with context. This is because they have additional cueing systems available, both syntactic and semantic, which help them predict and confirm words.

Matching Phonics Lessons to Text

Becoming a Nation of Readers advocates that "a high proportion of the words in the earliest selections children read should conform to the phonics they have already been taught. Otherwise they will not have enough opportunity to practice, extend, and refine their knowledge of letter-sound relationships" (Anderson et al., 1985, p. 47). However, this matching of the reading lesson to the phonics lesson is easier said than done. It is a balancing act to write books for beginning readers that are enjoyable and create enthusiasm, and use natural language, yet provide practice in sound-letter relationships that have been taught. It is this dual requirement that has made beginning reading so controversial for so many years.

> Phonics instruction that includes context, sentences, and whole text is not only more interesting, but children's identification of words improves with context.

In the past, one extreme was the Sullivan Readers, which devised a total match of targeted sounds to the text. To teach the short *a* sound, children read, "Dan can fan the man. Can Dan fan Nat? Dan can fan Nat. Can Dan fan a rat?" The correspondence was very high, but quality of the text was low. The text was actually more difficult to read because the content was contrived and the sentence patterns were unnatural. Going to the other extreme, some teachers have used a phonics book from one publisher and a basal or trade book from another and then started both of the books on page one and went forward. There was absolutely no connection between the phonics lessons and stories in the text. This was truly phonics in isolation and without application. Whole language advocates extolled books with predictable text. Beginning readers who start with predictable text do experience early success in "reading," but they often do not pay much attention to the print, which does not optimize word learning (Johnston, 1998).

> Where context is strong enough to allow quick and confident identification of the unfamiliar word, there is little incentive to pore over its spelling. And without studying the word's spelling, there is no opportunity for increasing its visual familiarity (Adams, 1991, p. 217).

In the middle position, some teachers are lucky enough to have a reading series that has coordinated the text and the phonics lessons and recommends corresponding trade books. However, many publishers decide to emphasize high-frequency words rather than words that are easily decoded. Anderson et al. (1985) cite two texts that could be read in first grade in approximately November.

"We have come, Grandma," said Ana.	Ray loads the boat.
"We have come to work with you."	He says, "I'll row."
"Come in," Grandma said.	Neal says, "We'll both row."
"Look in the book," said Grandma.	
"Mix this and this."	They leave, and Eve rides home alone.

Beginning readers who start with predictable text do experience early success in "reading," but they often do not pay much attention to the print.

The first text uses seventeen words of which only three to ten could be decoded entirely on the basis of letter-sound relationships, depending on one's definition of the rules. This program has chosen to start with high-frequency words. The second text has eighteen different words of which seventeen could be decoded entirely on the basis of sound relationships taught in the program. Neither story is very memorable, but then it is hard to write terrific stories with a limited vocabulary, whether that vocabulary is limited by high-frequency words or by reliable phonetic relationships.

Over the last decade, little books of twelve to sixteen pages have been published for beginning readers. The stories are simple, and the pictures help to carry the story line. They provide predictable elements with decodable text and basic sight words often featuring a key sound-letter correspondence. Oxford, Wright, Rigby, Sundance, Modern Curriculum Press, and Scholastic are some of the publishers. Several of the companies also have matching big books. The vocabulary from book to book in the series is not as repetitive as a basal so the children have to rely on their decoding abilities because the words are encountered less often.

However, most teachers use what they have to make as many matches as possible. Since children need a great deal of practice reading connected text to learn comprehension strategies and to solidify their word recognition skills, why not provide practice with stories that are memorable and make children want to read? Whatever the targeted letter-sound, it will probably come up several places in the story and the words and patterns can be noted. Certain trade books emphasize letters, and they make good books to read aloud, share, or use in small-group guided reading.

The teacher can also resequence the order of the phonics lessons to better match the stories being read. However the match is made, there must be application of the word recognition skills for the decoding process to be meaningful. Many phonics activities have been noted in this chapter. Now add to every paragraph, "and then children must apply this skill in connected text."

In determining which methods are used more often, it seems that elementary teachers are eminently practical and use a balanced approach. In a survey of 1,207 kindergarten through fifth-grade teachers, J. F. Baumann, et al. (1998, p. 641) found, "A majority of teachers embraced a balanced, eclectic approach to elementary reading instruction, blending phonics and holistic principles and practices." Specifically, 66% of the kindergarten through second-grade teachers used systematic instruction in synthetic phonics, 40% used analytic phonics, and 19% taught phonics on an as-needed basis. And, 67% of the kindergarten through second-grade teachers believed that instruction in phonics was essential, 32% thought it was important, and only 0.6% thought it was not important.

. . . it seems that elementary teachers are eminently practical and use a balanced approach.

In Morrow and Tracey's study (1997) of seventy-six preschool, kindergarten, first- and second-grade classrooms, they found that indirect methods (teaching sound-symbol relationships as they occurred in reading) were most often used in preschool classrooms. As children progressed through the grades, the instruction in phonics became more explicit.

Stahl and Miller (as cited in Stahl, 1992, p. 620) found whole-language programs to work well in kindergarten, but their effect was diminished in first grade where "more code-emphasis approaches seemed to produce better results." Morrow and Tracey attributed the low number of teachers using the combined approach to teachers being unaware of the method, choosing not to use it, or not making conscious decisions regarding the ways in which they teach phonics.

I would also add to the list that the time required to coordinate exciting and interesting books to explicit phonics lessons keeps many teachers from taking advantage of the best of both worlds. To provide a structured phonics program and to give kids the opportunity to apply their new skills in books that make them want to read is truly the balanced approach. Yet to find books that are exciting and motivating, to make sure they match the decoding skills being taught, and to not overwhelm the beginning reader is a balancing act. Trying to do all of these things well has created the debate about beginning reading instruction for more than a century.

Assessing Sound-Symbol Relationships

The first figure in the assessment chapter shows the BAF test, which uses a series of pseudowords to diagnose or test sound-symbol relationships. It is set up in categories of consonant letters, consonant digraphs, consonant clusters, and vowels. Although it is administered individually, a knowledgeable first or second grader can complete the test in about three minutes. It may not be authentic assessment, but it certainly is efficient and comprehensive. Because it is out of context and none is a sight word, the teacher knows that it is only the sound-letter correspondences that are being tested.

For a more informal assessment that uses context, try using *Good Zap, Little Grog* (Wilson, 1995). Young readers who know the system love the book, but those who only know sight words or are unsure of the sound-symbol relationships stumble through the text. The book is a good diagnostic tool that is fun for children to read.

> Zoodle oop, little Grog,
> give a hug; stretch and yawn
> The night moons are fading.
> There's shine on the lawn.

> In the dusk of the garden
> a wild fribbet humms,
> and all the blue zamblots
> are covered in flumms.

The objective of phonics instruction is to help children recognize words quickly and automatically so their cognitive energy can be spent on comprehension. The idea of merely sounding out words is only a partial view of the role of phonics. Children need to learn to recognize the patterns that are useful for both spelling and reading. A balanced approach combines immersing children in rich language by reading aloud to them and by providing them with a variety of texts, while explicitly and systematically teaching them the sound-symbol correspondences and connecting these to decodable texts. No wonder teaching first grade is such a challenging job!

To provide a structured phonics program and to give kids the opportunity to apply their new skills in books that make them want to read is truly the balanced approach.

Teaching and Learning Spelling

It is possible to spell a word correctly by chance,
or because someone prompts you,
but you are a scholar only if you spell it correctly
because you know how.

—ARISTOTLE

Spelling requires certain types of understandings in sequential stages, making it so developmental in nature that there has been relatively little controversy concerning good instruction. Spelling is not nearly as cognitively complex as reading. It is a skill of closer and closer approximation as new strategies are added to the student's spelling repertoire. In the first stages of learning to spell, children learn through discovery, experimentation, and instruction that posits that spelling is related to sound. Students learn predictable sound-symbol relationships simultaneously with beginning reading and writing activities. They also learn the broader concept that knowing how to spell is necessary to communicate in writing. In the later stages, when multiple strategies and finer discrimination are needed, students learn the complexities of spelling through explicit instruction and wide exposure to print, which serves as a model of conventional spelling. Spelling is applied whenever students write.

Spelling is not just a matter of simple memorization but a complex system that includes alphabet knowledge, sound-symbol relationships, visual memory, knowledge about common patterns and alternate patterns, and the peculiarities that the orthographic system uses to maintain sounds or alter sounds due to adjacent letters. Some words are spelled to retain the root word, despite their pronunciation, and others are spelled to reflect foreign derivation. There are also those words that defy any rational explanation at all, but, fortunately, there are not very many of them.

> **Spelling is a skill of closer and closer approximation as new strategies are added to the student's spelling repertoire.**

Stages of Spelling Development

J. Richard Gentry and Jean Gillet (1993, p. 21) have identified five successive stages in spelling that are "qualitatively different from the others and each indicative of a different mind set or cognitive awareness of how spelling works."

The Precommunicative Stage

Preschoolers start with scribble writing, which has no letters or symbols similar to letters, although several other aspects of writing-spelling in English are included. The children know that the scribbles "say something," and the scribbles are written in horizontal lines that, after a while, are written in a left-to-right direction.

Soon, children add letters or letter-like symbols. Some children naturally acquire these basic conventions if they have been lucky enough to grow up in a print-rich environment and have seen their parents reading newspapers and books and writing grocery lists and letters. They noticed the print on cereal boxes and logos of their favorite fast food restaurants and tried to reproduce those letters. The luckiest of children have had stories read to them and have seen and heard how print and speech are related. For students who have not had these experiences, their teacher may be their only model, and their first purposeful exposure to print may be in kindergarten.

As children begin to learn the letters of the alphabet, their spelling-writing takes on a new form. Symbols or numbers can be mixed in with uppercase and lowercase letters. To adults, it might look like a random collection of symbols usually with little or no spacing. The writer can often read it back immediately after it is written, but there is no pattern or correspondence to words or sounds. Some children use many letters while others use just a few that they have learned. Some start with marks that are similar to letters but are not accurate in directionality or form. However, this is the beginning of spelling: the realization that meaning is conveyed and words are written with a standard set of characters—the alphabet. This stage is typical of preschoolers from ages three to five.

The Semiphonic Stage

Semiphonic spellers make a huge leap in understanding when they grasp the alphabetic principle, the idea that a correspondence exists between letters and sounds. Children begin to spell by using the initial sound. An entire word may be represented with only one or two letters, perhaps representing the most significant sounds, but perhaps not.

> In the semiphonic stage, an entire word may be represented with only one or two letters, perhaps representing the most significant sounds, but perhaps not.

Consonant sounds are much easier to spell because most of the sounds are similar to the letter names. In general, learning letter names is extremely useful for beginning spellers, though the letters *g, q, w,* and *y* do not provide helpful sound hints from their names. Learning letter names is both a good predictor of early reading success and helpful in spelling. Vowels, the bane of the English language, are usually not included at this stage. As students progress through this stage, more and more of the sounds are represented by letters. Spellers at this stage are usually five- and six-year-olds.

The Phonetic Stage

In the phonetic stage, the sound-it-out strategy works best for children as they learn reasonably accurate letter representations of all the sounds.

Because they can quickly and phonetically spell any word in their speaking vocabulary, children can become prolific writers when they reach this stage. Phonetic spellers are usually six years old.

Their writing is quite readable. Ask any first-grade teacher if she can read "primary," which is almost like a predictable foreign language. She will answer, "Ys, I kan red pri-mr-e." Letters or letter groups that do not match conventional spelling are often written in predictable patterns because they are developmental patterns. Figure 3.1 shows typical phonetic spelling patterns.

Although these substitutions may look peculiar to adult readers, the reasoning is systematic and quite legitimate. Students will progress to the next stage when they learn that they must add other strategies besides sounding out in order to spell conventionally.

The Transitional Stage

At this stage, vowels appear in every syllable, vowels are connected to *l, m, n,* and *r,* and vowel sound alternative spellings (*ai, ee, a_e*) are learned, even if not always correctly applied. In some words, all the letters are present but in a rearranged order, as in *tlod* for *told,* or *gril* for *girl* and *Jhon* for *John.* Transitional spellers use correctly spelled words in greater abundance in their writing, especially if they read and write regularly. Typically, it is seven-, eight-, and nine-year-old children who are at the transitional stage.

> Students progress in the transitional stage when they stop relying on sound alone and realize that words must look right as well.

Students progress in the transitional stage when they stop relying on sound alone and realize that words must look right as well. Although English is basically a phonetic system, and sound is always the dominant feature of spelling, students must learn which representation of a sound is the standard spelling because there are several spelling alternatives that correspond to both consonant and vowel sounds. Which alternative is correct is just a matter of social convention, as in *go, know, load,* or *note.* Is the word *cake, caek,* or *kake*? The orthographic possibilities, however, are not endless. It is not likely to be *keik* (as in *weigh*) because that is uncommon. It is not going to be *cace, ceik,* or *kace* because *ce* has the /s/ sound, and it is not going to be *cayk* because *-ay* almost always occurs at the end of words. At this stage, students need to learn which are the possible alternatives, which ones are not possible, and eventually which one is correct.

SkyLight Training and Publishing Inc.

DEVELOPMENTAL SPELLING PATTERNS

Long vowels and short words are spelled by letter names.	oak	OK
	you	U
	are	R
Short vowels are spelled the closest to the letter names; thus, they seldom match conventional spelling.	bat	BUT
	bet	BAT
	bit	BET
	cot	CIT
	cut	COT
M or *n* before a consonant is dropped.	jump	JUP
	stamp	STAP
Vowels are dropped before *l, m, n,* or *r.*	atom	ATM
	open	OPN
	bird	BRD
The -*ed* endings are changed to *t* or just *d*.	stopped	STOPT
	timed	TIMD
Dr and *jr* sound the same.	dragon	JRAGON
Tr and *ch* sound the same.	truck	CHRUCK
D and *t* are confused as medial sounds.	ladder	LATER
	attitude	ADITUD

Figure 3.1   The above represent typical patterns used by early readers when spelling phonetically.

"Transitional spellers enter a developmental phase in which they need opportunities to look at words in specific and intent ways in order to internalize visual, and later semantic and etymological patterns" (Gentry and Gillet, 1993, p. 34). Conspicuous instruction of alternative patterns will help students become more aware of the possibilities.

The Conventional Stage

At the conventional stage, children have learned to integrate and apply several strategies, including regular and irregular sound-symbol relationships, visual memory, and alternate patterns. They are able to handle semantic demands, such as how to maintain the root word when adding endings. They know how to handle compounds, contractions, prefixes, suffixes, and double consonants in words such as *hopping*. They know how sound is affected by the position of a letter in a word, and they can differentiate many homophones, such as *they're*, *their*, and *there*. Typically, eight- and nine-year-olds are spelling at this stage.

Good spellers employ more strategies than poor spellers. The most common spelling strategy of poor spellers in fourth to sixth grade is phonetic analysis or sounding-out, while better spellers use a variety of strategies such as visual information, root words and affixes, and analogies to known words (Anderson as cited in Tompkins, 1997). Explicit instruction in multiple strategies is beneficial at this stage.

Good spellers are more likely to learn patterns than rules. Try these examples for pronunciation:

Metamere: Any of a longitudinal series of similar segments making up the body of a worm or crayfish.

Orpiment: Arsenic trisulfide having a lemon yellowish color that is used as a pigment.

Praenomen: In ancient Rome, a person's first name.

These three highly unusual words can be found in the dictionary. If you are unfamiliar with them, you probably pronounced them automatically by using analogy and pattern—not by recalling rules of spelling. For example, "set` a here" rhymes with *metamere*. The next word can be pronounced "oar` pi(t) meant," because the suffix *-ment* is familiar, and *or* is a real word. The prefix of *praenomen* can be pronounced like *Caesar*, and *-nomen* recalls the word *nomenclature*. Thus, teaching some rules may be helpful, but children and adults remember patterns better than rules. (See the Kathleen Brown study later in this chapter.)

As students progress toward expert spelling, they also learn historical or etymological demands, such as how to spell words derived from Latin or Greek (*psychology*) or words that keep their original foreign spelling (*llama, cello, trousseau*). Students continue to work on the exceptions and irregularities through eighth grade. According to a National Assessment of Educational Progress study, thirteen-year-olds can generally spell 97% of words correctly (Wilde, 1992).

Expert spellers have the ability to visually recall words. They can simply tell if a word looks right because they have the ability to retrieve the

Expert spellers can tell if a word looks right because they have the ability to retrieve the visual image.

visual image of the word from their memory. Poor spellers do not seem to have the visual coding mechanism that allows them to retrieve the image, and there is no evidence that it can be taught (Gentry and Gillet, 1993).

Teachers who understand the developmental nature of spelling can use that information to diagnose the work of their students. They can also choose appropriate strategies for helping students progress from stage to stage.

Should Spelling Be Taught Directly or Learned Indirectly?

Occasionally, the question arises as to whether spelling is worth teaching at all, because English is so irregular. However, it is not as irregular as might be thought. Frank May (1998, p. 195) states, "Nearly three-fourths of the time, English spelling follows regular patterns." Using Edward B. Fry's top 1,000 high-frequency words, the spelling pattern of vowel/single consonant words (rip) predicts the word's sound 86% of the time, short vowel/two consonants (risk) 89% of the time, long vowel/silent e (ripe) 81% of the time, double vowel (rain) 77%, and consonant/long vowel (go) 77%. The irregulars get so much attention that it is forgotten that most of the language is regular. Since spelling patterns in English are generally predictable, the teaching of spelling is worthwhile and necessary for clarity in written communication.

English has thousands of words. They can't all be taught, but just 100 words account for 50% of the words used in children's writing, 1,000 words account for 89%, 2,000 words for 95%, and 3,000 for 97% (Hillrich as cited in Murphy, 1997). If students are taught just 1,000 words, they could spell correctly 89% of the time, which is a good return on the teacher's and child's investments in the study of spelling.

Sandra Wilde (1992) takes a workable approach to teaching spelling directly and indirectly. She believes children informally learn to spell words with predictable patterns. All the consonant sound-symbol correlations that have consistent relationships, and most prefixes and suffixes, can be learned by reading and by writing with invented spelling. These generalizations come quickly and easily to students who are surrounded by print and who are given many opportunities to experiment on their own. Other words that are extremely low frequency, historical, or simply arbitrary are not worth spending much time on, according to Wilde.

> Since spelling patterns in English are generally predictable, the teaching of spelling is worthwhile and necessary for clarity in written communication.

ALTERNATE SPELLING PATTERNS FOR SOUNDS

Consonant Sound	Example					
/ch/	chew	watch				
/h/	he	who				
/j/	joy	gene	badge			
/k/	key	cap	lock	quill	hiccup	chord
/s/	sigh	kiss	cent	scissors		
/z/	zoo	buzz	as			
/zh/	beige	usual				

Figure 3.2

Consonant sounds that are inconsistent need to be taught. The spelling of the sound depends on its location within the word or on the adjacent letters. See Figure 3.2.

Short vowels, inconsistent consonant sounds, double consonants, silent letters, spelling variants of the same sound, orthographic patterns for adding prefixes or suffixes (dropping the final *e* before adding certain suffixes), and high-frequency words do need to be taught.

One example of a spelling pattern that needs to be taught is consonant sounds that are inconsistent, Figure 3.2. The spelling of the sound depends on its location within the word or depends on adjacent letters.

As I read the spelling research, a pair of very nontechnical terms occurred to me—the noticers and the non-noticers. Some students, as they read, notice all the patterns and all the irregularities. They seem intrigued by language and patterns and constantly compare their current notions with standard print. On the other hand, there are the non-noticers, students who may be bright and talented but never seem to notice the differences between their concepts and standard English conventions. Immersion in print-rich environments makes a difference, but they just don't pick up the nuances. Bringing the details to their attention makes a big difference.

I recently learned an excellent example of using a pattern to determine correct spelling. I have always struggled with words that end in -*able* and -*ible*. I never knew when to use which suffix. Sandra Wilde (1992) taught me the difference in twenty seconds. Words that end in -*able* include the following: workable, reliable, laughable, and remarkable. Words that end in *-ible* include: visible, possible, edible, and legible. Do you notice any pattern? Words ending with *-able* are usually those in which the root is "able" to stand on its own, although there are a few exceptions. I have three college degrees, I read voraciously, and I have been immersed in print all my life, but this simple pattern escaped my notice. Direct and explicit teaching is a huge help for non-noticers.

Kathleen Brown, Gale Sinatra, and Janiel Wagstaff (1996) also found that direct instruction helped non-noticers. Second graders were taught dozens of common rimes (*-ent, -at, -ight, -tion*) both explicitly and holistically throughout the school year. The researchers wanted to teach students to recognize and to spell particular words, but they also hoped that students would be able to notice patterns so they could identify and spell unfamiliar words. They took samples of students' writing at the beginning, middle, and end of the year to ascertain how often students were using spelling patterns in unfamiliar words that were analogous to patterns they had been taught.

High-achieving students were able to transfer the instructed pattern to new words 97% of the time by the end of the year. Low-achieving students were able to do it 87% of the time, nearly equaling their higher achieving peers. However, with rimes that had not been taught, it was a different story. High-achieving students were able to transfer spelling patterns of noninstructed rimes to new words 47% of the time by the end of the year, whereas low-achieving students were able to do it only 7% of the time. The non-noticers always benefit the most from direct instruction.

Activities to Encourage or Teach Spelling

The best way for young students to learn beginning spelling is through writing. Writing also happens to be the sole reason why anyone learns to spell. Invented spelling does not teach students how to spell correctly, but it does give them the underpinnings for spelling. It establishes the basic phonetic principles. As students experiment with representation of sounds in the words they write, they analyze and ponder, becoming totally involved in figuring out relationships. The words with which they practice are their words.

Invented, inventive, developmental, or approximated spelling frees young writers from being bound by absolute correctness. Invented spelling helps

> **Direct and explicit teaching is a huge help for non-noticers.**

to make children "noticers." S. S. Robinson (as cited in May, 1998) found that children's invented spelling was the best predictor of subsequent early reading success, perhaps because spelling strengthens children's phonemic awareness as they listen closely for sounds to give them clues about which letters to write. They also begin to generate hypotheses about how the general spelling-reading-writing system works. Invented spelling also allows writers to write fast enough so that the content can be remembered.

Young spellers need daily writing opportunities. They can write about their weekends, their families, or about a class project. They can write birthday cards, messages to their classmates, or stories about seasons or holidays. Students can write about the content they are learning or personal experiences. Since this type of writing is mostly practice and experimentation, it need not be graded.

Remember, however, that invented spelling is just the first step in a developmental process. Students need to become comfortable with the alphabetic principle—the idea that letters and sounds have a generally consistent relationship. The student's job is to move along on the continuum toward conventional spelling.

The teacher provides the encouragement to do that as she moves around the room asking questions, helping a student relate a sound to a letter, or perhaps having the child listen for a medial sound (the one in the middle), which is harder to identify. As students become more proficient at the basic relationships, the teacher may identify a vowel, help the child remember a high-frequency word he has seen in print, or compare a word in the child's writing to a word on a chart on the wall. It is an art to nudge a child to move along the developmental scale at just the right time, adding only those elements to the child's spelling for which he is ready. This is why it is essential that teachers understand how spelling and phonetic knowledge normally develop, and which parts will be learned informally and which parts need instruction.

A teacher is not offending a child's individuality when helping him to become a more proficient speller. Adding knowledge for the next stage of spelling is very different than marking every error in red and insisting on spelling perfection.

As young writers become more fluent through invented spelling, they also need to learn that there are other stages in the writing process—revising

> **Students need to become comfortable with the alphabetic principle—the idea that letters and sounds have a generally consistent relationship.**

and editing. Even young writers have to consider the reader. Wilde (1992) recommends that students go back and circle three words that might not be right. Students can confer with classmates, look at word walls and charts, and begin considering alternate patterns for the same sounds.

Learning Spelling Through Reading

Young spellers learn many words through wide reading. Even if children were exposed to a formal spelling program with twenty words every week from first grade to eighth grade, it would total only 5,760 words. Wilde (1992) estimates that the average literate adult can spell 80,000 words. The remainder are learned by sight, through reading, or by analogy. All the words ever needed cannot possibly be taught, but that does not mean it is not worthwhile to teach patterns and some specific words.

The average literate adult can spell 80,000 words.

Matching Sounds to Letters

Activities for beginning spellers are indistinguishable from phonics activities. In reading, students see letters and work out the sound. In spelling, students have the sound and work out the letters. One supports the other.

In **Matching Sounds**, students can match words with the initial sound of the teacher's word, or the teacher can match the sound of a student's word. Sometimes, it is fun for the teacher to respond and allow the student to decide if the teacher's response matched or not.

For **Letters and Words**, select a consonant that is being studied, write the letter on the board, and have students generate words that start with the sound. As the words are written, emphasize the beginning sound. Ask students to come to the board and underline the beginning letter and say the word. Later on, words that end with that sound and words that have the sound in the middle can be added.

Word Sorts

In a word sort, words are written on individual cards or paper strips. The words are then sorted or classified into categories. Word sorting is effective because it is manipulative and flexible (Zutell, 1998). Students can change their minds as they move the cards around as they see patterns and contrasts. They are actively engaged in problem solving, making generalizations, and discovering relationships in word sorts (Fresch and Wheaton, 1997).

If students make their own categories, it is an open sort, but if the categories are identified by the teacher, it is a closed sort. A set of cards may be developed to explore a single spelling issue, or a larger set of cards can be used for multiple sorts. A pocket chart works well so that all students can see the cards, and they are securely held in place. Although word sorts can be used at all developmental levels of spelling, those for beginning spellers should concentrate on beginning and ending consonants, blends, and then vowels when students reach the phonetic stage and are including all the sounds that they hear. Sorting actually works better for contrasting patterns and for discriminating the usual sound from an alternate sound.

Human Letters

Each child is randomly given a large individual letter that is part of a word such as *friend*. The teacher asks those children who are part of the word *in* to step forward; then those who are part of the word *end*, then *rid*, and finally *friend*. This idea also works well with a sentence strip that has been cut into individual words. If the sentence is from a book the children have read, they are more likely to see the application of the activity.

In each of the preceding activities, be sure to have children discuss their reasoning. Learning is a social process, and verbalization helps bring the concept formation to the conscious level. The right spelling is just the end product. The process of reaching the generalization is the real work.

Word Walls

Many teachers use word walls, or large charts of words, for references that can be accessed at a glance. The word wall might be organized alphabetically, by word families, or by topic. No one at any age likes to pull out the dictionary constantly, but children will gladly check a spelling on a chart that the teacher has prepared or that the class has developed. Some teachers like to prepare a laminated copy of the 100 most frequently used words (Horn, as cited in Tompkins, 1997, p. 115) for each student to keep at his desk (Figure 3.3). The more accessible the list, chart, or word wall, the greater the likelihood that it will be used. The 100 most frequently used words make up more than 50% of all the words children and adults use to write; therefore, it is a very handy list.

The correct spelling is just the end product. The process of reaching the generalization is the real work.

THE 100 MOST FREQUENTLY USED WORDS

a	about	after	all	am	an
and	are	around	as	at	back
be	because	but	by	came	can
could	day	did	didn't	do	don't
down	for	from	get	got	had
have	he	her	him	his	home
house	how	I	if	in	into
is	it	just	know	like	little
man	me	mother	my	no	not
now	of	on	one	or	our
out	over	people	put	said	saw
school	see	she	so	some	that
the	them	then	there	they	things
think	this	time	to	too	two
up	us	very	was	we	well
went	were	what	when	who	will
with	would	you	your		

Figure 3.3   From Horn, as cited in *Literacy for the 21st Century* by C. E. Tomkins.

The spelling words that are often posted on word walls are sight words in reading because they are phonetically irregular. The common but irregular words listed in Figure 3.4 are from Edward Fry's list of the top 240 high-frequency words. Most of these words continue to give students trouble through the middle grades. They may be learned by continuous exposure to reading because they are such high-frequency words, but explicit spelling instruction also helps.

Techniques for Transitional Spellers

Transitional spellers have conquered the basic sound-symbol relationships. Now they need to learn the alternate representations of the sounds

COMMON BUT IRREGULAR WORDS

of	they	one
some	could	people
great	because	does
know	again	own
come	though	answer
thought		

Figure 3.4

Teaching children to spell through analogies is a very powerful technique.

and the orthographic regulations. This kind of work requires finer discrimination, greater visual memory, and more specific instruction.

Wide Reading and Writing

Reading and writing continue to be immensely important for providing the information to build word concepts. Building concepts about word structure provides the intellectual glue necessary for words to stick in memory and be recognized in reading and produced in spelling (Zutell, 1998).

Alternate Spellings

Figure 3.5 lists the alternate spellings of all the consonants and vowels. They are considerable. Trying to teach these letters and sounds in isolation has given spelling a bad name. A much more reasonable, efficient way is to study word families and spelling by analogy.

Spelling by Analogy, Word Families, Onsets and Rimes, and Phonograms

Teaching children to spell (or read) vowel sounds and rhyming word segments through analogies is a very powerful technique that resurfaced in the 1930s, 1940s, 1970s, and 1990s, supported by practitioners' and researchers' beliefs. Some teachers may be more familiar with the terms "word families," "onsets and rimes," or "phonograms." One can quibble about nuances in definitions, but they are all similar in classroom usage.

ALTERNATE SPELLING PATTERNS FOR SOUNDS

Sound	Spellings	Examples	Sound	Spellings	Examples
long a	a-e	date	m	m	man
	a	angel		me	come
	ai	aid		mm	comment
	ay	day	n	n	no
ch	ch	church		ne	done
	t (u)	picture	long o	o	go
	tch	watch		o-e	note
	ti	question		ow	own
long e	ea	each		oa	load
	ee	feel	short o	o	office
	e	evil		a	all
	e-e	these		au	author
	ea-e	breathe		aw	saw
short e	e	end	oi	oi	oil
	ea	head		oy	boy
f	f	feel	long oo	u	cruel
	ff	sheriff		oo	noon
	ph	photograph		u-e	rule
j	ge	strange		o-e	lose
	g	general		ue	blue
	j	job		o	to
	dge	bridge		ou	group
k	c	call	short oo	oo	book
	k	keep		u	put
	x	expect, luxury		ou	could
	ck	black		o	woman
	qu	quite, bouquet	ou	ou	out
l	l	last		ow	cow
	ll	allow	s	s	sick
	le	automobile		ce	office

Figure 3.5 Alternate spellings of consonants and vowels. From *Literacy for the 21st Century: A Balanced Approach* by Gail Tompkins ©1997. Reprinted by permission of Prentice-Hall, Inc.

ALTERNATE SPELLING PATTERNS FOR SOUNDS

Sound	Spellings	Examples	Sound	Spellings	Examples
	c	city		i	onion
	ss	class		ue	value
	se	else		ew	few
	x (ks)	box	z	s	present
sh	ti	attention		se	applause
	sh	she		ze	gauze
	ci	ancient	syllabic l	le	able
	ssi	admission		al	animal
t	t	teacher		el	cancel
	te	definite		il	civil
	ed	furnished	syllabic n	en	written
	tt	attend		on	lesson
long u	u	union		an	important
	u-e	use		in	cousin
	ue	value	contractions		didn't
	ew	few		ain	certain
short u	u	ugly	r-controlled	er	her
	o	company		ur	church
	ou	country		ir	first
y	u	union		or	world
	u-e	use		ear	heard
	y	yes		our	courage

Figure 3.5   (continued)

The idea is that when a child learns one member of the family, she learns them all. They are also highly efficient for teaching vowel sounds.

To demonstrate the effectiveness of learning vowel sounds through word families, try to pronounce the vowel sounds in the following syllables: *ma, ma, di, di, sa, soa*. Now try the following: *ad, ade, im, ime, ap, oap*. Which was more helpful for reading or spelling the words *mad, made, dim, dime, sap, soap*? Onsets and rhymes are relatively easy to remember and splice back together (Adams, 1990). Word families are actually easier to remember than individual sounds.

SkyLight Training and Publishing Inc.

P. Bryant and U. Goswami (cited in Peterson and Haines, 1998) studied orthographic analogies and found that even beginning readers were able to make the inferences between known and unknown words. Ending rimes were the easiest to transfer to unknown words, but students could also make analogies about other words that started with the same first three letters, such as *beak* and *bean*.

In a famous 1970 study with 900 children, R. E. Wylie and D. D. Durrell (as cited in May, 1998) found that only 37 rimes are needed to generate 500 words frequently used by children in first through third grade. These common rimes and other less common but useful rimes are listed in the chart below.

Vowels, which are the scourge of spelling, are so difficult in English because there are sixteen vowel sounds but only five vowel letters, with a little help from *y* and *w*. Phonograms, onsets and rimes, spelling by analogy, and word families make up a rich strategy for learning to spell

WYLIE AND DURRELL'S RIMES TO GENERATE 500 WORDS

ack	ail	aim	ake	ale	ame	an	ank	ap	ash	at
ate	aw	ay	eat	ell	est	ice	ick	ide	ight	ill
in	ine	ing	ink	ip	it	ock	oke	op	ore	ot
uck	ug	ump	unk							

Less Common Rimes and Useful Endings

ace	ad	ade	age	ail	ait	al	all	am	and	ance
are	art	as	ask	aw	azy	eak	eam	ean	ear	eck
ed	een	eep	eet	em	en	end	er	et	ew	ib
ice	id	igh	ile	im	ime	imp	is	ish	ive	old
og	on	one	ong	ony	ood	ook	ool	orn	ose	ough
ould	ound	own	ub	ue	un	up	ut			
ed	ing	ie	ly	tion	y					

Figure 3.6 From R. E. Wylie and D. D. Durrell, as cited in *Reading as Communication* by Frank May.

ornery vowel sounds, for learning multiple words from a single lesson, and for developing a strategy that can be applied over and over again independently.

Hinky Pinkies

For sheer fun and language manipulation when studying word families, students can make up hinky pinkies. Hink pinks are a pair of one-syllable words that rhyme, hinky pinkies are a pair of two-syllable words that rhyme, and hinkity pinkities are a pair of three-syllable words that rhyme. They are structured into riddles. Developing riddles with the same spelling pattern is a real challenge. This can be an opportunity to study alternative spellings for rhyming words.

> What do you call a glass of Hawaiian Punch? A pink drink.
>
> What do you call a chubby cat? A flabby tabby.
>
> What disease describes high school seniors as they apply to college? Admission condition.

DSTA

A particularly good activity for learning spelling alternatives is Jerry Zutell's (1996) Directed Spelling Thinking Activity, or DSTA. It is patterned after Russell Stauffer's DRTA (see chapter 6). In a DSTA, students who are using but confusing a word pattern are given a pretest of sixteen to twenty words, which includes words from two or three contrasting patterns and a few exceptions. They might be consonant alternatives for /f/, such as *feet, laugh, sheriff*, and *graph*, or they could be vowel alternatives for long /a/, such as *raid, made*, and *say*. The words should all be in the students' speaking and reading vocabularies.

The group members then share their initial attempts and discuss their strategies and reasoning in attempting to spell the words. As students discuss the possible answers, they are actively engaged in discovering and thinking through the possibilities. Students may notice patterns or similarities and revise remaining words on the list. Only after discussion and a group prediction does the teacher present the correct spelling.

DSTA allows for active participation, concept development, and social learning, and it promotes attention to detail. It is also fun and a vivid contrast to many rote and dull spelling exercises.

Vowels are so difficult in English because there are sixteen vowel sounds but only five vowel letters.

Word Sorts at the Transitional Stage

Word sorts allow for active manipulation rather than memorization. They seem more appropriate at the transitional stage in spelling than at the earlier stages because the discriminations are of a finer nature. The word sort is an excellent tool for noticing small differences or close alternatives.

Sets of word cards can be prepared on index cards, sticky notes, or small slips of paper. The sturdier varieties once prepared can be used from year to year if labeled and kept in small sandwich bags. The teacher can set up category words at the top of each column, or students can decide on their own what the categories are. The rule of "used but confused" is helpful for deciding on the words. *Mad, made, bad, had, lad, pad, sad*, and *fade* would make a good beginning. While *glade, jade, wade*, and *spade* fit the rule, these words are less likely to be known and *wad* just doesn't fit at all. Adding *stayed, maid, played, laid*, and *paid* would make it more challenging for better spellers. Students must explain what the rule is and why each word fits in the category. This isn't quite as effective as DSTA because some children will sort by visual features unless they are required to pronounce and develop the rule.

> Word sorts seem more appropriate at the transitional stage because the discriminations are of a finer nature.

Spelling Rules and Orthographic Demands

Wilde (1992) cites Wheat's 1932 discovery that there are only four spelling rules consistent enough to be worth teaching.

1. When a word ends in a single vowel and single consonant, double the consonant before adding *-ed* or *-ing* if the word is monosyllabic or has stress on the final syllable.

2. When a word ends in a consonant and *y*, change the *y* to *i* before adding most suffixes except for those beginning with *i*.

3. When a word ends in a silent final *e*, drop the *e* before adding suffixes starting with a vowel. Dropping the *e* before *-ed* is intuitive and probably doesn't need to be taught.

4. Use *i* before *e*, except after *c*, or when sounded as *a* in *neighbor* and *weigh*, or in weird words such as *their*.

Memorizing for Visual Demands

Some spelling demons just need to be memorized. Gentry and Gillet (1993) gives the example of *carrot, karat, carat*, and *caret*. Sound-symbol, roots and meanings, and English orthographic patterns are of no help here. If assistance is needed, the four are the vegetable, the gem stone weight, the purity of gold, and the insert editing mark. When dealing with spelling demons, rote practice still works. Nancy Murphy (1997) claims the look-say-write method was first developed by E. Horn in 1919.

1. Look at the word and say it to yourself.
2. Close your eyes and try to see the word as you spell it to yourself.
3. Check to see if you were right.
4. Cover the word and write it.
5. Check to see if you were right.
6. Repeat steps 4 and 5 two more times.

Do not eliminate this strategy just because it is old and not structured like a game. The important thing is to have students write the words from memory, not just copy them. It may be one of the few activities that can strengthen visual memory. Because visual memory is so important, when students practice spelling words, they should write them rather than practice aloud (Matz, 1994).

Because visual memory is so important, when students practice spelling words, they should write them rather than practice aloud.

Multisensory Techniques

A multisensory technique is visual, auditory, kinesthetic, and tactile (VAKT), and it includes saying, writing, checking, and tracing the word, and then writing the word from memory. The belief supporting this technique is that students learn best when information is presented in different modalities. The method, originally developed by Grace Fernald in 1943, has been found to be successful with learning disabled students (Murphy, 1997). Murphy's study of third graders showed an 11% increase in correct spelling by students using the VAKT method as compared to students using traditional methods.

Text Resources

Students need to know how to use the dictionary to check spellings. Dictionaries come in an assortment of levels of difficulty from picture glossaries to college level. Having a selection of dictionaries helps to meet a variety of needs.

Semantic Demands

As children become conventional spellers, they need to learn the semantic demands of English spelling or those patterns that keep the meaning even though the sound or spelling changes. Although the meaning is constant, the sound changes in *sign, signal, design*, and *designate*. The real demons are those words in which the root changes, as in *wintry, forty*, and *curiosity*.

What About Spelling Tests?

Many teachers question the value of spelling tests from a spelling textbook because many of the words seem to be at an inappropriate level, or the correct spelling does not transfer to the student's everyday work.

One option is for students to select their own list for the week, usually ranging from five to ten words. They participate in spelling games, do group work on common patterns (there could actually be some), work with word families, rhyme, do dictionary activities, and proofread. Partners teach each other and record words they can spell in their personal spelling logs (Gentry and Gillet, 1993). While this sounds charming, it is a logistically difficult task and may ask more of children than they can manage.

A more balanced and manageable approach is for the teacher to have a base list of words of varying difficulty for the week. The words may be high-frequency words, words expected to be used in writing the following week, words from spelling textbooks, word families, words sharing a common visual pattern, words sharing a common pattern for prefixes or suffixes, or words from content areas. Content words are often developmentally inappropriate as spelling words so content-related words must be carefully chosen. Since children learn to spell by pattern rather than by word, lists that share a common feature are preferred. The anomalous sight words make great extra credit words. An excellent source for developing lists is Ed Henderson's *Teaching Spelling* (2nd edition, 1990, Boston: Houghton Mifflin), which includes an appendix of grade-level words categorized by patterns.

With the premise of a teacher-selected core list, there are several options. The teacher can select a core list that everyone must learn, there can be a core list and an optional list, there can be a core list and individually chosen words, or there can be optional words and individually chosen words. When students have different lists, the spelling test is given in partners. (There are some inherent problems with accuracy.)

A more balanced and manageable approach is for the teacher to have a base list of words of varying difficulty for the week.

The most workable plan that I have come across is an ingenious blend that includes self-choice, a range of difficulty, a way to eliminate studying known words, and an overall related list. It is from M. J. Fresch and A. Wheaton (1997). It starts with a pretest similar to the one in Figure 3.7. Students fold the paper along the dotted line and are given the pretest from words in the first column. For every word they spell correctly, students can choose a word from the second column. If the words in the pretest list are straightforward, inclusion students can be easily incorporated into the week's activity at an appropriate level. Children who consistently score above 80% can choose their own words, but they must be based on the pattern of the week. Students copy their list three times. List One goes home, List Two stays in school, and List Three can be cut apart for word-sorting activities.

For the list in Figure 3.7, small groups of children in my class did open word sorts for different types of plurals. They generated their own rules, and it didn't matter if all the students didn't have exactly the same words.

The small groups then gathered together to do a large sort modeled by the teacher as students added their insights and conclusions. This large sort was then added to the word wall.

The next day, students participated in a word hunt for about twenty minutes in which they searched their own reading materials for examples of this pattern. On the third day, students used their word list in writing. Fresch and Wheaton (1997, p. 28) suggest "These compositions [can] take on forms such as poetry, advertisements, riddles, limericks, and short stories . . . . The entire writing process is used as the texts are edited." The activities on the fourth day depended on the pattern and included editing, proofreading, dictionary work, compounds, letter scrambles, crosswords, or hidden words. Day five involved buddy testing.

In 1897, J.M. Rice wrote a journal article in *The Forum* entitled "The Futility of the Spelling Grind." If we use all that is known about teaching and learning spelling, perhaps at the close of this century, Rice's thoughts will no longer hold true.

If the words in the pretest list are straightforward, inclusion students can be easily incorporated into the week's activity.

SPELLING LIST

Pretest List	List From Which To Select
cones	studies
hunters	predators
desks	chairs
babies	ladies
berries	blueberries
puppies	guppies
bushes	airplanes
bunches	animals
branches	paintbrushes
inches	miles
taxes	penalties
classes	churches
dishes	radishes
watches	lunchboxes

_____
_____
_____
_____
_____
_____
_____
_____
_____
_____
_____
_____
_____
_____

Figure 3.7 From "Sort, Search, and Discover" by M. J. Fresch and A. Wheaton, *The Reading Teacher* 51, 1997.

Emergent Readers and Writers

Dear little child, this little book
Is less a primer than a key
To sunder gates where wonder waits
Your "Open Sesame!"

—RUPERT HUGHES

Learning how to read seems to happen in a moment of magic: One day a student does not know how to read, the next day he does. Although it may seem that way, learning to read and understanding what reading means actually happens over an extended period of time. Linda Teran Strommen and Barbara Fowles Mates (1997) conducted a three-year longitudinal study to explore young children's ideas about reading. Although the children reached the various stages at different ages, the progression of increased understanding of reading concepts was similar in all children.

A three-year-old's concept of reading does not match conventional concepts of what it means to read. In Strommen and Mates' study, the first idea developed by some of the readers was that reading is one aspect of a social routine. "We take a bath in the shower, and then we go to bed. We read the story, then when my light is off, I call Daddy," noted one three-year-old in the study (Strommen and Mates, p. 100). Reading is not yet a distinctive activity that can be separated from a social routine.

Students next come to perceive that reading is an interaction between a person and a book. For example, when asked to "read," children turn the pages and look at the pictures. Sometimes they do this silently; sometimes they comment on the pictures. These are the observable aspects of reading that lead children to believe that reading involves merely turning the pages and looking at the pictures.

Children subsequently notice that reading involves telling an event in sequence, but they think that the story is created by the reader through the pictures. In Strommen and Mates' study, the children who had reached this stage could identify words and letters as "something you can read," but they did not yet connect that knowledge to reading a story. Despite having little knowledge of text, children are willing to "read" because they are confident of their abilities to invent an organized account through the illustrations. Often children use the type of language and sentence patterns found in children's books. Sometimes their stories are close to the author's and sometimes not.

In the next stage, children discover that a book has a particular story. "However, to many children this meant that, although the meaning must remain the same, the choice of words need not be exact," according to Strommen and Mates (p. 102). At this stage, children can often "read" a favorite story from memory, matching the sequence to the pictures but

> Young children think that the story is created by the reader through the pictures.

changing the words with each retelling. Actual print is optional rather than essential to the process. They can even "read" their favorite books without the book being present or with their eyes closed.

In Strommen and Mates' study, children eventually realized that it is the print that tells the exact wording although they believed that reading from a text was an ability acquired when you "got big," a mysterious process acquired all at once that was not a matter of decoding. Strommen and Mates state, "When children achieved this insight they were generally able to read and write their own names, family names, and a few sight words . . . . Most could "sound out" some simple unfamiliar words. However, these skills did not constitute reading in the minds of these young children because they did not yet understand that the nature of the reading task is to use multiple strategies to interpret the language encoded by print" (p. 103).

At this stage, decoding skills were so incomplete and laborious that some children abandoned their efforts because it hindered the process of revealing the story. Although children understood that readers focused on print, they often had the idea that it was just an aid for memorizing the story. The idea that knowledge of sound and letters can enable a reader to read unfamiliar text was not quite established.

Children finally reached the stage of using multiple strategies, including pictures, letter-sound relationships, sight words, sentence patterns, and story meaning. One student who had finally gained the concept of reading told the researchers, "[To read] you sound out the letters, or you just know it."

Strommen and Mates' fascinating study reveals the complexity of knowledge children need before they are able to assemble an entire working concept of reading. It is also a reminder to teachers that children's concepts of reading may need to be readjusted so they can benefit from instruction. It's hard to motivate a child to learn the alphabet when he thinks he should be working on memorizing the story.

Early Literacy Experiences

Early experiences in literacy can have a profound impact when children begin to learn to read. Below are several simple yet effective examples.

> Early experiences in literacy can have a profound impact when children begin to learn to read.

Read-Alouds

"There is no substitute for a teacher who reads children good stories. It whets the appetite of children for reading and provides a model of skillful oral reading" (Anderson et al., 1985, p. 51). Hearing stories read immerses children in the more formal language of literature and helps them develop a sense of story structure. Read-alouds, especially those slightly above grade level, help children to learn new vocabulary simply by hearing the word used in context or from very short explanations by the teacher. It also helps to establish the conventional concept of reading—that the text tells the story or provides information. Many primary teachers read aloud to their classes several times a day. Kindergarten teachers say they can immediately tell which children have been read to by their parents because they are better able to focus on the story, ask questions, and listen with sustained attention. Listening comprehension is a moderately good predictor of reading comprehension (Anderson et al., 1985).

Before reading a book aloud, the teacher should ask for predictions about the story to generate interest and provide focus. Both during and after reading, the students need an opportunity to discuss the story and ask questions. This provides opportunities for thoughtful use of language and for language acquisition. A rather unexpected side effect is that repeated reading of favorite books may help to confirm in the minds of very young children that reading is memorizing. If the teacher reads from a variety of texts, it may contribute to a shift in the child's thinking. If the teacher covers the pictures and is still able to read, this may also give a jolt to other children's concepts about reading. When teachers read aloud to their classes, they model expert reading and fluency. This is especially important for children who have not had this experience in their homes.

> When teachers read aloud to their classes, they model expert reading and fluency.

Other Early Experiences with Language

The variety of language experiences traditionally used by early childhood and primary teachers serves several purposes. These activities help to develop language complexity and vocabulary, consolidate sentence patterns, and help children learn to listen to the sounds within words. Many activities were discussed in chapter 2 in the section on phonemic awareness. They included telling stories, using finger plays, having children retell stories, and interactively reading aloud stories of predictable patterns, rhyme, and repetition. More specific word studies include singing and chanting, discussing word meanings, talking about words, and learning riddles, rhymes, chants, and nursery rhymes. They are especially important for children who have little experience with stories and print or with the type of language used in school, or for children for whom English is a second language.

Print Awareness

As children participate in the above activities, they develop an awareness of print. Strommen and Mates' study reminds us that children do not automatically understand the nature of print but assume that the reader invents the story through the pictures. Children most often start by learning the letters of the alphabet but do not necessarily connect the letters with words that carry meaning. One child in the study talked about reading a story and then "doing" letters, which to him were two completely unrelated activities. The concept of words and the idea that the meaning is conveyed through words can be demonstrated in several ways. Big books are especially useful for demonstrating print as the teacher points to words as she reads or has a child use a pointer. Students also learn that print is read left to right and top to bottom. A print-rich environment of words can be developed by labeling classroom objects and developing class charts with names, jobs, birthdays, daily activities, and classroom news.

A print-rich environment can be developed in the classroom by labeling objects and making class charts with names, jobs, birthdays, daily activities, and classroom news.

I'm Really Reading and Writing

First experiences often involve shared reading and writing. Echo reading, patterned book reading, and language experience charts are the tools and techniques.

Echo Reading

With echo reading, the teacher first reads and discusses a story with the class. Then she reads a sentence or two, and the students repeat it using the same intonations. A big book or multiple copies of a story book can be used. Children have the opportunity of hearing the text read correctly before they read it themselves. Pointing to the words as they are read helps the children focus on the print instead of simply relying on auditory memory. For very young readers, this technique helps them establish the concept of what a word is and allows them to "read" an entire text. It certainly is a good technique for building confidence and fluency. Children who are a little more mature than most will incorporate some words into their sight vocabularies. Less experienced readers can echo read with more experienced partners, especially following a group session. As children become more familiar with letters, sounds, and words, they can share the task of reading with the teacher as they work out words and discuss the meaning.

Patterned Books

Children are able to "read" predictable books with the teacher from the very first day of school. The stories are simple and use a repeated pattern. Some patterned books rhyme, and others do not. A well-known example is *Brown Bear, Brown Bear, What Do You See?* by Bill Martin (1967). The pattern is repeated more than a dozen times.

> Brown bear, brown bear, what do you see?
>
> I see a red bird looking at me.
>
> Red bird, red bird, what do you see?
>
> I see a yellow duck looking at me.

Although first books are "read" from memory of the patterns, from known nursery rhymes, and from picture cues, children are able to sound like adult readers. They start reading with a feeling of accomplishment and confidence. Children develop word and print awareness, a sense of sentence and story, increase their vocabularies, learn a few sight words, and develop their first ideas about fluency. Because patterned books rely so heavily on auditory memory, they may not be the most suitable materials for teaching words that are retained by students unless the teacher conspicuously focuses students' attention on the deep processing of words and provides sufficient follow-through practice.

Language Experience Stories

Language experience stories are stories or texts "written" by the students themselves. After a book has been read or an activity has been completed, the entire class or a small group discusses it and decides what to write. In kindergarten and early first grade, the teacher usually does all the writing on chart paper as students dictate the sentences. As she writes, the teacher thinks aloud about starting on the left side, beginning with a capital, determining beginning sounds, leaving spaces between words, and including punctuation.

After it is completed, the teacher points to each word and reads the sentence out loud. The children echo read their story, which is relatively easy to read because they composed it. Individual children can be called upon to read single words or sentences.

Children are able to "read" predictable books with the teacher from the very first day of school.

Language experience stories are powerful tools for beginners because reading, writing, listening, and speaking are all integrated. Students see how their own ideas can be communicated and transformed into print. They learn concepts about words and sentences, see how print is arranged, and review letters. As children become more proficient, language experience stories serve as models for choosing topics, thinking of details, and coordinating letters and sounds.

Balanced Primary Reading

Effective teachers use balanced instruction in which a whole-part-whole model is used. Read-alouds, echo reading, patterned books, and language experience stories are all components of the first "whole" in whole-part-whole instruction. They help children develop a working concept for what literacy is. Emergent readers need this foundation before they start working on the parts, or they will not understand why the parts should be studied or how the parts fit together.

The "parts" of emergent literacy are the skills and strategies encompassed in four cueing systems used to identify words and comprehend meaning. They are graphophonics (the sound-symbol relationships and patterns), syntax (sentence patterns), semantics (the sense of the sentence and story), and sight words (words that can be recognized instantly without consciously applying phonics rules or patterns). Most young readers need systematic, explicit instruction in each of these systems. In balanced reading, the lessons are usually drawn from literature as the skills are modeled, explained, and illustrated in context. Some lessons, especially those on learning key words in depth, are out of context so that the reader focuses specifically on the skill to be learned.

Good readers use all of these systems, but the relationship among them is a bit lopsided in first grade because of the overwhelming importance of learning to identify words. However, if all the systems are not all taught and used, the reader will come to rely on one and not be successful.

Graphophonemic clues provide the sound-letter correspondences for identifying unknown words. If it sounds like a known word, the reader can identify it. Chapter 2 provided strategies for teaching phonemic awareness and phonics.

Syntactic clues are given by the structure of the sentence. The placement of a word in a sentence helps the reader to identify its function. When

> **Effective teachers use balanced instruction in which a whole-part-whole model is used.**

trying to identify a word, it cannot be just any real word; it has to fit the slot in the sentence. Do you remember the "tourmarands" sentence? *The squitly tourmarands vashornly blained the cloughts in the wroked knanflede.*

What did the tourmarands do?	They blained the cloughts.
Where did they do it?	In the wroked knanflede.
What kinds of tourmarands were they?	Squitly tourmarands.
How did the tourmarands blain the cloughts?	They did it vashornly.

Syntactical clues do not provide much help in precise word identification, but they do help in limiting the possibilities. English patterns, especially in primary text, tend to be very predictable.

Semantic cues are found in the context; they are also in the pictures. Successful readers continuously monitor their interpretation of the text to see if it makes sense. All readers must use previous experiences and their knowledge of language structure and vocabulary to make these interpretations. Fortunately, most primary text is straightforward and apparent. Meaningful context speeds word identification (Anderson et al., 1985) but does not provide reliable enough clues for exact word identification.

Sight words are not usually considered a cueing system. As the little girl in Strommen and Mates' study said, "You sound out the letters, or you just know it." Sight words seem to be "just known" and are the principal way that mature readers identify words. Sight words are the result of intensive word study and extensive reading.

After concentrated study of specific strategies, children need ample opportunity to practice and apply what they learned, which is the second "whole" in whole-part-whole instruction. Children can read in partners, or independently with books that the class has studied or books of their own choice. Choice in independent reading gives some control to students and strengthens their motivation. The National Academy of Sciences' report on preventing reading difficulties published by the National Research Council (Snow et al., 1998) recommends daily independent reading. Reading numerous easy books provides better practice than books with which the child has to struggle.

Even beginning readers can make good use of independent reading time when they are taught how to select books and how to pretend read or picture read. Children can pretend read by telling the story of a familiar story book, picture read by looking at a book with lots of pictures and

> Reading numerous easy books provides better practice than books with which the child has to struggle.

talking about all that they see, or actually read by reading the words (Cunningham et al., 1998).

Children love to share what they have read, and opportunities for children to tell or write about their books should be provided. In addition to giving the reader a chance to report, other children learn about books they might like to read.

Learning Words

As with first-grade reading instruction, the main focus of this chapter may seem a bit lopsided because it concentrates heavily on learning words rather than equally considering all four cueing systems. Hopefully, the last section on organizational practices in primary grades will help to integrate all the components of reading.

So much of first-grade reading has to do with learning how to identify words. Students must learn to recognize words quickly and automatically so they can focus their attention on the meaning. With skilled readers, a possible interpretation of a word is formed with just partial phonetic and contextual knowledge, and the remainder of the word is then analyzed and confirmed within 250 milliseconds (Anderson et al., 1985).

Beginning readers go through developmental stages in word recognition. Young children, before they learn any sound-symbol relationships, recognize words holistically by idiosyncratic features, such as the characteristics of a logo. Then, children gain partial knowledge of sounds and letters so they often confuse words starting with the same letter or with similar appearances. Next, they gain a working knowledge of sounds and letters and finally learn common patterns and irregularities culminating in the ability to pronounce any unfamiliar word.

Words that are to be learned are considered by teachers in terms of their decodability, frequency, repetition, and concreteness. **Decodable words** follow the regular patterns of sound-symbol relationships. They are words such as *can, then,* or *make*. **High-frequency words** occur the most often. Edward Fry and his colleagues developed a list of the top 100 high-frequency words, or "instant words," based on samples of 1,045 books in twelve subject areas in third through ninth grades (May, 1998). Teachers often concentrate on these words for instruction because they occur so often, and there is such a high return for the time spent learning these words. Unfortunately, many of them are irregular, such as *said* or *come,*

A possible interpretation of a word is formed and confirmed within 250 milliseconds.

and these irregular words require special attention. Significant **repetition** is needed to learn any word. With each repetition, words that are identified by only partial cues become more fully analyzed. Researchers believe that when a word is read, the visual code (letters) is stored in one part of the brain, the sounds in another, and the meaning in a different part. Repeated practice is needed to establish and strengthen these connections. There is mixed research about whether or not words that are more **concrete**, such as *table*, are learned more easily than abstract words such as *his*.

Only a few words are learned holistically in the sense that they are memorized as a unit. Simply memorizing words to become sight words is not an effective strategy. The strain on visual memory is too severe for learning a large number of words, and there is insufficient depth of processing to insure retention. As children learn phonetic relationships, they begin to analyze words. Those that are fully analyzed and seen repeatedly, especially in a variety of contexts, eventually become recognized and processed as a whole; in other words, they eventually become sight words.

Strategies for Learning Words

All the cueing systems aid readers in identifying words, including those that fall under implicit instruction. Strategies such as context, spelling, and environmental print are used in implicit instruction in which specific words are learned indirectly.

Context and sentence patterns help limit choices of words to those that are contextually and syntactically appropriate. However, students still need to learn to identify the exact word. Context is an insufficient and unreliable cueing system for word identification. Considerable evidence exists that only beginning and struggling readers rely upon context to identify words (Johnston, 1998). However, words make more sense when introduced in context. Children can see why it is worthwhile to learn and study a word. After word study, the text can be reread so that there is immediate application and transfer in context.

Another method that aids word identification is **spelling**. As spellers determine sound-letter relationships, they identify how words look in print. Chapter 3 offered several ideas for working with children who are learning how to spell.

The idea of **environmental print** involves primary teachers labeling

Edward Fry and his coleagues developed a list of the top 100 high-frequency words or "instant words" . . .

everything in the classroom. To be effective, the children's attention needs to be drawn to the print and the word analyzed. Labeled objects can always be used as examples. When working with *m*, the markers and the milk crate become perfect examples.

Specific and Conspicuous Word Study

Although implicit instruction is sufficient for some readers, most will need explicit instruction and extensive practice. There are many explicit techniques to help children learn to identify and to remember words. When studying words in depth, sometimes it works better to take away the other cueing systems, such as pictures and context. The teacher will eventually reassemble all of the parts for application, but focused concentration on learning words requires attention to print.

The primary method for precise identification of unknown words is through **phonics**, or decoding. Chapter 2 dealt extensively with strategies for identifying words through phonics. Other techniques are described below.

In first grade, **word walls** are usually composed of high-frequency words or key words for word families. About five words are worked with and learned each week. The posted words serve as a reference for beginning sounds, key words, spelling, or word recognition. Word walls can be effectively used for emergent readers, too. Janiel Wagstaff (1998) started a word wall with her emergent readers by using nursery rhymes. After reading, reciting, and dramatizing "Jack and Jill," they chose three key words, *Jack, water,* and *pail*. The teacher emphasized the initial sounds, and the children made the sounds and practiced writing the first letter. They searched for other words that began with those letters and reread the rhyme. The teacher posted the words below the alphabet with illustrations as cues and displayed "Jack and Jill" for rereading. Each week about three new words were added.

As described in her study, Francine Johnston (1998) used a **word bank** activity in conjunction with "little books," which are equivalent to primer texts. In this activity, students reread a little book every day for a week, but they were also given a text-only copy of the story. The students then selected words that they thought they knew by underlining them. The teacher held up an index card with one of the selected words printed on it. If the child could name the word, it went into his word bank. All known words were placed in the child's word bank. On the third day,

> The primary method for precise identification of unknown words is through phonics, or decoding.

children reread the words, used the book to identify others, and added more words to their banks. On the fourth day, the students read their words again and participated in a word study game. (The teacher asked, for example, "If you have a word that begins with *f*, hold it up. Hold up a word that rhymes with *not*.") Students who participated in the word bank study learned more words than those who used sentence strips or repeated reading. Again, it is depth of processing that produces retention. Johnston recommends discontinuing word banks when a child has 150 to 250 words because by then the child will have developed his own system of internally storing and retrieving words.

It is depth of processing that produces retention.

Always **review words** that have been studied. Words on a word wall or on index cards in a word bank make this task easier to do. When a child does not recognize a previously studied word, the teacher can place it in a group of words and ask her to find *look,* or ask her to read a sentence that contains the word. Having an additional clue may be enough to reactivate the word.

Students can be asked to **compare words** and make connections with words they are studying. They may be asked to think of another word that starts the same as *said*. What is a word that rhymes with *toy*? What is another word that starts and ends with the same letters as *rug*? Whatever the answer, it can be compared with the target word and analyzed for structure and pattern.

Originally suggested by Sylvia Ashton-Warner (as cited in May, 1998), **key words** are personal words that a child wants to know either because he has a need for them or finds them interesting. The teacher asks each child for a word and writes it down for him on an index card. Card collections can be kept in word banks, in word boxes, or on large snap-open key chains (which solves the spillage problem). The key words may be added to sight words or kept separately. The child works with the word by reviewing his collection, reading words with a partner, or making sentences with the word cards.

Great **word cards** can be made on the computer in a 72-point font. Five words will fit on a piece of paper. The words will look more like the text in a book than handwritten print. Producing word cards on a computer is especially useful when word cards are made for the whole class, or even for a small group of students. The drawback to this technique is that not all printers take heavy, durable paper. If the teacher has access to a duplicator that takes heavy paper, the computer-printed cards will serve as master copies.

To make life easier logistically, glue a library pocket in the back of little books or trade books into which all the word cards for that story can be permanently placed. Experienced teachers know to write the name of the book on the back of the card so that the leftovers lying on the floor can find their proper places.

As children learn a substantial number of words, they can use their words in a **word sort** for further analysis and study. Words can be sorted into a variety of categories, including the initial sounds, ending sounds, medial sounds, vowels, singulars and plurals, places, names, action words, or colors. Sorts can be done as a group activity or after each child has a set of words. As students become more sophisticated, the number of categories should be increased.

The teacher can turn **word games** into board games by using the insides of file folders as the boards. A series of squares drawn on the makeshift board with words written in them can act as the spaces that the children advance through as they play the game. Add a pair of dice and a set of tokens to move as game pieces. Students move the markers around the board as they correctly pronounce the words written in the spaces.

Words with Text Support

The previous activities have used mostly word study in isolation. Providing additional cueing systems can help children to consolidate and to apply their new knowledge.

Use **word cards with text support**. When studying words that have been taken from a story, allow students to keep their books open. Those students with only partial knowledge can use the book for additional clues to identify the words.

A short story or a passage can be rewritten on **sentence strips**. These are presented without the support of the pictures. The strips can be shuffled, and the students must reassemble the story in correct sequence. Large strips written on tagboard can be used in pocket charts as well as having small duplicated sentence strips written on paper for individual students. If the teacher makes a line down the edge of each child's paper with a different color marker before cutting it into strips, children can

As children learn a substantial number of words, they can use their words in a word sort *for further analysis and study.*

easily identify which strips are theirs when working with a partner or when they get spilled on the floor. Even beginning readers can use this technique with a memorized poem. Since students already know what the lines say, partial clues can be used to make the match and to put lines in order.

Individual sentence strips can also be cut into **word strips**. The words can be reassembled into the original sentence with the help of the book or rearranged into variations. With large cut-up sentence strips, the words can be given to different children who need to assemble themselves in a sentence sequence. The period can also be included on a separate card. After the children are in order, other students in the class read the sentence.

Connected flash cards are individual flash cards that make up a sentence when put together. It is easier to recognize the words with some context help, and they can be used to communicate messages:

| *Line* | *up* | *for* | *music.* |

Reassembling All the Parts with Connected Text

After isolated and supported word study, words need to be read in connected text. The teacher reminds students of techniques they have learned for identifying words and helps them choose among several strategies, such as those described below.

Connected text is needed for **combining syntax, semantics,** and **graphophonemics**. It is a way to support children during guided reading and to help them become consciously aware of strategies they can use to identify words. The following example is adapted from Sylvia Forsyth and Cathy Roller (1998) who used the book *Horace* (Crowley, 1982).

> Student: " 'No Horace, you can't come,' said Dad. So Horace _____."
>
> Teacher: "Okay, it has to be a noise he's making."
>
> Student: "Howled?"
>
> Teacher: "Did you see how I knew that?"
>
> Student: "No."
>
> Teacher: "I looked at Horace's face, and Dad just told him he couldn't come, so I was thinking about the meaning. And then I just thought, well, what's one word that he could do that starts with *h*?"

After isolated and supported word study, words need to be read in connected text.

Modeling of strategies is so important, especially when there are so many elements to combine.

Teachers worry about interrupting meaning when they provide corrective feedback of miscued words, but providing **corrective feedback** leads to significantly improved word recognition (Perkins, as cited in McCormick and Becker, 1996). In other studies that compared feedback to feedback with practice, the combined approach promoted better retention. When a student missed a word while reading a story, the teacher wrote it on a card. The cards were practiced until the passage could be read correctly (McCormick and Becker, 1996).

Students recognize words better when they have previously heard them in a story, a form of **preliminary modeling**. The teacher can read the story to the student, a partner can read it, or the student can listen to it from a tape recorder as she follows along in the text. The words also need to be practiced out of context to make sure the student was not just depending on auditory memory. Although these methods are more passive than repeated reading, gains are made.

During **repeated reading**, an individual student or partnered students read and reread the same passage or short story until fluency is achieved. Word errors decrease, reading time is shortened, and fluency increases. In a study by S. H. Dowhower (as cited in May, 1998) repeated reading resulted in significant improvement for second graders in reading rate, accuracy, comprehension, and the ability to read meaningful phrases. Reading gains even carried over to new but similar selections. Stories that have been read repeatedly are good candidates to be brought home for additional practice with the family.

Fluency and Reading Rate

Young readers need to become fluent in their reading. Fluency is defined by accuracy and speed (Samuels, 1997). If readers do not read rapidly enough, they lose their train of thought by the time they get to the end of the sentence. Average third graders can read an unfamiliar story at about 100 words per minute, but poor readers have a rate of only fifty to seventy words per minute. If a sixth grader cannot read 100 to 120 words per minute, he will not be able to attend to the meaning (Honig, 1997).

Reading with fluency is the second principle of reading. According to Anderson in *Becoming a Nation of Readers,* "Readers must be able to

> If readers do not read rapidly enough, they lose their train of thought by the time they get to the end of the sentence.

decode words quickly and accurately so that this process can coordinate fluidly with the process of constructing the meaning of the text" (Anderson et al., 1985, p. 10). Nonfluent reading, and thus laboriously slow reading, is a direct result of poor word recognition. It can also be the result of teachers or students overemphasizing correct word recognition to the detriment of other cueing systems such as sentence patterns and meaning. Lack of fluency is part of a vicious cycle. Poor word recognition hinders speed, which hinders comprehension. With loss of comprehension, students are less able to use the flow of language to help them predict upcoming words or ideas.

Repeated reading of the same text is very helpful in building fluency. This can be done untimed or timed (even young students can use a digital kitchen timer to record reading times). The teacher can record the decreasing reading times onto a graph, which is exciting for the reader to see. Repeated reading helps the student reach the stage of automaticity in word recognition, and comprehension also improves. To ensure the student is not just relying on his memory, ask a different comprehension question with each rereading.

Reading numerous easy books helps students become more fluent as does choral reading, readers' theater, and partner reading. New words become familiar and familiar words become set in memory. Being allowed to read a book to the class that has been practiced until it can be read fluently is another activity that is enjoyed by students.

> **Poor word recognition hinders speed, which hinders comprehension.**

Comprehension in the Primary Grades

Because word identification is so important in first grade, it is difficult for both students and teachers to remain focused on comprehension. Nevertheless, it is essential. Fortunately, much of the text read by beginners is straightforward.

Primary comprehension strategies are learned and practiced during guided reading through teacher modeling, explanation, and illustration. Primary strategies include monitoring for comprehension, predicting, connecting to prior knowledge, retelling, and using fix-up strategies when the text does not make sense. They can best be learned in the context of connected reading. During guided reading, the teacher should choose materials at the students' instructional levels, materials that might provide difficulties if read independently. Children learn to read increasingly difficult material because the teacher is there supporting the process.

Guided reading often starts with making links between known concepts and the story and connections between words studied and the text. These connections need to be made explicit for many students, especially in the primary grades when children are not used to the idea of searching their own backgrounds for familiar ideas that will help them interpret new ones. Next, students are asked to read silently to answer a question or for a particular purpose. Although oral reading is extremely valuable for diagnosis, when students read silently, everyone practices, not just the student whose turn it is. Comprehension strategies are modeled by the teacher and discussed with the class as the content of the story is revealed. Students practice and strengthen comprehension through extensive independent reading.

Monitoring for comprehension means balancing the cueing systems. If the phrase looks like *little red boot*, but the story is about sailing a toy on a pond, the reader needs to notice the conflict between the cueing systems and take a second look. Teachers can judge which systems the student is relying on too much by his miscues, that is, the occasions when the child's response does not match the text. The following figure and related explanation point out miscues and the reasons behind them.

Monitoring for comprehension means balancing the cueing systems.

MISCUES

Original text: James put the little red boat in the water.

Irene: The boy is sailing the boat in the pool in the park.

Mike: Jack puts the pretty little sailboat in the pond.

Julie: James put the late red boot in the water.

Lauren: Jamie pat the little ready beat in the wait.

Albert: James put the little red boat in the water.

Figure 4.1

Based on the example in Figure 4.1, we can determine what cueing systems each child is relying on too heavily. Irene is picture reading. She uses appropriate sentence patterns and makes sense, but she is not using any print cues, not even the number of words in the sentence. Mike is matching the number of words, using the picture and such partial clues as the *J* in James. He probably knows some of the other words by sight, such as *the* and *in*. He is monitoring for syntactic and semantic clues. Julie knows the words, but she is not monitoring for sense or using her prior knowledge. Lauren is relying solely on graphophonemic cues. She knows something about initial, medial, and final consonants, but she is not paying attention to sentence patterns or the meaning of the sentence. Albert reproduced the text exactly, but the teacher cannot tell which cueing systems he used.

Other basic comprehension strategies are appropriate for beginning readers. Making predictions about upcoming text and discussing related concepts prior to reading help children narrow their focus and identify new words that were just discussed. Repeated reading can often assist with comprehension as word identification problems are solved in prior readings. Retelling the story helps students to remember the sequence and sometimes to catch illogical interpretations. Children also love to demonstrate their comprehension of the story through dramatic interpretations.

> Repeated reading assists with comprehension as word identification problems are solved in prior readings.

Emergent Early Writing

Writing can begin on the first day of school. With teacher support, children should begin with shared writing, and later in the year, they can move toward guided writing. Eventually, they will become competent independent writers.

Modeled Writing

Learning about writing often starts by watching the teacher model the process as she verbalizes her thoughts about content, spelling, and mechanics. Primary teachers often start the day with a "morning message," in which the day's schedule, a list of special events, or a personal anecdote is communicated to the students by the teacher via a written format. Modeling writing about everyday occurrences lets children know that their daily happenings are suitable topics for writing. Children see how writers think and what the product looks like even if they cannot do it themselves yet. They need to see that overall broad concept first.

Shared Writing

Shared writing is among the very first writing experiences in which children participate. It is very similar to a language experience story except, as students begin to learn more about sound-symbol relationships and sight words, they are writers. After the topic is chosen by the students, a sentence is developed. Children are called upon to write the beginning letter, a blend, a vowel sound, the ending sound, or the rime part of a word-family word as the teacher guides the children in letter formation and matching letters to sounds. More difficult vowel sounds, /ou/, /ow/, /oo/, /igh/, are often written by the teacher.

It's a good idea to place white tape over any misprinting or misspelling. The child gets a second chance to rewrite the letter, and the finished story is quite legible. In contemporary educational jargon, the tape is placed over a "preconventional attempt." Letter formation needs to be taught. Children who use unusual directionality patterns will be handicapped when trying to learn cursive writing, which requires movement from left to right only.

Words are counted, spacing discussed, and capitals and punctuation are put into place. Sometimes the entire text is only a single sentence long as constructing it takes considerable time. "The power of the lesson lies not in the length of the text constructed but in the quality of the interaction" (Button, Johnson, and Furgerson, 1996, p. 449). The teacher can provide instruction at the exact point it is needed for accomplishing a relevant task. Student-generated stories are posted in the room for rereading or can be duplicated for at-home reading practice. Topics suitable for shared writing include transcribed nursery rhymes and poems, class observations of pets or plants, class rules, and stories modeled after patterned text.

After the shared writing is completed, the class reads the text in echo, choral, or real reading, depending on the maturity of the students. Many teachers also have students write their own copies of the day's text on white boards with markers or on primary paper on clip boards.

All students, regardless of their abilities, can participate in shared writing. When the teacher works through the process, rather than just taking dictation, close examination of print concepts and word analysis are encouraged. Children also learn about the process of composing and see themselves as successful writers.

> **Children who use unusual directionality patterns will be handicapped when trying to learn cursive writing.**

Developmental Stages of Writing

Primary students use all of the stages of writing—planning, drafting, revising, editing, and final publication. However, as expected, drafting is the most important.

Young children do not plan. They do not weigh one topic against another, nor do they anticipate a reader's response, or even plan the direction of the writing. Often the idea occurs through drawing. Making a drawing helps them to remember their ideas when they take time out to decide what letter is required for the word they want to write. Much of the content of their stories is expressed through their drawings (Calkins, 1986).

Students start writing by labeling pictures with a single declarative sentence. Next, they write "all about" stories. These are distinguished by several similar, related sentences: "I like pizza. I like steak. I like brownies. They are good." These stories are often written in book form with one sentence and one illustration on each page. Writers often vocalize while they write in order to hang onto their ideas or to sound out words. Narrative stories that have a sequence and action develop later in the first grade. Curiously, children begin writing narratives at about the same time they are able to draw figures in profile. Children who have been read to or read many books independently are more likely to write pieces that imitate the author's style.

The conventions of writing—spelling and punctuation—also develop in a predictable pattern. Emergent writing begins with scribble writing then progresses to using a combination of letters, numbers, and symbols. "My cat, Elliot, sleeps in the sun" might come out "FF3W+AA," for example. Throughout the first and second grade, writing evolves to approximate standard representations of words as children learn sound-symbol relationships and study conventional print and spelling.

Revision is not really a concept cherished and understood by most first graders. Children tend to write more pieces rather than longer pieces and seldom make any changes in previously written text. When the topic of a story goes astray, children often fix it by changing the title. Teachers can also encourage additions by asking questions. Although the student has the supporting details in mind, they are not on the paper. It takes too long to include everything. Asking the student to reread his work to another student or to the teacher also prompts new ideas and forces the child to reconsider her writing through the eyes of a reader.

Editing should be saved until the end if the children are using invented spelling. The constant spelling concerns of young writers often interrupt their thoughts. Students can use the word wall, word banks, or a checklist

> Curiously, children begin writing narratives at about the same time they are able to draw figures in profile.

to check (that is, "edit") their pieces. The important pieces of writing by students can be brought to the so-called publication stage via the teacher, who acts as editor in chief.

Balancing Leadership in the Writing Classroom

Balancing leadership roles in the classroom encourages good readers and writers. By combining student-selected topics and teacher-directed writing, balanced leadership can be achieved.

Self-Selected Writing

Self-selected writing usually takes place in a writers' workshop format. (See chapter 10 for a complete description.) Children who make some of their own choices are motivated to write, but choosing a topic is sometimes the hardest part. Once a child has declared his topic, there is less chance that he will sit there staring at a blank piece of paper.

Writing time starts when a mini-lesson on one aspect of the writing process is completed after which students draft independently or ask for assistance from peers. The teacher circulates, asking open-ended questions to encourage children to evaluate their own work to make it more complete and understandable.

Teacher-Directed Writing

Sometimes the teacher assigns a piece with a set topic. With a common assignment, specific lessons can be taught to the whole group or the whole class. Another advantage to teacher-selected topics is that students can hear other students' work and find out how they solved the same problems in writing.

Developing fluency and flexibility are the goals of primary writing, but children also need instruction in organization, mechanics, grammar, and usage. Although mini-lessons can be used in self-selected writing, it seems easier to integrate direct instruction when the same assignment is written by everyone. Some lessons can be applied to any piece, but other lessons fit better with certain types of writing assignments.

Balancing leadership in the classroom encourages good readers and writers.

Genres and Purposes in Primary Writing

Primary writers need to write for a variety of purposes. A list of ideas serving various purposes follows in Figure 4.2. (Duke and Stewart, 1997).

PURPOSES OF WRITING

Writing for Obtaining and Communicating Information

morning message	lunch counts	lunch choices
cards	notes	weekend news
surveys	labeling	journals

Writing for Literary Response and Expression

retelling stories	story recommendations
favorite scenes	story extensions based on theme or topic
poems	expression of personal events
story maps	writing original stories

dialogue journals in which the student and teacher respond back and forth

Writing for Learning and Reflection

exit slips or quick writes about what was learned in a content lesson

reflecting about classroom conflicts

listing or grouping content area facts

Writing for Problem Solving and Application

letters requesting a solution to a dilemma

researching a problem and writing the solution

brainstorming topics and writing the list

brainstorming what is known about a topic or problem and writing the list

Figure 4.2   Adapted from "Standards in Action in a First-Grade Classroom" by N. Duke and B. Stewart in *The Reading Teacher* 51 (3), 1997.

Organizational Patterns for Instruction

Emergent literacy instruction can be organized in many ways. The traditional three-group organization did provide targeted instruction, but students spent two-thirds of their time in independent seat work and were placed in slow-, average-, and fast-reading groups with little chance of ever "catching up." Two good plans for reading organization are the Four Block plan developed by Patricia Cunningham et al. (1998) and Integrated Code Instruction by Diana Lapp and James Flood (1997). Both are balanced approaches because skills instruction is combined with whole text reading, the language arts are integrated, and leadership is balanced between teacher and students.

Four Block

Cunningham recommends that language arts instructional time, usually $2\,^1/_4$ to $2\,^1/_2$ hours daily, be divided evenly into four blocks—guided reading, self-selected reading, writing, and working with words, each receiving about thirty to forty minutes of instruction.

Guided reading may use basals, trade books, and big books. "The purposes of this block are to expose children to a wide range of literature, teach comprehension strategies, and teach children how to read materials that become increasingly more difficult" (Cunningham et al., 1998, p. 653). Early in the year, the guided reading block includes choral, echo, and other types of shared reading. Children act out stories, read and reread individually, read and reread with partners, and read and reread with small groups. As the year progresses, children read more independently with teacher guidance or with partners. (See chapter 6 for a full description of guided reading.) Guided reading includes making predictions, studying vocabulary, discussing, learning and practicing comprehension strategies, and working on writing activities connected to the text. Because it is the most difficult block for accommodating individual differences, teachers choose two selections each week, one at grade level and one that is easier. Each selection is read several times for different purposes using different formats such as guided reading, partner reading, and independent reading. Teacher supported groups change daily and do not include just the low readers.

Self-selected reading works in a readers' workshop fashion. Children make their own choices about what they want to read and respond to. The teacher reads a book aloud during this segment, and students have

> Developing fluency and flexibility are the goals of primary writing.

time to tell their classmates about books that they have read. Because the range of abilities is already wide in a first-grade class, it is important to have available a variety of books written at different reading levels.

The writing block is carried out in a writer's workshop fashion with children choosing their own topics. (See chapter 10 for a full description of a writers' workshop.) The teacher provides a ten-minute mini-lesson, and students get to share their work at the end. After drafting four or five pieces, one is brought to publication with standard conventions.

Working with words makes use of all the techniques from phonics instruction, spelling, and the strategies listed in the section "Learning Words." This block always includes adding to and working with words on the word wall.

Language arts instruction time can be divided into four blocks—called the Four Block plan.

The instruction is integrated in several ways. Words are chosen that appeared in guided reading selections. Books written by the same author or that match the theme of guided reading can be offered during self-selected reading, and writing topics can be suggested that are coordinated with the theme. The daily routine allows children to anticipate an opportunity to write and makes children less dependent on the teacher's directions. It is a strong model of shared leadership.

Integrated Code Instruction

Lapp and Flood describe a typical set of lessons that might occur in a classroom, which integrates skill instruction with literature as well as integrating the language arts. These lessons, based on *I Went Walking* (Williams, 1997), would take place over several days. The teacher first told her class about a walk she and her dog, Clifford, had taken. She introduced the book and asked the children to make predictions about the story based on the pictures. The teacher read the story aloud, and the class discussed the events and checked their predictions. As the teacher reread the book, she asked the children to listen for all the color words. Students joined in on the second reading.

Next, the teacher and children wrote a list of the color words on the board and discussed how the author had used them. The teacher and class returned to the book, looked at the sentences, counted the number of words in each sentence, and noted other print cues such as punctuation, directionality, and capitalization. They matched sight words in the story with words on the word wall. Since two of the words belonged to the *-at* family, the class developed a list of *-at* words, read the list, and discussed the rhyme and common spelling pattern. They added *cat* to the word wall as a key word for the family. The teacher and students reread the story, sharing additional thoughts.

The students copied all the *-at* words for a word bank and took turns reading the word cards to partners. They reread the story with a partner and dramatized a section of the walk. While the students were working with partners, the teacher met with small groups to reinforce comprehension as well as sequence, directionality, sight and color words, concepts of print, awareness of letters, phonograms, or sounds based on the needs of the group. Some students retold the story.

Extension activities for the students included word matching, retelling with sentence strips, cloze sentences, writing additional sentences that fit the pattern of the book, role playing, drawing, and writing about what they would like to see on a walk. While the students worked on these extension activities, the teacher worked with individuals at text, sentence, word, or letter levels. The students could also take home a copy of the story and read orally for thirty minutes each night.

This type of lesson may be more integrated than Four Block, but it is harder to plan and requires good record keeping and a conscious balancing of the types of activities.

Texts Are Constructed for Different Purposes

Teachers often have the option of choosing which texts to use. All texts are not created equally. A reading texts is written based on the author's or publisher's philosophy of what would make it easy for children to learn to read. Some books were not constructed with instruction in mind. All types of texts have advantages and disadvantages.

Patterned texts make it possible to immediately "read" from picture clues, patterns, and memory while learning some of the words. Word learning is assumed to happen as children read and reread the text, but evidence for this is limited (Johnston, 1998). So much of the book is "read" by repeating the pattern from memory that children's attention is often not sufficiently focused on the text. Children may be able to easily recognize the words from context while the pattern is present, but they do not learn and retain the words unless the teacher specifically uses the text

All texts are not created equally.

to teach sound-letter relationships or word analysis. Context is seldom sufficient for thoroughly learning a word.

When teaching with a set of patterned books, Johnston also found insufficient repetition of words. Although this seems contradictory on the surface, the set of words used in one patterned book may be completely different than the set used in another. Also, the key word, the one that is different within the pattern, may appear only once; for example, "I saw a robin, I saw a cat, I saw a lion." Certain words may be used to make the story charming or creative, such as *possum*, but may not occur in text again for quite some time. Over half of the words (52%) in the predictable books used by Johnston occurred only once. While basals no longer have the controlled vocabulary they once had, words do appear with greater frequency in basals. Johnston concluded that beginners are more likely to learn words that are repeated and are easily decodable, and those words were not the most common words in the predictable books used in her study.

Literature-based instruction can be described as using aesthetically constructed text (Cole, 1998) to read for enjoyment and appreciation, not specifically to teach reading. Many basals and primary anthologies have switched to these stories to the delight of many children. In these books, the language is rich and varied and has greater structural complexity that can be appreciated by children who have the backgrounds to understand it. The majority of children are successful in literature-based instruction.

Old basals and supplementary books, such as the "I-Can-Read" series, can be thought of as beginner-oriented text (Cole, 1998). They may not have thrilling stories, style, or beautiful language, but they do have certain advantages, especially for struggling readers. Cole found they offer repetition, simple language, simple sentence structure with fewer words per sentence, fewer words on a page, larger print fonts, and new sentences that begin on a new line, which is helpful to some readers. While these texts may not prove very interesting or engaging to most children, their simplicity and controlled vocabulary can provide success for young readers who are overwhelmed by too much vocabulary and what must seem to them a tangled web of long and complicated sentences. Although *Where the Wild Things Are* (Sendak, 1964) is loved by thousands of children, it has sixty-seven words within one sentence strewn across four pages (Cole, 1998), which can be daunting for some

> Old basals offer repetition, simple sentence structure with fewer words per sentence, fewer words on a page, larger print fonts, and new sentences that begin on a new line, which is helpful to some readers.

children. Cole argues that the kind of language structure offered in beginner-oriented texts may prove to be the segue into fluency for struggling readers.

Beginner-oriented texts come in two varieties: those that emphasize high-frequency words and those that emphasize decodable (phonetically regular) words. Students who use books with decodable words can identify more new words independently, but they have some difficulty with the high-frequency words because so many are irregular. Students who learn with high-frequency readers are quicker to identify the words they have been taught, but they have more difficulty with new words that have not been studied. Clearly, both types of words need to be taught.

Aesthetic and beginner texts differ noticeably in vocabulary. While aesthetically constructed texts use vivid verbs such as *demanded, tucked, wailed, observed,* and *capture,* the beginner-oriented texts settled for *said, put, saw, went, came,* and *hop,* all of higher frequency and easier to decode. Aesthetically constructed texts were rich in adverbs and adjectives (*generous, frightened, plump*) while beginner-oriented texts stuck to simple sentences with little elaboration (*big, red*). The aesthetic texts used idiomatic language and compound and complex sentences whereas the beginner-oriented texts did not. The books used by Cole in her comparison were not unusual; she included books by Eric Carle, Steven Kellog, and several that had won awards for exemplary children's literature.

Another type of text for beginner readers is the "little book" developed by several publishers over the last decade. These books are written on preprimer, primer, and first-grade levels. They offer a rich opportunity for practice unlike the old primers in basal series, which had little or no supplementary materials containing additional connected text. Some are specifically written in decodable text while others specifically concentrate on high-frequency vocabulary. Some start with predictable text and progress to text that is less predictable and then to more decodable text. Some are meant for shared rather than independent reading. The teacher needs to ascertain what was the intent of the author and the publisher before choosing a series of the little books.

Teachers who understand how beginning texts are constructed may be able to choose texts to match the needs of their students. If the text, no matter how it is structured, conforms to the concepts in phonics and word study that have been taught, children can apply their lessons. Unfortu-

> **Beginner-oriented texts come in two varieties: those that emphasize high-frequency words and those that emphasize decodable (phonetically regular) words.**

nately most basals do not do a very good job in matching skills and text. It is usually easier for teachers to structure word study lessons to match the text than to find texts that match a program of word study.

Success in First Grade Is Critical

First-grade success in reading and writing is critical. Despite teachers' unfailing optimism that a poor student will catch up, this is generally the exception, not the rule. Although there will always be a range of abilities, prior experiences, values, and motivation among first-grade children, teachers need to ensure that young children have a solid foundation. When learning to read becomes frustrating, children avoid the task and limit their opportunities to improve.

There are several key strategies for maximizing early success. With emergent readers, phonemic awareness is critical for learning the alphabetic principle. At the same time, children need to develop an appropriate concept of reading and a willingness to read. These are developed simultaneously in a balanced program.

Young readers who have learned how to rapidly and automatically decode will have enough cognitive energy to focus their attention on comprehension, which requires engaged thinking. To become an automatic decoder requires explicit instruction and significant practice in connected text. When engaging literature is used, children are likely to develop an interest in reading. Children who read extensively (which almost always means willingly) develop larger vocabularies, learn more concepts, and have greater opportunity to practice comprehension strategies than those who don't. Young readers who have ample opportunity to write improve in both spelling and reading. By integrating the language arts, one process strengthens another.

Research suggests that students who are having the hardest time benefit the most from focused, organized instruction. Those kids who are at risk and those who always seem a little vague about the whole process do better with a straightforward approach. In a report from the National Academy of Sciences commissioned by the U.S. Department of Education and the U.S. Department of Health and Human Services (Snow, Burns, and Griffin, 1998, p. 3), the blue ribbon panel advises, "There is little evidence that children experiencing difficulties learning to read, even those with identifiable learning disabilities, need radically different sorts

Despite teachers' unfailing optimism that a poor student will catch up, this is generally the exception, not the rule.

of supports than children at low risk, although they may need much more intensive support. Excellent instruction is the best intervention for children who demonstrate problems in learning to read."

Excellent instruction is the best intervention for all children who are learning how to read.

Students who are having the hardest time benefit the most from focused, organized instruction.

Patterns for Teaching with Literature

*O for a Booke and a shadie nooke, eyther
in-a-doore or out:*
*With the grene leaves whisp'ring overhede, or
the Streete cries all about.*
*Where I maie Reade all at my ease, both of
the Newe and Olde;*
*For a jollie goode Booke whereon to looke is
better to me than Golde.*

—JOHN WILSON

ow much time do children spend reading books, both in school and at home? Several studies have been conducted in which researchers have recorded the actual amount of time students spent in reading connected text, that is, stories or books. The results are absolutely staggering.

In 1984, John Goodlad (as cited in Atwell, 1987) found that students in kindergarten through sixth grade spent only 6% of their day actually reading, junior high students spent 3%, and high school students spent 2%. In a study for the U.S. Department of Education, R.C. Anderson, E. H. Hiebert, J. A. Scott, and I. A. G. Wilkinson (1985) cited findings that up to 70% of the time allocated for reading instruction was spent on activities related to worksheets. Only 10% of that time was spent on independent reading of text in primary classes, and fifteen minutes per school day were spent reading in the middle grades.

Voluntary reading outside of school fared no better. Richard Anderson, Paul T. Wilson, and Linda G. Fielding (1988) found that half of the fifth-graders in their study read for four minutes a day outside of school. The other 50% read even less. As teens enter the time of their lives when social concerns occupy much of their thoughts, the amount of time that is spent reading is diminished even further. This is especially dismal since another finding of Anderson et al. in their 1985 study was that the more whole text that was read by children, the more their reading improved. Fielding, Wilson, and Anderson (as cited in Tunnell and Jacobs, 1989) found that the amount of leisure time spent reading books was the best and most consistent predictor of standardized comprehension test performance, size of vocabulary, and gains in reading achievement between second and fifth grade. Children clearly need an opportunity to spend significant time reading, and nothing can match reading quality children's literature.

Teaching with literature has many advantages and advocates. The language is more natural and predictable, and students who read literature in the primary grades are not so perplexed when they encounter increasingly complex narratives at the early elementary level. Timothy Rasinski and Diane E. Deford (as cited in Tunnell and Jacobs, 1989) found that children in a literature-based program believed reading to be more of a meaning related activity than did children who learned to read in a basal or mastery-learning program. Students in a literature-based reading/writing program in fifth grade not only scored well on standardized tests

Students in kindergarten through sixth grade spent only 6% of their day actually reading.

but showed a marked improvement in attitude (Tunnell and Jacobs, 1989). And once again, the more whole text that is read by children, the more their reading improves.

Literature-based programs have also been successfully used with remedial readers (Humphrey et al., 1997; Tunnell and Jacobs, 1989). Tunnell cites a 1987 study by Larrick of high-risk kindergarten students in New York, in which 92% came from non-English speaking homes, 96% lived below the poverty level, and 80% spoke no English upon entering school. They were provided opportunities to read in unpressured, pleasurable ways, and they were immersed in children's literature and in language experience. By reading the spring of first grade, all were reading English, and 60% were reading above grade level.

Best of all, literature provides models of ethical responsibility, inspiration, aesthetic experiences, and social cohesion (May, 1998). Literature offers a look at characters of depth whom we can admire or despise with a passion. It takes us away to another time and place where we are not able to go to vicariously explore adventurous situations that we might be afraid to try on our own. It gives us insight into our own character and the character of others, so we can understand how other cultures function when our own experiences are limited or restricted.

> **Literature provides models of ethical responsibility, inspiration, aesthetic experiences, and social cohesion.**

Literature is not just the rambling of dead English authors. There is a multitude of wonderful books starting at the primary reading level that can hearten and inspire children. Hundreds of poignant books with themes of friendship, family life, ingenuity, coming of age, prejudice, peer pressure, survival, and immigration are waiting for children to pick them up and read. Children need different role models from those they see daily in the media! See the last section of this chapter for resources for choosing exceptional children's literature.

A last advantage of literature is the exquisite language and artwork found in special books. The plot of *The Secret Garden* by Frances Hodgson Burnett could be summarized in a paragraph, but children love to listen to the lyrical language. They eagerly visualize the book's interpretation of the coming of spring, and they come to love the characters. It is a terrific book to read aloud. All in all, teaching with literature beats "The cat sat on the tan mat," an actual bit of text from a 1970s reader.

Literature study should start in the primary grades, and a literature-based program starts with read-alouds. Children who have been read to extensively as preschoolers develop phonemic awareness, print awareness, a sense of story, and occasionally learn to read without formal instruction. Primary teachers can provide this experience for all children as well as provide models of expert reading by reading aloud daily to their classes. Read-alouds need to be interactive, with the students given the opportunity to predict and discuss the characters and sequence of the story. Children who from an early age learn to love a good story have a headstart toward becoming first-rate readers. While learning to read, students should have access to a wide variety of books, including those with patterns, those with decodable print, those with captivating artwork, and especially those with great stories for extended periods of independent reading. In a balanced reading program, primary teachers teach vocabulary and comprehension mainly from children's literature. Many decoding skills can be taught in context, and most teachers are integrating the literature with a systematic component of phonics and word analysis. The teacher can then show how those lessons can be applied to real books.

In teaching reading with literature for a balanced reading program, teachers use three basic patterns. These patterns are whole group instruction, or the novel focus unit; small group instruction and discussion, as in the literature circle; and independent reading, as in readers' workshop or silent sustained reading. Each pattern has its place. The novel unit allows for the most direct instruction and for guided reading at an instructional level. Literature circles represent a small group activity, and, therefore, teacher instruction is diffused. However, literature circles allow for choice, for student-directed activities, for the use of social interaction and the exchange of ideas in small group discussions, and for extended periods of uninterrupted reading. Readers' workshop and silent sustained reading allow for the greatest choice, the most opportunity to read, and the least direct instruction and limited peer interaction. When a teacher uses all three forms of literature-based instruction, a balance is struck between the teacher and student in terms of choice and leadership.

One of the constraints in a literature-based program is that there are few prepared teaching materials, such as vocabulary lists, questions, or assessment materials. Sometimes this is a blessing because many basal materials from the past proved boring and focused on inconsequential skills, but it can be difficult to start from scratch or to depend on ideas from a teacher's personal repertoire. Commercially developed literature-related materials vary considerably in quality, but they can often provide a start-

For a balanced reading program, teachers use the novel focus unit, literature circles, and readers' workshop.

ing point. An advantage is that activities prepared by the teacher can be tailored to the needs of the class.

Literature Focus Units and Novel Focus Units

During a literature focus unit, the entire class studies one work of literature in depth. Generally designed for younger students, a literature focus unit highlights one main piece of literature but uses a set of related texts such as books by the same author, books with the same theme, or versions of the same story. For older students, novel focus units, in which the class focuses on a single novel, work well. Both literature-based units and novel focus units provide a means to integrate language arts instruction so that reading, writing, listening, and speaking are all taught and practiced together in a thoughtful manner with each skill enriching the others. Literature units can be broadened with interdisciplinary activities.

> **Novel focus units provide a means to integrate language arts instruction.**

Because the teacher provides whole class instruction and guided reading throughout the process, the book chosen can be at the general instructional level of the class. The teacher cycles daily through prereading, reading, and responding activities with younger students and on a longer cycle with older students. The book needs to be rich enough in content and theme so that it is worth studying for a two- to four-week period by the entire class. The following strategies and activities are part of teaching literature-based units.

Scaffolded Reading

No matter what the book, it won't be at everyone's instructional level, which is why the teacher uses guided reading and then structured activities to help students during independent reading. Jody Brown Podl (1995) calls this guided independent reading, which even she admits is an oxymoron, but one that every teacher will understand. The more academic term is scaffolding. "Scaffolding—providing support to help learners bridge the gap between what they know and can do and the intended goal—is frequently singled out as one of the most effective instructional techniques available" (Graves, Graves, and Braaten, 1996, p. 14). Scaffolding allows a student to carry out a task (in this case, comprehending a novel) that would be beyond him if he were unassisted. With assistance, all students can participate in the class novel, which suggests to the students that everyone belongs and everyone can participate in this class. When special education students are included in the classroom, this technique becomes much more important.

The teacher plans all the normal activities for prereading, reading, and postreading with the selected novel, which could be considered scaffolding for the entire class. (Specific techniques for guided reading and strategic reading are detailed in chapters 6 and 7.) She also plans alternate activities or additional activities—called differentiated scaffolded reading experiences—for students who need greater assistance.

M. F. Graves, B. B. Graves and S. Braaten (1996) offer an idea in regard to guided reading with a targeted group that never occurred to me in twenty-five years of teaching. The usual problem is that when the teacher pulls aside, offers extra support, or does guided reading with a targeted group, it takes about twice as long as independent silent reading. The targeted group could end up with most of the reading assignment left to do, which the rest of the class had finished in their independent silent reading. Though the lessons the small group did with the teacher were worthwhile and instructive, the targeted group, which sometimes struggles the most and takes the longest to read, ends up with extra work. Graves et al. suggest "modifying the text," in which the teacher provides a summary of the remainder of the chapter, so the small-group students can start even with their classmates tomorrow. Although they may not have read as much as the other students, they worked as hard, they studied a section in depth, and they should not be penalized for being slow readers.

Or, while the teacher does guided reading with the targeted group, other groups can participate in oral shared reading and discussion, which minimizes separating the students. Students who have learned techniques of the literature circle can handle this quite independently once they understand the expectations. The teacher can also suggest that anyone who wants to read in the guided group can join the teacher. Good readers, poor readers, and those who simply feel in a more social mood that day can join the group.

In addition to pulling a group aside for guided reading, the teacher can provide a study guide for the selected novel to act as a virtual teacher while students read silently. Study guides can also be offered to other students who prefer a little extra guidance for finding and interpreting the most important parts. Study guides can provide definitions of vocabulary words, briefly explain concepts in the book that may be beyond a student's experience, or draw a student's attention to specific events in

> The teacher can provide a study guide for the selected novel to act as a virtual teacher while students read silently.

the narrative. It is preferable to put these questions in the order of the story so students have a purpose for reading. For example, if students read three to five pages without finding an answer, they know they need to backtrack because they have not closely monitored their comprehension and have missed a crucial point. Learning to self-monitor is one of the most important reading strategies. Study guides can be based on the needs of the students or on special difficulties presented by the text. Either way, they remove obstacles before they become a problem.

Students who need the extra scaffolding will probably be able to participate in all of the postreading activities, although it is an excellent idea to check on their comprehension to make sure they're on the right track before they start on a concluding activity. Some reteaching may be necessary.

Specific Skills and Strategies for Learning to Read

Any skill or strategy taught with a basal can be taught with a novel. However, when extensive novel study is used, teachers must be aware of the variety of comprehension strategies that need to be learned and make sure that balanced instruction accompanies the literature. Beginning teachers might want to consult a teacher's manual of a basal series, a scope and sequence chart, or state-wide standards to make sure that students are participating in the breadth and depth of experiences embodied in a successful reading program.

Essential Questions and Grand Conversations

Guided discussions with the whole group, conducted while the book is underway and after it is completed, can teach students to explore a novel in depth. In guided discussion, children can raise issues, clarify their thoughts, and test their ideas against their classmates' ideas (Burroughs, 1993). This is the time when children can explore what the Great Books Foundation calls essential questions or what Gail E. Tompkins (1997) calls grand conversations.

Essential questions are inference questions that could have more than one answer. The student must use the facts from the book combined with his own knowledge to interpret the story. Students sit in a circle so they can discuss their interpretations with each other while the teacher facilitates the conversation but gives no answers. Students use their books to prove their points or highlight which clues brought them to a certain conclusion. Everyone must participate at some time during the discussion. With this technique, the teacher starts with the essential question. For example, for the story "The Parsley Garden" by William Saroyan, the essential question could be, "Why did Al react so strongly after he was caught stealing the hammer?" For "The Veldt" by Ray Bradbury, "Why aren't the children upset when the psychologist comes back to see them in the nursery." For "Through the Tunnel" by Doris Lessing, "Was it an act of maturity or immaturity for the boy to swim through the underwater tunnel?"

These questions may seem straightforward, but they aren't. They are critical or essential to the story. Students must use the text, infer motivations, make judgments, and evaluate the circumstances. The questions aren't just about the characters in the story. They are about prejudice, retribution, pride, selfishness, being spoiled, growing up, independence, and risk taking, which are useful and interesting topics for students. Essential questions are more than just questions essential to the story; they are essential to life.

Grand conversations are similar to essential questions. Sometimes students start with a quickwrite to recall the story or to rehearse answers. Grand conversations are broader and may focus on illustrations, authors, comparisons, or literary elements as well as an interpretation of the story.

In guided higher-order discussions, children learn to analyze, interpret, and synthesize as they have an opportunity to hear someone else's reasoning and compare their answers with their classmates. My favorite example is Meghan. Near the end of a Great Books circle, I asked everyone to offer a final opinion. Meghan was the last. I asked her if it was difficult or easy to be the last to give her opinion. She said at first, when she knew she would be the last respondent, she thought it would be so easy because she could hear everyone else's opinion first, but when there were so many contradictory but good ideas and such sound reasoning, it was difficult. She changed her mind four times before it was her turn—an act of cognitive dissonance! She learned that making judgments takes time, thought, and consideration of multiple viewpoints. Not a bad lesson to learn.

There are a host of other ideas for responding to literature at the end of the readers' workshop section in this chapter. Most responses could be used effectively in any of the organizational patterns.

Essential questions are critical to the story. Students must use the text, infer motivations, make judgments, and evaluate the circumstances.

Integrated Language Arts

The literature focus unit is a good vehicle for teaching all the aspects of literacy in an integrated manner, which is one of the principles of balanced reading. Students can write about what they are reading, discuss it, and listen to the observations of other students. Most importantly, they can think about the meaning and application of ideas they encountered in the novel. Is there any novel for which a teacher couldn't dream up a dozen connected writing opportunities?

Two teachers who taught the same grade but lived in different states developed a clever idea for reading-writing integration. They arranged to teach the same novel at the same time. Students in each class were assigned pen pals from the other class. As they proceeded through the book, they wrote to their pen pals explaining what they thought of the book and recounted different activities that their class had done. Next time you're at a conference, see if you can find a colleague who teaches the same book and might be willing to teach it on the same time schedule.

Literature Circles

The second part of a balanced literature-based reading program is the use of literature circles. Groups of four to eight students read and study a single book together. There are many possible variations, but the two key features are that students choose their own books and the groups are heterogeneous. A student's first choice for a book may not always pan out, because enough students have to select that book so that a group can be formed. Thus, some teachers offer a limited selection of books to ensure greater agreement, or sometimes children make multiple choices from a larger selection.

Reading is done independently, but study and discussion are collaborative. The groups can be led by the teacher or by the students, but either way, the students must take substantial responsibility because the teacher will have to monitor three to six groups.

Some teachers alternate days for literature circles with days of more direct instruction, but continuity is a real advantage. Have you ever read for several days straight during the summer or while on vacation and thought it was absolutely luxurious not to have to read piecemeal? There is an enjoyment to reading literature nonstop and then having a good chat about what you read.

In literature circles, groups of students choose their own books, and these student groups are heterogeneous in nature.

The following account of initiating literature circles is an adaption from an article I wrote called "Changing the Classroom Climate with Literature Circles" for the *Journal of Adolescent and Adult Literature* (October, 1998, pp. 124–129; reprinted with permission). It describes a sixth-grade class in a suburban setting. Students were given as much choice and student control as possible. It is one version of teaching literature circles.

Changing the Classroom Climate with Literature Circles

Kenneth is leading a discussion using questions that he developed himself. Four other students in his group are answering his questions, giving their opinions or predictions, and finding proof. Suzanne is silently reading *Island of the Blue Dolphins*, Libby is reading *The Light in the Forest*, and Evan is reading *Julie of the Wolves*. [After] twenty minutes, Kenneth's small discussion group is finished, and soon Suzanne is sharing some of her favorite passages [from] *Blue Dolphins* with four of her classmates, while Evan and Libby continue reading their own books. The class (all students' names are pseudonyms) is using literature circles to strengthen literacy skills and change the climate of the classroom.

> Literature circles incorporate several features that can change the classroom climate to be more cooperative, responsible, and pleasurable while encouraging growth in reading.

Literature circles incorporate several features that can change the classroom climate to be more cooperative, responsible, and pleasurable while encouraging growth in reading. These features include student choice, groups of [students with] mixed ability, student management of small interactive groups, and substantial time to read during the school day.

Literature circles offer to students a limited selection of books around a central theme, not just a random offering of novels. Six titles seem to be a perfect number. The sixth-grade unit described above was based around a survival theme, using *Sign of the Beaver, Sarah Bishop, Hatchet, Julie of the Wolves, The Light in the Forest,* and *Island of the Blue Dolphins*. The entire class had already read *The Cay* and was familiar with the survival theme.

The students in this class, located in an affluent, middle class, suburban U.S. area, were all able to read near or above grade level. In a classroom with a wider range of reading abilities, books of diverse reading levels would need to be offered.

The Power of Choice

The teacher began with short book talks that included information about the characters and plots and the length and complexity of the books. The class was familiar with *Sarah Bishop* and *Sign of the Beaver* [because] they had previously read excerpts. After testimonials were given by a few students who had read some of the other books, students chose two possibilities to read. For middle school students, it seemed to work better to have them make rapid choices so that students picked a book that really interested them, rather than wait until after they had seen what their friends had chosen.

With literature circles, students are able to make several of their own decisions, which is motivating to reluctant readers and gives students a feeling of control over part of their learning.

The power of choice was one of [Linda B.] Gambrell's most consistent findings about reading motivation. "The research related to self-selection of reading materials supports the notion that the books and stories that children find 'most interesting' are those they have selected for their own reasons and purposes" (Gambrell, 1996, p. 21).

The next step was for the teacher to determine groups and balance them with a mix whenever possible. Because each child had made two initial choices, it was relatively easy to honor choices and establish groups of four or five students. Gender of the main character seemed to have only a moderate effect on choice so each literature circle was composed of equal numbers of boys and girls. With heterogeneous groups, when a section was challenging, there was always someone who could help. The exciting, can't-wait-to-see-what-happens-next plots also helped. Strong interest can transcend reading levels (Hunt, 1997).

[Batya E.] Elbaum, [Jeanne Shay] Schumm, and [Sharon] Vaughn (1997) concluded that middle grade students, both good readers and poor readers, preferred working in mixed-ability groups and in mixed-ability pairs over either whole-class instruction or individual work. The students perceived that in mixed-ability groups, students helped each other more, learned more, and enjoyed being in the group more.

When groups met for the first time, their job was to determine their own homework assignments for the next two weeks. Some groups chose to read shorter amounts each day for the full fourteen days, but other

> With literature circles, students make several of their own decisions, which is motivating to reluctant readers.

groups chose to read more daily so that they did not have homework over the weekends or any holiday that occurred during this time period.

Some groups divided by pages, and some divided by chapters. Everyone then copied the agreed upon schedule into his assignment notebook and gave a copy to the teacher.

Choosing Roles in the Literature Circles

Each group received a packet of role assignments. Each student chose one of five different roles, Discussion Director, Vocabulary Enricher, Passage Picker, Illustrator, or Quotation Chooser.

The Discussion Director had to develop four discussion questions, which could not be answered just by finding the "right" passage in the book. They were "Why did . . . .," "What do you think . . . .," or "Predict how or what . . . ." The class had practiced developing higher level questions with a previous story. Formulating higher level questions was not a skill that came easily to many students; instruction and practice were necessary.

The Vocabulary Enricher chose five unknown vocabulary words, found the definitions, and taught them to the group. Four interesting, surprising, or significant passages were chosen by the Passage Picker who could share them with the group in a variety of ways. The Illustrator drew a favorite scene, and the Quotation Chooser selected several quotations and asked the group to identify the speaker.

After roles were chosen, the teacher laid out a schedule for the days the groups would meet with their discussion circles. On a typical day, everyone read silently for the first five minutes. This was really a necessity to allow for transition, for everyone to settle in, for minor problems to be solved, and for establishing a quiet atmosphere in the room. Then Group A met with the teacher for twenty minutes while the other five groups read silently. Group A returned to reading while Group B met with the teacher. Groups C, D, E, and F read silently for the entire period. The next day, groups C and D met with the teacher while everyone else read silently, and the pattern continued for two weeks.

The Power of Social Interaction

The social interaction that takes place in a literature circle is a key component of its success. To be able to verbalize the content, to listen to other

The social interaction that takes place in a literature circle is a key component of its success.

SkyLight Training and Publishing Inc.

modes of thinking, and to hear other perspectives contribute to deepening comprehension.

Literature study moved from an individual act of creating meaning to a social act of negotiating meaning among students. The main character in *The Light in the Forest* initiated the most discussion, [because] his acts were interpreted as everything from bratty to trying to adapt to changing cultural expectations.

The students liked the intimacy of the small reading group because it allowed more opportunity to participate . . . . Smaller groups allow more opportunity for active involvement, which also changes the classroom climate.

Students enjoy the more relaxed atmosphere of belonging to a "book club" and working in a congenial setting where discussion is allowed and even encouraged. Because relationship goals are very important to pre-adolescents, a program designed to attend to both social and academic goals can be very engaging (Hicks, 1997). [Katharine] Samway and Whang (1991) found that students who are socially comfortable begin to feel free enough to take the risk of sharing their ideas. For students who have had fewer positive and successful experiences with reading than this group had, small group discussions may be even more beneficial.

As each group finished its discussion, the students received a packet for the next round, and each student had to pick a role that had not been done before. They were reminded of their next meeting date, and they wrote down their new assignments. Much to the teacher's surprise, many students had completed their books in six school days, and several started another book that their classmates were reading.

Finding Time for a Pleasurable Book

Appreciation of literature and time to read in school often appear in curriculum guides but seldom appear in lesson plan books. Literature circles are an opportunity for both, as well as for social interactions about literature. If teachers really want to develop lifelong readers, then they need to allow students to have an opportunity to experience reading interesting books just for the pleasure of it.

The students were able to read the books in this unit independently. They were not the kinds of books that involved heavy symbolism or those that

Appreciation of literature and time to read in school often appear in curriculum guides but seldom appear in lesson plan books.

required extensive background knowledge. Those types of books need mediated reading with a teacher to activate prior knowledge and to guide interpretation. Literature circles work best when the books are meant to be enjoyed.

The Teacher's Role

Because this was the class' first encounter with literature circles, the teacher was a part of each circle. She kept the group on task, established a pattern for taking turns, encouraged students to talk with each other rather than to her alone, and sometimes answered when called upon by the Discussion Director who generally took charge of the group. [During discussion, if a particularly interesting question arose or debate ensued over some point, the teacher asked students to document their opinions and bring it to the next literature circle.] If students are not taught the patterns and the responsibilities of literature circles, they tend to lose focus and wander off task. It is important that an adult is present as groups learn the process. [Ann] Brown (1997) suggests that even with experienced groups, the teacher should hold a short debriefing at the end of each session for students to assess listening behaviors, interactions, and the types of questions that were asked.

For literature circles to run smoothly, much preparation is needed. Six sets of related books must be available in sufficient quantities, role sheets must be ready, and expectations for students' responsibility must be clarified. The process also works better when the teacher has read all of the books. Although there are experts who say it is not necessary for the teacher to read the books to be able to facilitate a good discussion, assessment of the comments and facilitation of the discussion proceed with much greater grace and accuracy when the teacher knows the books well.

Literature circles should be one of several organizational patterns in a teacher's repertoire because so many aspects of building a positive classroom climate are incorporated into this method of sharing literature. When students are allowed to make their own choices about what they read, to prepare their own lessons, and to take charge of discussions with their peers, it changes the climate of the classroom. The teacher is no longer the sole commander of the students' fates.

Student choice, social interaction in a heterogeneous group, and a substantial amount of time to read during the school day lead to motivation

> Discussion and assessment proceed with much greater grace and accuracy when the teacher knows the books well.

that has a powerful effect on achievement. [End of "Changing the Classroom Climate with Literature Circles."]

But Did They Get It?

"Changing the Classroom Climate with Literature Circles" does not address evaluation to any large degree. The whole process might feel a little slippery to a teacher who is used to keeping her thumb on the pulse of every student. I always want to slip in a worksheet or at least one set of individually answered questions, despite the fact that the kids were self-directed and were actually excited about reading.

Remember a few pages back thinking about the joy of reading without interruption? Could you imagine having to stop and answer a dozen questions or make a story map before being able to go on to the next chapter? Perhaps, at least once in a while, we should let our students enjoy reading the way that adults do if we really want them to spend a lifetime enjoying reading.

Since literature circles are just one part of a balanced literature program, teachers should be grateful for the benefits that literature circles provide, which include motivation from having freedom of choice, social interaction in a heterogeneous group, a chance to discuss and listen in a real conversation about a book as opposed to a question-and-answer session, improvement of the classroom climate, and sufficient quiet time for reading an entire book. Students are developing questions, learning vocabulary, visualizing the scenes, picking favorite passages, and making connections.

However, when in doubt after meeting with a group, if the teacher still thinks the students need to probe for greater depth, or someone is not fulfilling his responsibilities, she can always ask that a specific assignment be prepared by the next group meeting.

Direct instruction of strategies and guided reading of challenging materials can be done when literature circles have concluded. It is exceedingly difficult to teach lessons from three to six different books simultaneously. This is one reason that literature circles should only be part of a balanced literature-based reading program. At the end of this chapter are examples of role sheets for literature circles for upper grade students (Figures 5.1 through 5.4).

> **Once in a while, we should let students enjoy reading the way adults do if we really want them to spend a lifetime enjoying reading.**

Silent Sustained Reading, DEAR, and USSR

Independent reading is the third part of a balanced literature-based reading program. R. C. Anderson et al. (1985) found that children who engage in a long-range program of sustained silent reading perform better on achievement tests than those who do not. Silent Sustained reading (SSR) Drop Everything and Read (DEAR), and Uninterrupted Silent Sustained Reading (USSR) can address the need for uninterrupted reading time as well as the extensive differences in reading abilities and in interests found in every classroom. Self-selection in SSR is an element that contributes to positive attitudes and motivation toward reading, so much so that Tunnell and Jacobs (1989, p. 476) state, "Sustained silent reading is unsuccessful unless children are allowed to read books of their own choosing."

Allocating time to read in school validates the idea that reading is important. Everyone must read, including the teacher, and a considerable number of books at a variety of reading levels must be available. J. S. Fractor, M. C. Woodruff, M. G. Martinez, and W. H. Teale (as cited in May, 1998) recommend that the teacher have in the classroom library at least eight books per child, develop a procedure for keeping books organized, and designate a special classroom area large enough to accommodate five children for silent reading. SSR can be successfully used from kindergarten through high school. A more structured version of SSR that includes reader response is called readers' workshop.

Readers' Workshop

Nancie Atwell (1987) popularized readers' workshops. In a readers' workshop, each student is allowed to read books of his own choice and at his own pace. Atwell wanted kids to read the way adults do, making their own choices and learning to love what they read, and she also wanted her students to experience modeling so she read when they did and discussed her own reading experiences with her students. Her rules for using readers' workshop help explain how the procedure works (Atwell, 1987).

1. Students must read for the entire period.

2. They cannot do homework or read any material for another course. Reading workshop is not a study hall.

> Children who engage in a long-range program of sustained silent reading perform better on achievement tests than those who do not.

3. They must read a book (no magazines or newspapers in which text competes with pictures), preferably one that tells a story. In other words, they must read novels, histories, or biographies, as opposed to books of lists or facts in which readers can't sustain attention, build up speed and fluency, or grow to love good stories.

4. They must have a book in their possession when the bell rings. This is the main responsibility involved in coming prepared to this class. (Students who need help finding a book or who finish a book during the workshop are obvious exceptions.)

5. They may not talk to or disturb others.

6. They may sit or recline wherever they'd like as long as feet don't go up on furniture and rule #5 is maintained.

7. There are no lavatory or water fountain sign-outs to disturb the teacher or other readers. In an emergency, they may simply slip out and slip back in again as quietly as possible.

8. A student who's absent can make up time and receive points by reading at home, during study hall (with a note from a parent or study hall teacher), or after school.

Atwell decided to make the reading of books the central activity of her classroom. It was what she wanted students to value most so she made time for it in school and did not relegate it to homework. "Periods of silent independent reading are perhaps the strongest experience I can provide students to demonstrate the value of literacy" (1987, p. 157).

I also changed my practices a few years ago. Reading is now done in school. The responses and assignments are done as homework. I was not as philosophical as Atwell about making the highest priorities the most visible at school. I just noticed that greater comprehension was demonstrated when the reading was done at school. Making a Venn diagram, drawing a story map, or making a sequence timeline is more reasonable homework against a background of screaming siblings and a blaring television, and they can be sandwiched between soccer practice and dinner more easily than reading. Reading with comprehension takes sustained attention and quiet.

For her version of sustained silent reading, Atwell starts with a ten minute lesson. It might be an introduction to an author or a genre. All students might read and discuss an opening of a chapter or book, or they might talk about a reading process. As the students begin to read, the teacher

> Nancie Atwell decided to make the reading of books the central activity of her classroom.

moves around the room, settling initial problems, and conferencing with students. Once everyone is settled, she settles into a quiet corner of the room for more in-depth conferences with students.

Responding with Conferences and Journals

Some teachers confer with students during the workshop time, asking open-ended questions. This is a good choice for younger students. However, for older students, dialogue journals can be used as well. Oral conferences are rather spontaneous, so they are often not particularly thoughtful, or worse, they turn into boring summaries. Atwell speculated that written responses in a dialogue journal might help her students respond at deeper, more critical levels because they would have more time to consider their responses. She modeled her answers and encouraged students to respond at an interpretive level rather than at a recall level.

Although written dialogue journals can provide insights into students' thinking and teach them to be more reflective, responding in writing may take even more of the teacher's time than conferencing orally. Teachers handle this in different ways. Some only respond to a portion of their students each day, rotating the sections. Some have students write back and forth to each other, and some teachers combine teacher and student responses.

Ideas for Responding to Literature

Whether students are reading with the whole class, reading separate books in literature circles, or reading independently, they need a way to share their thoughts. Responses also provide a means for the teacher to peer into the process of comprehension and assess the students' progress.

Responding During Reading

To encourage reflectiveness or to calm teacher anxieties about comprehension, some teachers end the day with a general exit slip. The questions apply to any book being read.

1. What is the biggest problem that the main character has encountered so far?

2. What is the best part of the book up to this point?

3. What questions would you like to ask the author?

4. Describe the setting of the section you read today.

5. Which character are you most like? How have you felt or acted the same?

6. Find the paragraph you wish you had written. Copy the first three sentences.

7. Make a prediction about what is going to happen next.

Responding After Reading

After reading, students can respond to what they have read in written form. They can write responses in the form of letters, diaries, journals, newspaper articles, postcards, retellings, summaries, or poetry. Or, they can critique in the form of recommendations, advice columns, and book reviews. They might also think of questions they might like to ask the author. Younger students can make an ABC book, a sequence time line, or a chart; or, they can play with the language by making riddles, hinky pinkies, or analogies.

Students can also respond orally to what they have read. They can make a variety of creative presentations, from puppet shows to news shows. They can turn a portion of the text into a script for readers' theatre, write a song, or stage a tableaux. A tableaux is a silent scene from the book, in which several children stand frozen in the scene. Each child, one at a time, unfreezes and speaks to explain something about the character he is portraying.

Finally, students can respond visually with a project requiring art work. They can draw the sequence of the plot in a cartoon format, make a collage, or create a pop-up book. Other art-related activities include inventing a board game, developing a CD or a book cover, creating a six-sided cube with scenes or story elements, producing a scrapbook of a character, or making masks of the characters. More complicated projects might include making a story wheel, constructing a weaving (story strips woven together), or creating a quilt of the story as a group project.

Though these activities are great fun and give students an opportunity to think about and interpret the story, the ultimate purpose of literature study is *to teach reading*. The extension activities, such as puppet shows, field trips, bulletin boards, board games, and movies, are appropriate and

Though activities can be great fun and give students an opportunity to think about and interpret the story, the ultimate purpose of literature study is to *teach reading*.

supportive, but reading is the primary objective. That is where the bulk of the time needs to be spent.

Choosing Children's Literature

There are several resources to help teachers choose quality children's literature. Books that win prestigious awards make good candidates. For example, the Newberry Medal is given yearly for the most distinguished contribution to American literature for children. The award has been given by the American Library Association since 1922. The Caldecott award is given yearly for the most distinguished American picture book for children. It is also awarded by the American Library Association and has been given since 1938.

The October issue of *The Reading Teacher* magazine offers an annotated listing of new books. Called Children's Choices, the list features books chosen by children. In November, *The Reading Teacher* features books that teachers find to be exceptional. Also, Children's Books is a regular feature in each issue of *The Reading Teacher.*

Don't overlook commercial catalogs when looking for books. They are divided by interest level, reading level, by author, by genres, and by themes. The issue of quality is not addressed, but catalogs are certainly helpful when trying to narrow the field and find a book for a specific purpose.

Literature for Today's Young Adults by K. L. Donelson and A. D. Nilsen (Scott Foresman, 1989) is a 588-page book that lists and discusses young adult books. Sketches of authors' lives, discussions of genres, and teaching suggestions make this a great reference. Nancie Atwell's *List of Favorite Adolescent Fiction* features more than 200 books, both old and new, which are rated 8, 9, or 10 on a ten-point scale by her eighth-graders. The list can be found in Atwell's *In the Middle: Writing, Reading, and Learning with Adolescents* (Heinemann, 1987, Appendix G, pp. 272-275).

Teaching with literature, with a whole class, with literature circles, or with independent reading offers excellent opportunities to incorporate all the aspects of a balanced literacy program. Skills and strategies can be taught and applied within the context of engaging reading materials, the language arts can be integrated, and there is opportunity to balance teacher and student choice and leadership.

> Skills and strategies can be taught and applied within the context of engaging reading materials.

DISCUSSION DIRECTOR

Name:_____   Book:_____

Tomorrow's Assignment: p._____ to p._____

Your job is to develop a list of questions that your group will discuss about this part of the book. Usually the best questions come from your own reactions and concerns. Develop questions that require a discussion, <u>not just a detail</u>. Use the sample questions below to help you.

Discussion Questions for Tomorrow's Assignment:

1. _____
   _____

2. _____
   _____

3. _____
   _____

4. _____
   _____

Sample Questions:

How did you feel while reading this part?

Did this section remind anyone of similar experiences of their own?

What do you think caused_____?

What questions did you have when you finished this section?

Did anything in this section surprise you or turn out differently than you expected?

Why do you think the author had _____ happen in the story?

How would the story have changed if the author had not let_____ happen?

If you had been _____, how would you have _____?

How are the characters developing or changing?

How is _____ different from _____?

Predict what you think will happen next.

What part did you like best? Least?

Summarize what happened in this part of the book.

Figure 5.1   Role sheet for a literature circle: Discussion Director.

SkyLight Training and Publishing Inc.

VOCABULARY ENRICHER

Name:_____ Book:_____

Assignment: p._____ to p._____

Find four words in the reading assignment that you don't know or you think an average student wouldn't know. Look up a definition that would make sense in that sentence. You may make up your own sentence or write the sentence that was in the book.

1. Word:_____ p._____

Definition:_____

Did you use a ___ dictionary or guess from _____ context clues?

Sentence:_____

2. Word:_____ p._____

Definition:_____

Did you use a ___ dictionary or guess from _____ context clues?

Sentence:_____

3. Word:_____ p._____

Definition:_____

Did you use a ___ dictionary or guess from _____ context clues?

Sentence:_____

4. Word:_____ p._____

Definition:_____

Did you use a ___ dictionary or guess from _____ context clues?

Sentence:_____

Now teach these words to your group or have them guess the meanings from the context.

Figure 5.2   Role sheet for a literature circle: Vocabulary Enricher.

SkyLight Training and Publishing Inc.

PASSAGE PICKER

Name:_____

Tomorrow's assignment: p._____ to p._____

Passage Picker: Pick three paragraphs or passages from the assigned reading and choose a plan for the paragraphs to be shared with the group.

	Reason for Picking	Reading Plan
1. Page _____ Passage begins with these words: _____		
2. Page _____ Passage begins with these words: _____		
3. Page _____ Passage begins with these words: _____		

Reasons for picking a passage

Exciting

Surprising

Funny

Scary

Significant

Vivid with details

Good dialogue

Reading/sharing plan

1. Passage picker reads aloud

2. Picker has someone else read aloud

3. Everyone reads silently

4. Then everyone comments on the passage

Figure 5.3   Role sheet for a literature circle: Passage Picker.

CREATIVE CONNECTOR

Name:_____

Tomorrow's assignment: p._____ to p._____

Of what does this reading assignment remind you? It might be something else we have done in this class, something from another class, a story or a book you have read, or a movie you have seen.

My Connections

1. _____ What's the connection? _____

_____

2. _____ What's the connection? _____

_____

3. _____ What's the connection? _____

_____

Questions to Ask Your Literature Circle

Ask your group to make connections also. Help them to think by asking them two questions.

Samples:

Does this remind you of something else we've done in class?

Do any of these ideas connect to something you've studied in another class?

Do you recall a time when _____?

Has something similar happened in your life?

Questions:

1. _____

_____

2. _____

_____

Figure 5.4   Role sheet for a literature circle: Creative Connector.

SkyLight Training and Publishing Inc.

Guided Reading

Instruction enlarges the natural powers of the mind.

—Horace

Guided reading is the bridge between direct instruction and independent reading. It is the stage in which teachers and children share the responsibility of constructing meaning. During guided reading, children read silently and the teacher reads alongside them. She provides support and prompting as students try out reading strategies and discuss the process of comprehending written text. Guided reading is the vehicle through which strategies are learned within the context of literature or other authentic text.

During guided reading, the teacher sets a purpose for reading a short passage, allows for silent reading time, and then discusses content and strategies with the class. The teacher may ask a student to prove an answer by finding the relevant passage in the text, or she may ask a child how a certain conclusion was reached. Perhaps a prediction is made; there is more silent reading, new questions are asked, and additional content and strategies are discussed. This whole process helps to make thinking visible. The class proceeds in this manner until the entire section is read. The procedure moves along slowly, but it is a strategy rich with opportunities for students who are learning to comprehend.

With guided reading, a teacher works with a group of children who are reading material at their instructional levels. Independent-level materials can be read successfully without any teacher intervention or guidance, but instructional-level materials include some new or unpracticed reading strategies that might present obstacles if students read on their own.

Guided reading allows for monitored practice and support in all aspects of comprehension, including reading for a purpose, predicting and confirming or rejecting, finding information, connecting prior knowledge, monitoring and adjusting strategies, making inferences and connections, and thinking about implications. "It encourages students to read beyond the superficial and to assume control for considering and assimilating what they read" (Mooney, 1995, p. 75).

Guided reading is extremely helpful to students who have defined reading only as fluent pronunciation—those students who are word callers. They have an opportunity to experience what it is like to make comprehension the primary activity during reading, and they have a teacher to guide the process. Guided reading is also very beneficial for students who have a difficult time focusing on printed material for a sustained period of time. They have expert leadership and direction from the teacher as to what they should pay attention to while reading silently, and they have a

> Guided reading is the bridge between direct instruction and independent reading.

defined shorter period of time for concentrated reading. As an added benefit, no student "reads" passively for very long before being prompted to recall, think about, or apply what was read. Guided reading encourages the habit of thinking while reading. Some students do think reading and thinking are separate entities!

Although some researchers (Strech, 1995) define guided reading as being conducted only with small groups, the process is suitable for whole-class instruction. Even when reading with an entire class, guided reading has high student involvement because everyone reads with a purpose and is ready with an answer or an opinion. Older students can write down some or all of the answers to ensure high involvement and on-task behavior. As students read the next section silently, the teacher can check on the responses of various students.

Another way the teacher can ensure high involvement during guided reading is to call on all students equally, regardless of ability or achievement. Having equal opportunities to respond was found to contribute to higher student achievement in the Teacher Expectations and Student Achievement (TESA) study sponsored by the Phi Delta Kappa organization. Sam Kerman and his associates found that "students with poorer learning histories are often called on less, giving them less opportunity for involvement" (as cited by Joyce and Showers, 1995, p. 80). Gradually the students became less involved and felt less valued. Calling on every student every day improves the climate of the class as well as keeping each student on his toes. Everyone knows he or she will be expected to respond at some time during the class, and the answer will be valued.

What Kind of Questions Should the Teacher Ask During Guided Reading?

The answer: All kinds of questions. This is how children learn to broaden their definitions of reading beyond fluent pronunciation. Students need to realize that reading is inseparable from thinking. Adult readers know that reading is a thoughtful process and that comprehension of the text requires attending to the meaning. Since not all children have yet reached this conclusion, they need modeling, guidance, and practice.

To be able to ask a broad range of questions, the teacher must be aware of the different levels of comprehension and questioning. Those levels are literal, inferential, and critical.

> Guided reading encourages the habit of thinking while reading.

Literal Questions

Literal comprehension questions ask what the author said, that is, the explicit meaning. It is sometimes called "reading the lines" because the answer can often be found in a single line of the text. They are the who, what, when, and where questions. If the class were reading the children's classic *The Tale of Peter Rabbit* by Beatrix Potter, for example, the questions might be: Who were Peter's brothers and sisters? Or, where did Mrs. Rabbit tell her children not to go?

Taffy Raphael (1986) called these type of questions "right there questions" because the answers are right there in the text. They can be underlined or copied. Often the same words that make up the answer are found in the question. There is usually a single right answer that comes directly from the text.

During guided reading, the teacher not only asks questions and receives answers but asks, "How did you know that?" Students demonstrate how to find literal answers, how to substitute a synonym in the question to match the answer in the text, and perhaps they explain to the class a concept they already knew that helped them understand the answer. When students are exposed to this kind of modeling and supportive scaffolding, they begin to better understand the process as well as the content.

Literal Rearranged Questions

There is a second tier to literal comprehension questions—literal rearranged questions. The entire answer is in the text but not all in one location. These types of questions show relationships in the text such as cause and effect, sequence, comparison and contrast, or topic and subtopic. Not every type of relationship is in every passage. Returning to *Peter Rabbit*, the questions might be: What happened after Mr. McGregor first saw Peter? Or, where were all the places that Peter hid from Mr. McGregor?

Raphael called these "think and search questions" because the answer has to be found in more than one place in the text. The student has to think about what is being asked, such as the effect, and then search for the cause. Literal rearranged questions are more difficult than simple literal recall questions. The child whose strategy was to scan the text to find words that were similar to the question and copy down the sentence is now stymied because that technique will no longer work. He soon realizes

> Literal questions ask what the author said, that is, the explicit meaning.

that the entire text must be read to find both bits of information necessary to solve the problem.

Inferential Questions

Inferential questions require that a student base his answer on the text but must also use past experience, common sense, or schema to find a reasonable answer to the question. Because the child must use both the text and personal experience, the inferential answer is not a wild guess. The answer must be probable, not just possible. Making inferences or interpretations is a higher and more difficult level of comprehension than looking for the answers in the text because students must use two elements intertwined with each other. The teacher might ask: Was Peter naughty or just curious? Or, when the old mouse couldn't tell Peter where the gate was, why do you think Peter started to cry? Raphael called these types of questions "author and me questions" because the answers are not solely in the text. The reader must interact with the text and draw upon her own experiences.

Authors cannot tell the reader every little detail. They expect that the reader will be able to fill in missing information or "read between the lines." Imagine the line, "While Jenny got ready for school, she thought about her big presentation." The author expects that the reader can fill in the details about Jenny's regimen for getting ready for school. Some children approach reading in a straightforward manner and think their only task is to parrot what the text said, but they miss all the information "between the lines." Authors also expect readers to understand basic human emotional reactions and apply what they have learned about how people act and react to the characters in the story. In *The Sign of the Beaver* (Speare, 1983), Matt will not use his new crutch until after the Indians have left his cabin. The author expects that the reader knows Matt was embarrassed to try out something new and possibly difficult while strangers were watching him, so the author never directly says that Matt was embarrassed.

Inferential or interpretive questions also include identifying the theme or moral, generalizing, and drawing conclusions. Another inferential task is imagining how the story would be different if it were told from another character's point of view. Questions that require interpretation or inference are by definition more abstract than literal questions. Because they are abstract, many children will not be able to answer inferential questions independently without modeling by the teacher. Some younger

> Because the child must use both the text and personal experience, the answer to an inferential question is not a wild guess.

children may not be able to answer inferential questions at all without direct cueing. A cue for *The Tale of Peter Rabbit* might be, "How have you acted when you were really, really afraid?" Guided reading gives students scaffolding, cues, and clues about what information to use to draw an inference. It also gives them a chance to hear the process used by other students for assembling information from two sources into one answer.

Some readers, whatever their ages, do well with inferential questions because they always think and relate to their own experiences as they read, prefer the big picture, and cannot be bothered with small details— the answers to the picky literal questions.

Critical comprehension can be thought of as "reading beyond the lines."

Helping Children Become Inferential Readers

Activating prior knowledge, or in some cases supplying background knowledge, can help students become inferential readers. The teacher should choose concepts from the stories that are likely to be obstacles to comprehension. Concepts are more helpful than vocabulary. For example, a class was reading *The Cay* by T. Taylor (1969) in which a small blind boy and an old man are marooned on a Caribbean island surrounded by coral. To the young students, coral was a lacy delicate object sometimes found in fish tanks or jewelry but certainly nothing that could rip out the bottom of a boat. When the teacher supplied information about different Caribbean corals, the class then understood why local fishing boats, which may have been capable of rescuing the characters, would not be sailing near the characters' island.

Direct teaching of a concept, listening to other children who have experienced similar occurrences, or searching one's own memory all bring background knowledge to the foreground so when the passage is read, both the text and the background can be woven together for deeper comprehension.

Critical Questions

Critical questions go beyond the text, asking questions of opinion, significance, or judgment. Critical comprehension can be thought of as "reading beyond the lines." Raphael called them "on my own questions" because the answers are not found in the book at all. These questions ask the reader to think about and use her own experiences. The text material provides a jumping off spot and can contribute to the reader confirming, altering, or rejecting previous beliefs. Concerning *Peter Rabbit*, the teacher might ask: What kind of problems might happen if you went into someone's garden without his permission? Or, should children be punished when they disobey their parents?

These types of questions can open up interesting and lively classroom discussions. They are often too complex, too abstract, or just too long for younger children to write out the answers. But, what a shame if young children didn't have an opportunity to discuss questions that require a critical response. If the teacher didn't give the class the opportunity to extend reading beyond the stated text, how else would they come to the realization that written text can provide the impetus for examining one's own beliefs?

Guided reading provides children with an opportunity to broaden their definitions of what reading entails and gives them an opportunity to participate in monitored practice at all the levels of comprehension. As children read and discuss, they receive support and clues from an expert reader to guide them through the process. Guided reading also allows for breaking down the text into manageable segments so children can concentrate on limited content and strategies.

Getting Started with Guided Reading

A good place to start guided reading is with a "fat" question, that is, a critical query, such as: What happened when you were some place you shouldn't have been? Encourage personal stories and guide the children to some of the concepts that will be encountered, such as the feeling of fright, hiding to avoid being caught, disobeying a parent who had the child's safety in mind, and getting out of the fix.

First, the teacher needs to set a purpose and a length for the passage to be read. For example: Read the first column on page 46 and find out what the rabbit family was going to do for the day. When the class has finished reading silently, it is time to ask questions.

> What was all of the rabbit family going to do that day?
>
> Who were Peter's brothers and sisters?
>
> Where did Mrs. Rabbit tell her children not to go?
>
> Why did Mrs. Rabbit tell her children not to go into Mr. McGregor's garden?

If the teacher didn't give the class the opportunity to extend reading beyond the stated text, how else would they come to the realization that written text can provide the impetus for examining one's own beliefs?

Be sure to ask how students found the answers, what information they used to reach the conclusions, what they knew that was similar, and how they knew what a sand-bank was. Reflecting on and naming the comprehension strategies makes guided reading powerful. Otherwise, it is just a question and answer period led by the teacher. Remember that the final objective is to develop independent readers who pose questions to themselves while reading.

Move on to the next section and have the children read the remainder of the page to find out what Peter did.

What did Peter do?

Was Peter naughty or just curious?

Why did Mr. McGregor want to chase nice little Peter out of his garden?

What kind of problems might happen if you went into someone's garden without his permission?

Answers can be oral, or some of the answers can be written down. As the teacher walks around the room while the students are reading, she can glance at written answers to assess comprehension of all of the children, not just those who had an opportunity to answer aloud.

Directed Reading Thinking Activity (DRTA)

When prediction becomes a central feature of guided reading, the process becomes DRTA, the Directed Reading Thinking Activity, originally developed by Russell Stauffer in 1969. It has never gone out of use. The teacher starts by asking the students to speculate what the story or passage might be about. Many possible answers are given before the students read to support or refute their predictions (Nessel, 1989).

Predicting is a very powerful motivational and thinking tool. Children love to predict and then read to find out if they were right. They typically approach story predictions as a puzzle, trying out different solutions and hoping their favorite prediction will be the one chosen by the author. Sometimes their predictions are much more interesting than the author's! The process of prediction teaches students to set their own purposes for reading and not to passively accept whatever passes before their eyes, whether it seems sensible or not.

Predicting requires that students think logically about the direction of the story, and then use their own experiences in conjunction with the text to

> When prediction becomes a central feature of guided reading, the process becomes DRTA—the Directed Reading Thinking Activity.

hypothesize. They can call upon their memories of similar stories, personal experiences, and plots of movies to justify their predictions. Once students understand that a single "right" answer is not needed and any reasonable, justifiable answer will be accepted, they will volunteer and support or challenge other predictions with enthusiasm. After the students complete reading the passage, the teacher asks if students want to stay with their original predictions or change their minds.

Multiple literal recall questions are usually not necessary because children must justify their opinions by recalling important points (Nessel, 1989). After finishing a DRTA lesson, the teacher may decide to go back to the story to use it again to teach or refine other skills or strategies. This second reading may be a better time for noticing multiple meanings of words, common suffixes, or text features. To do all this on the first reading interrupts the flow of the story and thus disrupts comprehension. This extending and refining of skills was originally recommended by Stauffer to encourage accuracy in reading in addition to speculation, but the second step sometimes falls by the wayside.

For *Peter Rabbit*, the teacher might ask: What do you think Mr. McGregor will do to Peter? Some will predict capture, and some will imagine a great chase, and some will use the fact that Mrs. McGregor baked Peter's father into a pie to predict his demise. Encourage several predictions and have the children explain what brought them to those conclusions. Then let the students read to find out what did happen to Peter. The enthusiasm of the students will be surprising.

Visualization

Another interesting and enjoyable strategy to use in guided reading is visualization. Young readers need to realize that good readers develop pictures in their heads about what the characters look like, what the appearance of the setting is, and whether the character walks with mincing steps or long strides. Good readers start to build pictures in their minds and adjust their visualizations as additional information is given by the author. When the student recalls information, some of it is attached to the picture he has visualized for himself. There is a dramatic scene in *Roll of Thunder, Hear My Cry,* by M. Taylor (1977), in which the father, Mr. Logan, is run over by his own wagon while trying to change a wheel during a storm. When a group of students in one of my classes was asked about what happened, a big debate ensued over where the father was

Good readers develop pictures in their heads about what the characters look like, what the appearance of the setting is, and whether the character walks with mincing steps or long strides.

standing, and if the wagon rolled forward or backward when the horse reared up. The imagery attached to that scene enhanced the readers' memories until they were absolutely positive that the author had stated the facts exactly as they "saw" them.

Some children are totally startled when asked: What kind of flowers were in the pots that Peter knocked over? Or, what color was the wheelbarrow on which Peter climbed? Their first response is always that the text didn't say, but as each student begins to build an image in her mind's eye, the entire event is redrawn, as well as the color of the wheelbarrow. The facts, the sequence, and the image are all strengthened.

Closing Up the Lesson with Critical Questions

Once the students have examined the story of Peter Rabbit, don't stop there. The critical questions remind children that they should think about what they read in a larger context than just the story. And, critical questions can be the most intriguing to ask and answer. For example: Should children be punished when they disobey their parents?

This question could lead to quite a discussion. There will be all kinds of provisos and opinions. Be sure to bring Peter and his experience back into the discussion, because there is a good lesson to be learned. Children do not automatically transfer the lesson from the story to their own lives unless the teacher provides a specific bridge. David Perkins and Gavriel Salomon (1988) state that teachers can help students transfer information learned in one context (the story) to a more generalized setting (their lives) by asking students how what they learned from one topic might apply elsewhere. Guiding students to explore in detail the similarities and differences between the two situations also facilitates transfer. The children who kick each other as they leave the classroom after reading a story about respect and human kindness did not have a teacher who encouraged transfer!

Guided Reading on the Overhead

An enjoyable variation of guided reading can be done with the whole class on the overhead with a story typed and photocopied onto a transparency. Choose a short story, preferably one that is unpredictable or could have several possible twists. Divide it into sections, sometimes stopping in the middle of a sentence. "And then he saw a . . . ." Be sure to type it large enough so the story can be easily seen.

> The critical questions remind children that they should think about what they read in a larger context than just the story.

Cover the unread sections one at a time and invite the class to read along as the teacher asks for predictions and justifications, visualizations, and inferences. Be sure to ask at what point students changed their minds and their predictions. For students who are timid about guessing, the teacher can ask: "Do you think that Claire is right, or do you agree with Jason?" because it is important that everyone is involved. Everyone can participate in the predicting because no one can read ahead. Everyone can listen to the reasoning. All will have a guess and be anxious to read the author's ending.

The drawback to guided reading is that it is very time consuming, but that seems such a minor disadvantage. Can you think of a better way for teaching children to develop and practice their reading skills while using literature, to broaden their definitions of reading, and to be fully involved in a worthwhile classroom activity? What better way to make literacy emerge?

Skinny questions answer who, what, when, and where, but the fat questions answer why or how.

Guiding Children Toward Greater Independence with Reciprocal Reading

Why should the teacher be the only one asking questions? Independent readers must learn to ask questions of themselves as they read. The teacher can provide the bridge toward this goal by asking the students to develop questions for materials that the class is reading or studying. This takes a great deal of practice and modeling because children tend to flock to the trivia questions.

The procedure for reciprocal reading is to have the students read a small section from their books. How short "a small section" is depends on the grade level. It could range from a single sentence to several paragraphs. The teacher then poses some questions to be answered and draws the students' attention to the types of questions that were asked.

Students are then asked to develop questions according to criteria such as fact or discussion questions. They don't have to know as much about the underlying levels of comprehension as the teacher has to know; they can usually do quite well by just defining the types of questions as skinny questions and fat questions, or fact questions and discussion questions. Knowing the difference takes some time, but a simple definition could be that skinny questions answer who, what, when, and where, but the fat questions answer why or how. Another simple definition is that skinny questions can be answered in one sentence and have only one answer, but fat questions require more than one sentence and may have several reasonable answers.

A useful progression of steps leading toward greater independence starts with the teacher asking questions and modeling the question types. Then the whole class can participate in developing, critiquing, and answering questions as they read the story. The teacher can guide question development by prompting, "What would you like to know about what happens next?" A student might respond, "What does the monster do after the fog horn is turned off?"

Cooperative group work follows as students ask each other questions. Everyone gets to have a turn more often so greater proficiency at developing questions is attained and participation is more active. Janice Almasi (1995) found that peer-led discussions were very powerful. Her award winning doctoral dissertation of 1994 found that there was richer and more complex interaction between peers than there was during teacher-led discussions. Also, there was greater retention of the thinking processes in which the students engaged.

> Janice Almasi found that there was richer and more complex interaction between peers than there was during teacher-led discussions.

Students can progress to working in pairs and finally to reading independently as they ask themselves questions. This takes time for the various levels of practice, but the gradual progression leads easily toward making self-questioning a habit.

For variety, there are two interesting permutations. For a written assignment in responding to reading, ask the children to write questions instead of answers. The questions by themselves will give the teacher a good indication of comprehension. A team challenge might follow. The other alternative for the teacher willing to put herself in the learner's role is to ask the students to develop questions that the teacher has to answer. If the teacher proves her answers by reading the relevant parts of the text or by explaining the reasoning process, it becomes another way of modeling what good readers do.

Think-Alouds

Although think-alouds are not normally thought of as guided reading, they accomplish many of the same purposes as guided reading does. In a think-aloud, the teacher reads a passage and thinks aloud while reading, thus modeling the processing of an expert reader in order to identify the specific strategies being used (Kucan and Beck, 1997). The teacher may wonder aloud about what will happen next and then make a prediction. As she reads further in the passage, she can identify when the prediction was confirmed or rejected and predict again. Monitoring of comprehension can be demonstrated when something is misread or a thought is lost. This modeling makes comprehension strategies more explicit to the learner. Students see and hear strategies for self-correction and learn that even expert readers may have to redirect, reread, or reconsider. Demonstration broadens the students' definitions of what a good reader does in the same way as guided reading helps to broaden the readers' definitions.

Beth Davey (1983) suggested the five most important strategies for modeling in think-alouds were predicting, visualizing, making analogies, expressing confusion, and demonstrating fix-up strategies such as rereading. The natural progression for think-alouds is the same as that for reciprocal reading; children read in pairs and think aloud to each other and then read independently and think by themselves.

Guided reading provides support for the reader while reading silently. It helps to broaden the definition of what an expert reader does while reading. It explicitly demonstrates and allows for discussion of the underpinnings and strategies of reading comprehension while using authentic text. It provides the bridge to becoming an expert, independent reader.

Guided reading provides the bridge to becoming an expert, independent reader.

GUIDED READING PLANNER

Prediction before reading
Text features to notice _____

First section p. ___ to p. ___
Prediction question: _____

Literal question: _____
Prove it. How did you know?

Literal rearranged question: _____
Where did you find the two parts? How do they fit together?

Inferential question: _____
How did you know that? Why is that a likely answer?

Second section p. ___ to p. ___
Prediction question: _____

Literal question: _____
Prove it. How did you know?

Literal rearranged question: _____
Where did you find the two parts? How do they fit together?

Inferential question: _____
How did you know that? Why is that a likely answer?

Critical question: _____
Why do you think so?

Last section p. ___ to p. ___

Prediction question: _____

Literal question: _____
Prove it. How did you know?

Literal rearranged question: _____
Where did you find the two parts? How do they fit together?

Inferential question: _____
How did you know that? Why is that a likely answer?

Critical question: _____
Why do you think so?

Figure 6.1

SkyLight Training and Publishing Inc.

CHAPTER

7

Helping Students Become Strategic Readers

The sagacious reader who is capable
of reading between these lines
what does not stand written in them,
but nevertheless implied,
will be able to form some conception.

—Johann Wolfgang von Goethe

C omprehending meaning is the heart and soul of reading, and learning to fully comprehend written text is complex. It is a task so intricate that it takes several years to become a mature reader who can handle simultaneously and almost automatically the multitude of tasks involved in reading comprehension.

Because reading is so automatic for most adults, it is difficult to imagine, much less to imagine teaching, all of the tasks that are involved in comprehension. Yet, take out an old high school or college foreign language text and start reading a passage. You will find yourself consciously, not automatically, using the skills and strategies of reading. You may find yourself reduced to subvocalizing and sounding out words that have slipped from sight vocabulary. You will consciously use context clues, reread, read ahead, skip, come back, read again, remember root words, and problem solve. You will predict and reject and recall situations from your past experience to figure out the meaning. It is a good experience to read in a partially remembered foreign language to see how reading strategies are problem-solving strategies, enabling the reader to construct meaning from the text. But you are an experienced reader, and you know the most important strategy of all: It is supposed to make sense and convey meaning.

Factors Affecting Comprehension

Comprehension is affected by the ability to recognize words quickly and automatically, the background and knowledge that the reader brings to the task, the familiarity of the reader with the content and vocabulary of the text, the complexity of the style in which the text is written, the ability of the reader to organize information, and the motivation of the reader. All of these components must be orchestrated together for good comprehension. If any component is missing, comprehension will be inhibited.

Fluency and Automaticity in Word Recognition

To comprehend material, students must be able to decode fast enough and automatically enough to keep the content in short-term memory so that meaning can be constructed. If the reader is not fluent and automatic in decoding skills, he forgets the beginning of the sentence by the time he gets to the end. Fluency doesn't ensure comprehension, but comprehension is difficult without fluency. If decoding is not automatic, reading becomes a long and laborious task that requires constant rereading.

Fluency doesn't ensure comprehension, but comprehension is difficult without fluency.

Background, Prior Knowledge, and Schema

Another factor that affects comprehension is the reader's prior knowledge. When the reader can recognize nearly every word in the passage but does not have a clue as to the meaning, there is often a mismatch between the reader's and author's schemas. "A schema as we define the term is an organized cognitive structure of related knowledge, ideas, emotions, and actions that has been internalized and that guides and controls a person's use of subsequent information and response to experience" (Goodman and Goodman, 1998, p. 115).

In other words, a schema is composed of personal background knowledge, and it acts as a filing system that has been set up to organize past experiences and interpret future experiences. For example, a restaurant schema includes tablecloths, menus, waiters, price ranges, and favorite dishes, so as we read, "Elena walked into the restaurant and was escorted to a table," we do not expect that the escort is going to sit down with her. A reader's schema helps him understand new text, make connections, and conjure up pictures while reading. Schemas also include attitudes that will influence judgments about what is read.

It is always an exercise in humility when I read a computer catalog. According to my Mac catalog, "For easy and affordable expansion of your 10Base-T twisted pair network, the DaynaSTAR MiniHub-5 and MiniHub-8 are quick and reliable solutions. Small and lightweight, these hubs have 5 or 8 RJ45 ports, and both include an extra cross over RJ45 port that can be used for hub-to-hub connections without a special cross over cable or connector." (MacWarehouse, 1998, p. 62). I can read every word in the catalog, but I am not familiar with the content. My schema doesn't match the author's. There is even a picture to help me, but I still have no idea. Having no idea what I am reading about is a major block to my comprehension.

When a student's schema matches the author's, it is likely that the text will make more sense, and the student will better comprehend and recall the material. When schema doesn't match, the student is reduced to recalling the information on a rote basis. He cannot make any judgment about the material because it is not really understood. A match between schemas may be through similar background knowledge, or it may be through familiarity with a type of text organization such as narrative structure or the type of organization found in scientific papers.

> When schema doesn't match, the student is reduced to recalling information on a rote basis.

Lack of matching schema is usually not as severe as mine with the computer catalog, but even small mismatches can produce unexpected results. One of my students who wrote about *Sarah Bishop* (O'Dell, 1980) discussed putting a jacket on a deer because the book said that Sarah had dressed a deer. Another student mentioned that an Indian visitor of Sarah's was sick because the text said he was ill at ease. Another, in a retelling, said that Ulysses poked out the eye of the Cyclops with a spear dipped in oregano because she had read the spear was of seasoned wood. These students formed images based on their past knowledge and in remembering the passages swore there were jackets, flu symptoms, and herbs. Some mismatches totally block comprehension, especially if it is an unknown concept, and some mismatches just change the details. Because readers construct meaning based on what they already know and try to integrate new ideas into their systems, the same text can have different interpretations for different readers. Providing background or connections for students increases comprehension.

> **Readers construct meaning based on what they already know and try to integrate new ideas into their systems.**

Difficulty of the Text

The difficulty of the text also affects comprehension. For young students, five unknown words on a single page may mean the book is too difficult for independent reading. Although determining the level of difficulty is often done by counting unknown words, organizational patterns and sentence complexity affect comprehension too. This is especially true in content area textbooks, such as science texts or social studies books.

Determination, Willpower, and Interest

The text, the reader, and an interaction between the two make up the elements of reading. Thus, the attitude and interest of the reader are important factors. "Teachers have long recognized that motivation is at the heart of many of the pervasive problems we face in educating today's children" (Gambrell, 1996, p. 17). The determination of the reader to be a problem-solver when the going gets tough is a factor in comprehension. Students who have an advantage in reading are those who are able to concentrate, see learning as a delightful puzzle to be solved, use a little elbow grease, see a purpose for learning to read, have adult models to imitate, and are risk takers.

High interest can often overcome difficult text. Strong interest can frequently help the reader to transcend his independent and instructional levels of reading (Hunt, 1996–97). Providing motivating situations and interesting content and tasks may be the most challenging and important responsibilities of any teacher.

Capable and Less Capable Readers

The difference between good and poor readers is often seen in the good reader's ability to use a variety of strategies. When one doesn't work, he tries another. Other characteristics of good readers are fluency, the ability to decode rapidly, large vocabularies, the understanding of organizational patterns, the idea that reading is a meaning creating process, and the ability to monitor and use fix-up strategies (Tompkins, 1997).

Less capable readers are more likely to focus on decoding rather than meaning, and as they get older, more likely to focus on a single detail rather than on the whole. They use the same procedures, no matter what the task. When immature readers were asked to read two stories, one just for fun and the other for preparation for a test, they did not adjust their reading strategies. The skilled readers did. "As a result, the immature readers did not remember any more of the story they were supposed to study than the one they were supposed to read for fun" (Anderson et al., 1985, p. 13).

> [Less capable readers] seem reluctant to use unfamiliar strategies or those that require much effort. They do not seem to be motivated or to expect that they will be successful. Less capable readers and writers don't understand or use all the stages of the reading and writing processes effectively. They do not monitor their reading and writing. Or if they do use strategies, they remain dependent on primitive strategies. For example, as they read, less successful readers seldom look ahead or back into the text to clarify misunderstandings or make plans. Or, when they come to an unfamiliar word, they often stop reading unsure of what to do. They may try to sound out an unfamiliar word, but if that is unsuccessful they give up. In contrast capable readers know several strategies, and if one strategy isn't successful they try another (Tompkins, 1997, pp. 136–137).

Reading Strategies

Reading strategies are those skills and thinking patterns that help the reader to solve the problems of constructing meaning. Not all strategies are used equally at every level of reading, nor are all strategies used in reading every type of text, but the strategic reader has a variety of techniques at his disposal and can intentionally select which ones to use and

The difference between good and poor readers is often seen in the good reader's ability to use a variety of strategies.

can determine when to use them. The proficient reader may not even be aware of using strategies until something goes awry with meaning. It is essential that reading instruction make students aware of strategic reading tactics so they can plan, evaluate, and regulate their own thinking (Tompkins, 1997).

Which strategies do good readers need and use? The first group of strategies includes the basic problem-solving strategies; that is, what good readers do to construct meaning from text. These include:

1. Linking one's background knowledge to the text.
2. Figuring out unknown words.
3. Visualizing.
4. Monitoring comprehension.
5. Predicting and then confirming or rejecting the prediction.
6. Stating main ideas or retelling important information.
7. Organizing ideas into patterns.
8. Using fix-up strategies when the text doesn't make sense.

The second group of strategies includes those that readers use for higher-level thinking:

1. Inferring.
2. Generalizing.
3. Evaluating.

Finally, the third group of strategies involves attitudes and dispositions held by good readers:

1. Understanding that reading is meaningful communication.
2. Desiring to read.
3. Seeing the need to read.
4. Having the willingness to expend considerable time and effort to become proficient.

(The three groups of strategies are derived from the work of Brown, El-Dinary, and Pressley, 1996; May, 1998; and Tompkins, 1997.)

Knowing how and when to use reading strategies requires instruction and the will to learn. Extensive research shows that when teachers explicitly teach strategies, students learn more. In explicit teaching, the teacher

The proficient reader may not even be aware of using strategies until something goes awry with meaning.

models the application of the strategy, carefully explaining to students what is being learned, why it is being learned, when it will be used, and how it will be used (McIntyre, 1996). When strategies are taught using whole text and literature, the approach to teaching comprehension is balanced. The sequence for reading instruction includes the following:

1. Teacher modeling, explanation, and instruction.

2. Guided practice, in which teacher and students share responsibility for constructing meaning, but students gradually assume more independence.

3. Opportunities for discussion among students and with the teacher.

4. Independent practice with feedback and scaffolding.

5. Ample time for practice.

6. Application of the strategies in real reading situations.

Teaching comprehension strategies takes considerable modeling, talking through, and thinking aloud. It requires asking: How did you know that? What clues did you use? What were you thinking about? And, how did you connect that? Learning how to extract meaning is a process that requires active participation and metacognition (thinking about how something is known or came to be understood). If the comprehension strategy is not consciously known, then the student will not be able to transfer that skill to a future application. In other words, the student not only has to be able to do "it", but has to know what "it" is, and when to do "it" again. Perhaps the most difficult part of teaching strategic reading is remembering that the content of the story is not what is really being taught. It is only the vehicle for learning the process.

Learning how to comprehend is enhanced when there is social interaction. As students hear the teacher explaining how she came to that understanding or listen to other students explaining how they reached a conclusion, they begin to understand the process. Vygotsky is famous for this kind of thinking—that with guided practice and observing the thinking of others, individual students will then be able to do a task by themselves.

> **With guided practice and by observing the thinking of others, individual students will be able to do a task by themselves.**

Strategies to Teach Prior to Reading the Text

Three types of activities are useful prior to reading the text. They are teaching unfamiliar concepts and content, teaching unfamiliar vocabulary, and providing pictures for visualizing the setting. All enhance comprehension. If the teacher instructs students how to link their own background to new content, how to use context clues, and how to develop images in their own minds, students begin to turn these skills into problem-solving strategies that they will use independently.

Teaching Unfamiliar Concepts and Content

Providing background information, new concepts, synonyms, connections, and simple examples can supply the big picture for readers so that the details fit into a comprehensible whole. People are able to learn the most when they already know 90% of what they are reading. Think of this as having a hook on which to hang new information or a file folder into which new information can be placed. This is obviously important for reading textbooks in which entirely new content is encountered, but it is also important in fiction, especially with stories that are set in other time periods and cultures, or stories that use concepts from an adult realm in which children do not normally participate. Concepts that are unfamiliar to children such as mortgages, organic fertilizers, or patents may need to be pretaught. When the teacher explains these ideas prior to reading, because the author didn't, comprehension is improved.

A teacher needs to carefully consider what content, setting, or concepts may cause a problem. Not everything should be pretaught, only those concepts that will block comprehension of the material.

Linking Background to New Content

Children need to develop the strategy of searching their own schemas when encountering new material. To teach this strategy, the teacher needs to take a slightly different tactic than providing the background. She needs to probe the experiences of the class and help students make their own connections.

To prepare for reading about Hermes in Greek mythology, students were asked to recall where they had seen Hermes' symbols. Their responses included: The winged feet are the symbol of a tire company; the Detroit Red Wings use a logo of a shoe with wings; Hermes is in a Saturn car commercial; his staff is on the Blue Cross logo; and a staff with intertwined snakes is used on the sign at a drugstore. The students' responses helped them realize that the mythological characters were not completely

> Children need to develop the strategy of searching their own schemas when encountering new material.

unknown to them, and they could make connections to aid their comprehension and to improve recall.

Prereading discussion is one of the most useful activities for activating prior knowledge or developing concepts. Relating anything to any film is productive, because young students seem to know every movie ever produced. One student will say, "Have you ever seen this movie? Well, it's like that." And, a chorus of now-understanding heads will nod in unison. Calling on every student during a discussion validates everyone's experiences as well as keeping everyone involved. For those who do not wish to or are unable to offer examples of their own, the teacher can offer choice questions such as, "Do you think Tony's story or Kaitlyn's story is the better example? How does her story relate to our discussion?"

The difficulty with whole class discussion is that it is all verbal interchange and those students with something else on their minds or those who have auditory deficits may still miss the connections. The following activities offer greater opportunity for student participation.

KWL was developed by Donna Ogle (1986). It is a three-part activity in which students describe what they already *know* about a subject, what they *want* to know, and then what they *learned*. It is perfect for nonfiction material, but it can also be used for unfamiliar concepts or settings in fiction. The best use seems to be in small groups in which plenty of discussion and interchange can occur, ensuring more active participation. The *W* can be changed to *T* to represent "*Think* you know for sure" for middle school students who often say they don't want to know anything about the topic.

Used prior to reading, an **anticipation guide** deals on a general level with the issues in an upcoming reading selection. It consists of a list of statements that reflect the underlying issues in the text. The statements are usually written in an ambiguous fashion so there can be both agreement and disagreement, which generally leads to discussion among the students. Each student gets a copy of the anticipation guide. They respond to the statements independently and then develop a set of cooperative answers. The teacher can ask for a consensus, or she can ask for students to check off whether they agree or disagree with a statement after explaining the rationale for their answers. Selected issues can be discussed with the whole class or a poll can be taken to ascertain opinions. "Children who are orphaned are best left in the care of a family

> Calling on every student during discussion validates everyone's experiences as well as keeping everyone involved.

member," could be an anticipation guide sentence for an upcoming selection about a child who becomes the responsibility of an uncaring relative.

Unknown Vocabulary Words

It is a great aid to comprehension to understand vocabulary such as *disdainfully,* but if the word can be skipped over without affecting comprehension of the story, then it is not a critical word for preteaching. The greater the importance of a word to understanding the story, the more it needs to be explained and connected prior to reading. Apprentice represents a concept, and the relationship between the midwife and the girl in *The Midwife's Apprentice* (Cushman, 1995) might not be understood without knowledge of what apprenticeship entails.

Unknown words can be figured out through the strategy of context clues. Context clues may be at the sentence level or at the story level. Learning how to pick out print clues and meaning clues can be explicitly taught. Reminders, questions, or hints while students are reading whole texts provide scaffolding until using context becomes an independent strategy. Chapter 8 gives many ideas for teaching vocabulary, including context clues.

Visualizing the Setting

Unfamiliar settings and times can be easily imagined when the teacher provides pictures. When reading about a story set in Japan, when trying to imagine Kubla Khan's court, when reading about rural Mississippi in the 1930s, it helps the reader to have a picture in her head, so she can see the characters moving through the setting rather than on an empty stage or misplaced in a setting that looks more like her own neighborhood. Clothing, mountain ranges, architecture, and unusual tools and foods come alive. Maps can serve the same purpose. These pictures are not always easy to find, but they are well worth the search.

Visualizing aids memory and deepens comprehension. Zhicheng Zhang (1993, p. 9) claims that visual images are retained longer than verbal recall. "Visual images may effectively transfer large chunks of information to long-term memory and may also act as the most potent device to aid recall of verbal material." The brain's storage capacity for visual information exceeds its capacity for verbal material (Oxford, as cited in Zhang).

> If the word can be skipped over without affecting comprehension of the story, then it is not a critical word for preteaching.

Although the teacher may initially supply pictures of the setting, students need to continue envisioning the scene, adding new props as the story progresses. To make visualization a strategy, prompt students to keep imagining and have students share the images that they see. There will be an amazing variety. The following example is a response by a sixth grader to "Which scene in the chapter could you visualize the best?" Notice how the writer adds homes that look more like his than the homes of ancient Greece, but there is also no doubt that the writer can imagine Ulysses' longing to reach home as he sees the distant familiar sights.

> In *Keeper of the Winds*, I could visualize Ulysses and his crew almost reaching their hometown. I saw Ulysses' castle on the top of the mountain. I also saw the large red brick houses with the smoke coming out. Along with that I saw people walking on the dirt road. You could see the port with ships lined all around and the mates were working hard on them. In the distance you could see people farming their land.

Drawing scenes also helps students deepen the images as students return to the text to get the details that they want to include. A single scene can be drawn, or a series can be depicted, which helps to firm up the sequence.

Comprehension Skills and Strategies During Reading

Guided reading allows for strategy instruction and constant interchange among teacher and students, but what about providing scaffolding or support during silent reading? Independent reading is perhaps the most difficult time to try to assess reading strategies because the entire complex process is happening silently and without many outward signs. One strategy students must use when reading silently is to monitor their own comprehension.

Monitoring Comprehension

Monitoring comprehension includes paying attention to what one has just read and judging if it is sensible and consistent. M. Grabe and S. Mann (as cited in Anderson et al., 1985) provide an example of consistent and inconsistent paragraphs. Poor readers do not notice the inconsistency because they are not monitoring.

Guided reading allows for strategy instruction and constant interchange among teacher and students.

All the people who work on this ship get along very well. The people who make a lot of money and the people who don't make much are still friends. The officers treat me as an equal. We often eat our meals together. I guess we are just one big happy family.

All the people who work on this ship get along very well. The people who make a lot of money and the people who don't make much are still friends. The officers treat me like dirt. We often eat our meals together. I guess we are just one big happy family.

Anderson et al. (1985) in the nationally commissioned report *Becoming a Nation of Readers*, proposes that poor readers do not adequately control the way they read or perhaps they do not see the point of reading and thus do not monitor as they read. Some students are just "doing school" and glide on through the text without constructing meaning—without connecting what passes before their eyes with actually thinking about what they are reading.

To help students develop the strategy of monitoring comprehension, the teacher can use guided reading, which is a read and respond, read and respond technique. During silent reading, she can provide a virtual teacher, that is, a study guide, a set of questions, or specific times to stop and think. These can be thought of as written prompts or reminders, similar to what a teacher might ask during guided reading, so that the student can never go too far without constructing meaning.

Embedded questions are questions that are actually written in the middle of the text and not at the end of the passage. The advantage is that the questions are asked just after the child has read a relatively short passage. If he cannot respond to the question, the reader immediately goes back to what was just read and finds or formulates the answer. Very few texts are written this way, with embedded questions, but no matter. The teacher can alter the text in order to provide guidance. The teacher can accomplish this in two ways, with stop and go questions or with embedded question markers in the text.

With **stop and go questions**, the student reads a question and then reads the text until the answer is found or a clue for a response is encountered. When a student knows the question and reads until encountering the answer, he finds himself reading for a purpose rather than just aimlessly wandering through the text. This aids comprehension considerably. Stop and go questions are the only way to really develop the strategy of making predictions during silent reading.

> Some students are just "doing school" and glide through the text without constructing meaning.

The questions should be in order and not have page numbers. When page numbers are included, it encourages students to scan or skip pages on which no answers are to be found. If the child reads several pages without finding the answer, he has to use a fix-up strategy such as rereading or reconsidering.

When I've asked students if they prefer the stop and go style, or if they prefer reading straight through and answering questions at the end, it is always about a 50-50 split. However, it is almost always the weakest readers who prefer the stop and go style because it provides a nudge toward continuing to concentrate on the passage and to continually monitor what is being read. Their success rate is improved with support.

A second method to encourage self-monitoring during silent reading is to insert **embedded markers** (in the form of numbers) in the text that match numbered questions, listed on a separate piece of paper. To show students where the embedded numbers go in the text, the teacher can reproduce the text on an overhead transparency. The students then copy the numbers into their own texts where indicated. Or, if a teacher has infinite time she could insert the numbers into the students' texts herself.

An adaptation from Marguerite Henry's *King of the Wind* (1951, pp. 91-94) provides an example. The story tells of a carter who forces a horse named Sham to pull a load too heavy for one animal up an incline. The cruelty of the act is witnessed by a crowd of onlookers who are silently fearful for Sham. Sham's burden is too great, and he falls to his knees between the shafts of the cart. The carter wants to force the horse to his feet by setting fire to a log braced under Sham's tail. A Quaker named Jethro Coke steps forward and offers a handful of gold coins for the struggling horse. The hard-hearted carter accepts the money. A young boy helps unharness Sham as the crowd applauds and cheers because the horse's life has been saved.

The teacher embeds numbers throughout a copy of the actual story that correspond to the following steps:

1. Make a prediction.
2. Tell what is happening.
3. Make a prediction.
4. Was your prediction right?
5. Visualize the scene.

> When a student knows a question and reads until encountering the answer, he finds himself reading for a purpose rather than just aimlessly wandering through the text.

However, if students require more scaffolding, the teacher can use **question markers** that are more specific, with the steps written in parentheses following the question:

1. Will Sham make it up the hill? (prediction)

2. Why didn't any of the passersby stop the driver from using his whip? (fact question)

3. What is the Quaker going to do? (prediction)

4. Was your prediction right or wrong? (confirm or reject prediction)

5. Why was there laughter and clapping? Who might have been watching? (visualization and inference)

The teacher can also use both these formats simultaneously, distributing the complete questions to students who need greater prompting, and giving the more independent version to students who are able to read with less prompting. The students might not even notice there are two versions.

Embedded markers are another method to encourage self-monitoring during silent reading.

As students need less guidance during silent reading to identify strategies or responses in the text, they can determine their own responses. **Say something** and **write something** make excellent bridges. Say something is done with partner reading. As students finish an entire page, each partner must turn to the other and *say something*. *Write something* is a single sentence written at the end of each page and is done independently.

Usually, but not always, the "somethings" are summaries of the plot. This technique also serves to help students monitor their comprehension so they don't get too far before they realize that they have not understood. The more practice that students have in reacting to text rather than just summarizing, the more likely they will respond at the end of the page with a question, a reaction, or an interpretation. For example, from *King of the Wind*:

p. 38 Agba runs into a camel dealer who recognizes he is a stable boy from the royal stables.

p. 39 Agba is revived with camel milk with honey. If he liked it, will Sham?

p. 40 Sham is weak and thin. I bet he gets well, or there will be no story.

p. 41 Sham loves the camel milk and honey. Agba promises him he will be King of the Wind.

Good readers will have more complex responses, but less mature readers will at least have the literal plot and will be able to fully participate in a guided discussion with higher-level questioning. Write something provides an excellent assessment of comprehension and is easily checked by the teacher. As an added benefit, it makes a good foundation for learning to write a summary.

The teacher can extend this activity by having children compare and evaluate the short summaries. Using children's work as models is often more interesting than teacher modeling. Students can explicitly explain and demonstrate how they came to their answers as well as showing their work.

With **reading logs**, students are free to respond when and with what information they choose, making this activity the most open-ended type of response to reading. Again the more opportunities students have to work with reacting to text rather than just summarizing, the more likely they will respond with connections, inferences, questions about what will happen, and personal responses. Teachers can encourage higher-level responses by responding to the logs with higher-level answers or by asking students to respond to starter stems, such as, "The most interesting part was . . .", "This reminds me of another story where . . . .", "The scene that I see most vividly in my mind is . . . .", or "The main character must have been feeling . . . because . . . ."

> **Reading logs make for the most open-ended type of response to reading.**

Predicting and Confirming or Rejecting the Prediction

Predicting is another strategy that good readers use while they are reading. It is a strategy that functions at two levels: predicting the next word or phrase in a sentence or predicting the next event in a story. Good readers predict at the sentence level all the time, which helps with word recognition.

Alex had smooth black hair reaching to his _____. The reader who is predicting is expecting *ears, shoulders, collar, waist* or any noun that could act as a marker for hair length. Successful prediction requires being aware of the meaning (semantic cues) and of regular English sentence patterns (syntactic cues). As the first letter comes into view, *Alex had smooth black hair reaching to his s*_____, the reader also adds graphophonic cues and within a microsecond confirms *shoulders*.

Because good readers make predictions based on what they expect will follow they sometimes mismatch the text, especially in oral reading, because the brain and eye spans are always ahead of the voice. Good readers, if they have substituted one part of speech for another when reading orally, are able to change the remaining parts of speech in the sentence, maintain the intended meaning, and read the whole sentence in fluent correct English patterns (Weaver, 1998).

A **cloze** exercise is an excellent way to practice predicting using semantic and syntactic cues. Cloze passages (from the word closure) omit every eighth word and substitute a blank. The entire first and last sentences are left intact. Any answer that makes sense is acceptable. Because cloze requires constructing meaning from an incomplete story and feels like a puzzle, students pay very close attention to the content. It is a good exercise for partners because of the social interaction as they discuss choices and help each other notice when a word does not fit with the meaning or with the syntax of the sentence.

When preparing a cloze exercise, do not use a word bank at the bottom of the page except with very young readers, because students will be deprived of using several comprehension strategies, and the idea of "one correct answer" is reinforced.

With cloze passages, semantic and syntactic clues are used to fill in the missing words. The reader uses past knowledge and infers time and place. He reads ahead to use all of the context clues that are available, and then he goes back to correct himself after coming across additional information. The reader predicts, confirms, and rejects—all valuable strategies in reading.

The second level of prediction is **predicting at the story level**. A student who predicts is more likely to monitor her own comprehension because she wonders if her prediction is going to be the choice made by the author. Some predicting is more like self-questioning: I wonder why he did that? That seems strange. I bet he doesn't have any friends. Students' prior knowledge may significantly influence what they wonder and predict (Zhang, 1993).

One method for practicing predicting is to reproduce a story and cut it into sections, only distributing one section at a time. Another method is to reproduce the story on an overhead transparency showing only one section at a time. A prediction tree can be used for responses (Figure 7.1).

> A student who predicts is more likely to monitor her own comprehension because she wonders if her prediction is going to be the choice made by the author.

PREDICTION TREE

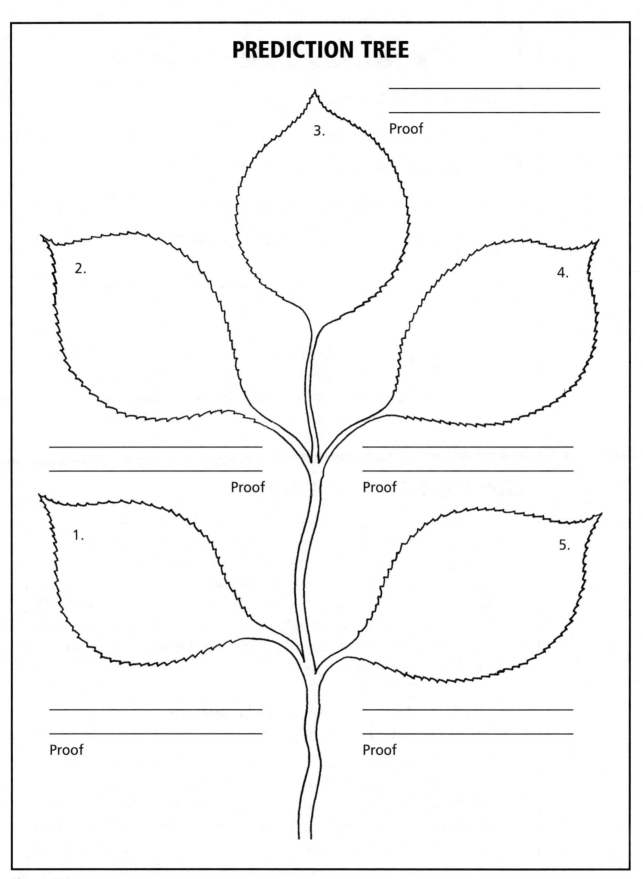

Figure 7.1

RETELLING INSTRUCTIONAL CHART

To RETELL part of a story, try...

Putting the story into your own words.

Saying the ideas in the order they happened in the story.

Including all the most important events and ideas.

Using the book to help you remember events or ideas.

Figure 7.2

A retelling instructional chart, as in Figure 7.2, helps young readers improve their comprehension.

After reading a section, the student must make a prediction. Being required to write it down ensures that everyone will actually predict, and it encourages more active participation. The probability of the prediction can be discussed as well as which clues were used to draw that conclusion.

Strategies After Reading

Strategies can be taught or practiced before, during, or after reading the selection. Most of the preceding strategies were suitable for before or during reading but could be used at any time. The following reading strategies and teaching activities can be used during guided reading or after reading as students go back and analyze in greater depth what they have read. The reader eventually orchestrates all the strategies for simultaneous use, but explicit teaching of individual strategies helps students identify and apply the strategies.

Stating Main Ideas and Retelling Important Information

A strategy that good readers use is to group information according to the main idea or around central events so that the content is easier to remember. This is not so easy to do. Young readers start by retelling the story. Retelling improves comprehension, sense of story structure, and oral language. James Baumann, Helene Hooten, and Patricia White (1996) suggest using a retelling instructional chart, as illustrated in Figure 7.2.

The next step is to state the main idea. Being able to state the main idea is more difficult than retelling because it requires combining, evaluating, and sometimes inferring information. Poor readers have a difficult time relating all the bits of information to each other and deciding what is the main idea. They can tell you several of the details but not combine them into a meaningful whole. To relate the bits of information into a main idea sentence, try this summary format.

> Summary Format: Somebody? Wanted? But? So?

> Example: *Goldilocks wanted* to see what was in the house, *but* the bears returned and frightened her, *so* she ran away.

The **write something** technique can also provide good practice for identifying main ideas, especially when the "something" is a one-sentence summary less than one written line in length. To make the ideas this short, students must paraphrase, which is another way to manipulate information and improve recall. Whole class processing and evaluation of the "somethings" helps students understand why one piece of information or one event may be more critical than others. Retelling or summarizing the events of a story are important methods for assessing comprehension.

> When bits of information are tied together into chunks, it helps the reader to see the relationships.

Organizing Ideas into Patterns

Good readers group ideas into organizational patterns such as cause and effect, comparison and contrast, and topic and subtopic. Good readers also sequence story events. When bits of information are tied together into chunks, it helps the reader to see the relationships among the various pieces of information. Good readers summarize and paraphrase in order to group and manipulate the information. This also fosters understanding and memory. Look at the following list for thirty seconds and then try to write it from memory: Oranges, rye bread, pick up blouse at cleaners, compost recycling bags, mustard, drop off pants at the cleaners, spackle, sliced ham.

Most adults who are successful with this experiment categorize or group—grocery story, cleaners, and hardware store. They also count the number of items. Most children try to memorize without a structure. Students need to be taught what the organizational patterns are and how they function.

Story mapping is an enjoyable way to practice **sequencing**. It can be done in a written format, as in Figure 7.3, or in a picture format. In written form, it looks like a simple outline (Routman, 1991, p. 96).

STORY MAP

Title: _____

Setting: _____

Characters: _____

Problem: _____

Event 1: _____

Event 2: _____

Event 3: _____

Resolution: _____

Figure 7.3

Story mapping is an enjoyable way to practice sequencing, as in Figure 7.3.

In picture form, the story map can be a series of pictures depicting the major events of the story connected by arrows in a flow chart. Pictures can also be arranged in a tic-tac-toe grid with the first line for the beginning of the story, the middle line for the middle, and the bottom line for the ending. For a whole novel, chapters can be assigned to groups that draw several scenes per chapter. As children visualize the scenes, they also unscramble the sequence and determine cause and effect.

Direct teaching of the elements of literature, or story grammar (opening event, characters, problem, resolution, setting, theme), does not seem to have much effect on comprehension (May, 1998) perhaps because each is being identified as a separate entity without connecting relationships.

The Venn diagram (see Figure 10.6 for an example) is a perfect vehicle for students to **compare and contrast**. They use it to see the similarities and differences between characters, settings, and even stories. It is a set of overlapping circles with the similarities listed in the overlap.

Cause and effect is a more difficult concept than sequencing or comparing and contrasting, because it often involves inference. It is also a more complex way of thinking for young students. Students who are not accustomed to thinking in this pattern may simply list adjoining events, whether the events have any relationship to each other or not. Once the teacher has directly taught what is meant by cause and effect relationships, most stories and informational texts can be used for practicing this organizational strategy because characters have motivations for their actions or one event dominoes into another.

An effective way for students to become more aware of cause and effect relationships in literature is to use a two-column worksheet that lists cause situations in one column and effects in the other. One side of each pair is left blank so the student fills in either the cause or effect. These questions are at the literal rearranged or inferential levels.

Topic and subtopic is more often found in nonfiction books. Webs or incomplete outlines are effective graphic organizers for helping students become cognizant of which details go with which main ideas. When students use the topic and subtopic organizational pattern in their own writing, it can have a positive impact on reading comprehension (Shanahan, 1997b).

Using Fix-up Strategies When the Text Doesn't Make Sense

Read aloud the following paragraph as an experiment:

> The Boat
>
> A man was building a boat in his
> cellar. As soon as he had finished
> the boot, he tried to take it through the
> the cellar door. It would not go though
> the door. So he had to take it a part.
> He should of planed better (Schwartz, 1997, p. 41).

Did you notice the conflicting word and meaning cues in the passage? Did you detect *boot* for *boat*, the double *the, though* for *through, a part* for *apart, should of* for *should've,* and *planed* for *planned*? You probably fixed the errors as you read for meaning.

Good readers who are monitoring their comprehension use fix-up strategies when the text does not make sense, usually because the reader has miscued rather than because the text was incoherent. Corrective action may mean rereading a section, skipping the part or word that is unclear

> Good readers who are monitoring their comprehension use fix-up strategies when the text does not make sense.

hoping that future information will clarify the problem, or just rethinking. Good readers go back and read more carefully, consider everything they know about the topic or root words, look at the pictures, get help from another source, or ask someone. These behaviors can be more easily seen during oral reading when the reader self-corrects after using a fix-up strategy.

Poor readers aren't aware that the text is not making sense, and when they realize they have a problem, they are unsure of what action to take. Often, they just keep going. Frequent questioning of the reader, through guided reading or the virtual teacher, can help those without fix-up strategies, because they need to first realize that they didn't understand. Explicit teaching of fix-up strategies is necessary for these students. The teacher can help students learn to apply fix-up strategies by questioning rather than correcting:

> Student: One of the chefs hailed the other captains.
>
> Teacher: Was he calling them for dinner in the middle of the battle?
>
> Student: (Puzzled, then rereads.) One of the chiefs hailed the other captains.

For those students who want to jump in and correct their classmates, the teacher can ask them to offer a problem-solving clue instead. R. M. Schwartz (1997) suggests posting the following reminder in the class-room to let students know that the ultimate task is to obtain meaning, not get every word correct the first time.

Readers know that:

1. Good readers think about meaning.

2. All readers make mistakes.

3. Good readers notice and fix some mistakes.

Strategies for Higher-Level Thinking: Inferring, Generalizing, Evaluating

Mature readers go beyond the printed lines: They infer, generalize, and evaluate. Students need to be explicitly taught what an inference is and that good readers are supposed to make inferences while reading. To infer, readers must combine what is in the text with their own knowledge.

It comes as a revelation to young readers that the author has not directly stated everything that he wishes the reader to know.

Young readers assume that everything that needs to be said has been said by the author, and in order to answer the teacher's questions, they need only to look back to find the relevant section in the text. It comes as a revelation that the author has not directly stated everything that he wishes the reader to know. Good readers use their prior knowledge to fill in the gaps that the author has left. Students who do not think beyond the concrete level benefit greatly from hearing how other students used their own knowledge—knowledge the concrete thinker also possesses—to put together two or more pieces of information to form an inference.

Character motivation seems to be one area in particular that requires making inferences because authors often choose to show motivation through action rather than through direct explanation. When teachers ask, "Why did the character do that?", students appear stymied until the teacher asks, "If you were in that situation, what would you do?" It is as if they think book characters act completely differently than real people do.

Good readers also generalize and evaluate what they read, but they sometimes need help in isolating details. Graphic organizers help to make details visible and separate from the tangle of information in the story. Two good examples are Shanahan's Character Perspective Chart (1997a) and the decision-making chart.

Character perspective charting goes beyond a simple story map, which lists only the elements of the story. Perspective charting asks students to consider the problem, goal, reaction, and theme from the perspectives of different characters. Charting helps to identify the conflicts of the story and makes the elements visible for comparison. Interpretation rather than simple summarization is the result. Figure 7.4 is from *The Big Orange Splot* by Daniel Pinkwater (1977).

Another graphic organizer that makes the conflict visible is the decision-making chart. Not only must conflicting reasons be identified, but the student must also make a personal choice about the conflict and identify the best reason for the decision. In Figure 7.5, the student must decide if Ulysses should stay with Calypso or continue his journey home.

Graphic organizers help students identify critical information and evaluate decisions. They are excellent bridges between guided reading and independent critical reading.

Graphic organizers are excellent bridges between guided reading and independent critical readings.

CHARACTER PERSPECTIVE CHART
The Big Orange Splot

Main character: Who is the main character? Mr. Plumbean	Main character: Who is the main character? Mr. Plumbean's Neighbor
Setting: Where and when does the story take place? Plumbean's Neighborhood	Setting: Where and when does the story take place? Plumbean's Neighborhood
Problem: What is the main character's problem? Plumbean's neighbors pester him	Problem: What is the main character's problem? Bird drops paint on Plumbean's house
Goal: What is the main character's goal? What does the character want? To decorate his house and get neighbors to leave him alone	Goal: What is the main character's goal? What does the character want? To make neighborhood all the same again
Attempt: What does the main character do to solve the problem or get the goal? Decorates house and talks to each neighbor	Attempt: What does the main character do to solve the problem or get the goal? Try to convince him to change then each changes to be like him
Outcome: What does the main character do to solve the problem or get the goal? Plumbean's house looks like his dreams and neighbors accept it	Outcome: What does the main character do to solve the problem or get the goal? All houses in neighborhood are decorated in same way
Reaction: How does the main character feel about the outcome? Happy	Reaction: How does the main character feel about the outcome? Happy
Theme: What point did the author want to make? Follow your dreams	Theme: What point did the author want to make? It is important to be the same

Figure 7.4 From Timothy Shanahan and Sherrell Shanahan (May 1997). "Character Perspective Charting: Helping Children to Develop a More Complete Conception of Story." *The Reading Teacher,* 50 (8), 668–677. Reprinted with permission of Timothy Shanahan and the International Reading Assoc. All rights reserved.

DECISION-MAKING CHART: ULYSSES

Calypso

Should Ulysses Return Home?

Ulysses should stay with Calypso because . . .

1. He would not grow old. (immortal)

2. At home he would live on memories.

3. He would be kicked out of his castle.

4. She'd make him her eternal consort.

5. His home will be wherever Titan's rule.

6. His other son would kill him.

Ulysses should return home because . . .

1. He should see his son.

2. His wife is being faithful.

3. He could be turned into an animal by Calypso.

4. His things are being taken.

5. He has been gone for 20 years.

6. He has paid for blinding Polyphemous, Poseidon's son.

Your conclusion:

Return home.

Best reason:

His wife is being faithful to him.

Maggie

Figure 7.5 Graphic Organizer: Decision-making Chart.

SkyLight Training and Publishing Inc.

Strategies for Influencing the Attitude and Motivation of Readers

Attitude and motivation also contribute to the success or lack of success of the reader. Attitudes and dispositions cannot be taught, but they can be influenced.

The most critical attitude or realization is knowing that reading is meaningful communication. This attitude is influenced by observing expert modeling, by being encouraged to constantly seek meaning, both in guided and independent reading, and from discussion and social interaction about reading.

Good students understand that they can learn by reading. They realize that school is not an isolated set of events unconnected to each other and unconnected to the outside world, and what they are learning about is of personal, real use. They are willing to alter or expand their preconceived notions—to be open-minded—abandoning, modifying, or reforming their schemas as new information is added. Teachers who connect the content that is read by the class to their daily events, experiences, and future lives can influence those students who seem to think the entire extent of their job is to fill in all the blanks on a worksheet.

Reading requires the skill and the will to read. Reading is a complex task that requires years of sustained attention and practice in order to become proficient, but for children who love to read, it is a pleasure every step of the way. One of the balance points in reading instruction is providing both cognitive instruction and an emphasis on motivation and social interaction (Gambrell, 1996). The deepest motivation is intrinsic, but a teacher can set up a climate that makes motivation more likely to develop.

Interest

Of all the materials available, choose the most interesting books and stories for instruction. "Research findings indicate that both good and poor readers perform significantly better on high interest as compared with low interest materials" (Asher as cited in Fink, 1998, p. 389). Great stories foster the love of reading, and many children first became hooked on reading when their teacher read aloud to them. Interest enhanced comprehension with fifth-grade readers, even with materials that were difficult (Renninger as cited in Wigfield and Guthrie, 1997). Rosalie Fink

Reading requires the skill and the will to read.

(1998) interviewed adult dyslexics who became very successful in their fields. They all became avid readers, usually between the ages of 10 and 12, because they became interested in a particular genre.

Long materials—books—are usually better than short materials because the flow of ideas is continuous and the interest is already present at the start of each day's lesson. Background has been developed so the concepts, settings, and characters are easy to understand. With a series of unrelated short stories, interest, schema, and concepts have to be rebuilt every day. This may be the best reason for not using a lot of worksheets; they just aren't interesting, and the class has to start from scratch each time.

Choice

Another way to encourage interest is to allow students to have some choice in the materials that they read. Self-choice is one of the strongest components in literature circles, readers' workshops, and silent sustained reading. As mentioned in previous chapters, students consider the most interesting books to be those chosen by them. Choice implies that there should be a wide variety of books available from which to choose, so classrooms need to be well supplied.

Success

Motivation is influenced by success. Allan Wigfield and John T. Guthrie (1997) found several factors of motivation that correlated with reading achievement. Several were related to success—a feeling of efficacy (positive self-evaluation of competence), challenge (satisfaction of mastering material), a desire for competition, and social recognition. Students' self-concepts as readers are linked to reading achievement (Gambrell, 1996). Motivation and success enhance each other, but it is difficult to maintain motivation if a reader is not successful.

Teachers need to set up situations in which success is more likely to occur. For example, providing choice in reading materials will contribute to the students' success, as will scaffolded or supported instruction. A particularly good first question for struggling readers is: Tell me something about the story. Even struggling readers can answer successfully in front of the class or reading group, and the teacher is able to ascertain something about which strategies the student is using.

A way to encourage interest is to allow students to have some choice in the materials they read.

Providing Time

Many children really do like reading, and they are willing to spend time and effort to learn to read. However, they are not willing to give up basketball, phone calls, video games, friends, and internet chat rooms. Family scheduling conflicts or just plain family conflicts also make it difficult for many students to read at home. The teacher who schedules uninterrupted extended periods of reading in school gives students opportunities that they may not be able to arrange for themselves.

Social Opportunity to Discuss Books

Reading is an individual and isolated activity, and this is one of the reasons it is so unappealing to many children. If given an opportunity to talk about books that they are reading, they become motivated and improve comprehension. The opportunity to share thoughts about material read was another motivating factor found in Wigfield and Guthrie's study. Teachers who communicate thoughts about their own personal reading become role models as they share their enthusiasm.

The Teacher

The teacher does make a difference. "Studies indicate that about 15% of the variation among children in reading achievement at the end of the school year is attributable to factors that relate to the skill and effectiveness of the teacher" (Anderson et al., 1985, p. 86). The teacher who understands the complexity of the reading process, teaches strategies, and fosters a love of reading will make a difference in the success of her students.

The teacher who schedules uninterrupted extended periods of reading in school gives students opportunities that they may not be able to arrange for themselves.

Increasing Vocabulary

*Words are the soul's ambassadors, who go
Abroad upon her errands to and fro.*

—J. HOWELL, "OF WORDS"

Substantial knowledge of vocabulary provides many benefits to the speaker, listener, reader, and writer. It is the single most powerful predictor of how well a reader understands text, with a correlation factor of .71 (Thorndike, as cited in May, 1998). This means that seven of every ten good readers also have good vocabularies. Thus, it might seem reasonable to teach list after list of vocabulary words in order to improve reading comprehension.

However, it is a correlation, not a cause. Both vocabulary and reading comprehension depend on verbal abilities, but wide reading increases vocabulary—not the other way around. Vocabulary is only one of the factors that influence reading comprehension. Background knowledge, motivation, text organization, and self-monitoring are also important. Yet, readers can miss the whole point of a passage if they do not understand key vocabulary words, and they certainly can miss the nuances if they do not understand certain words. Vocabulary *is* important.

Our use of the word *vocabulary* will focus on reading vocabulary, which means acquiring new meanings for words in print that are not in the student's speaking vocabulary. Identifying known words in print should be thought of as word recognition. This chapter will focus on how definitions and new word usage are learned: how vocabulary is learned from reading; and how vocabulary can be learned for reading. Linking vocabulary study with reading is a strong strategy because new words are encountered in meaningful context, and there are many opportunities for using those words in responses to reading.

The idea of teaching vocabulary for its own sake, outside of any context, does not match anything that is known about long-term learning and worthwhile use of class time. "To separate word knowledge from reading . . . is in essence weakening a natural bond" (Laflamme, 1997). Out- of-context learning of vocabulary seems best suited for calendars featuring the word of the day.

> As an average child matures, he will learn an additional 3,000–4,000 words per year, but only 400 are formally taught in school.

Vocabulary Development

Jeanne Chall (as cited in Irvin, 1990) estimated that typical first graders understand and use about 6,000 different words. As an average child matures, he will learn an additional 3,000–4,000 words per year, according to various research studies, but only about 400 are formally taught in school. How are the remainder learned? Some come from direct experience. Students who play sports learn *dribble, offensive, bunt*, and *clutch*.

Some words are discovered by watching television. Every child in the United States knows the word *morph* from watching commercials, cartoons, and the Nickelodeon channel, and hopefully one day, they will learn *metamorphosis.* Also, many new words come from daily conversation. "Billy, you're just *exasperating*!"

However, most vocabulary is learned through reading. Almost without exception, those people who read widely have large vocabularies. The use of multiple modalities provide one of the advantages in learning words from reading: The word is seen, it is read in meaningful context, and it is heard as most readers mentally pronounce new words to decide if they are already in the reader's meaning vocabulary. W. E. Nagy (1988) provides fascinating statistics about vocabulary acquisition. Readers learn only about one word in twenty through context, but an average fifth grader who reads for about twenty-five minutes a day will encounter 20,000 unfamiliar words a year. That accounts for 1,000 new words learned each year through reading.

Depth of Word Knowledge

There are several levels of word knowledge. There are words that we have never seen or heard before, words that we remember having seen or heard but are unsure of the meaning, words that we have a general idea about, words that we are fairly sure about, and words that we know well and can use correctly. Well-known words can stimulate mental images and emotions as well as verbal recall. It is only through many exposures in varying contexts that words are thoroughly learned. Ten to twenty-four exposures are required to gain comprehensive knowledge of a word.

> A variety of contexts is important for learning connotative meanings or for learning multiple meanings of words.

A variety of contexts is important for learning connotative meanings or for learning multiple meanings of words, such as *run* fast, a *run* in my stocking, the blood *ran* through his veins, home *run*, *run* away, *run* to the store, my horse *ran* last, the car *ran* over the nail, the car *ran* out of gas, the rain *ran* down the window, the colors *ran* into each other, *run* a red light, *ran* late, *ran* low, the *running board* on the Dodge, *run* the blockade, *run* for election, *ran* me ragged, rum *runner*, *ran* into difficulties, etc. The more encounters with a word, the greater the depth of understanding.

Is It Worthwhile to Teach Vocabulary?

Because so much of vocabulary is learned through wide reading, is it worthwhile to teach vocabulary at all? Yes, it is worthwhile, using both direct and indirect methods. As students study literature and content areas, there are words that are critical to comprehending the text. Teaching meaning vocabulary used to be considered the domain of the intermediate and upper grades, but with the introduction of trade books in primary grades, reading vocabulary is no longer controlled. Words outside of the reader's speaking vocabulary are now encountered more frequently in the lower grades. Direct teaching of those crucial words helps students to understand the text.

Which Words Are Most Easily Learned?

W. B. Elley (1996) found that the words most easily learned were those that were repeated often, those accompanied by illustrations, and those accompanied by meaning clues. Words that were connected to the plot, that were vivid, or that were associated with a familiar concept were also easily learned. For example, the post-test scores from Elley's studies showed a 40% gain for *parasol*, but little gain was shown for *anguish*.

One reason why *parasol* was easily learned is that it is a synonym for the more common word *umbrella*. Synonyms are easy to learn because the concept is already known. Words that are already known but have different and new meanings are more difficult; for example, *acute angle* and *acute pain*. Words such as *integrity, epidemic,* or *glorify* represent new concepts. They do not have single word synonyms, or they require background knowledge. Some words are used only in certain contexts. *Balmy* means warm, but it can't be used in the context of reheating dinner. "I'm going to put this chicken in the microwave to make it a little *balmier*." Concept words require more explanation and more usage in varied contexts.

Indirect Teaching of Vocabulary

Indirect teaching of vocabulary is elusive to define or measure. For example, primary students learn many new words when their teacher reads aloud to them, although the foremost reason for reading aloud is to learn to love stories and to learn a sense of story or expositional text. Nevertheless, children also learn new vocabulary as they listen to the story and match the events to the picture. The effect of indirect teaching of vocabulary is not as deep as the effect of direct teaching, but it is still significant.

The studies by Elley illustrate the differences between direct and indirect teaching. A short story was read aloud to seven-year-olds. The story took about ten minutes to read, contained twenty unfamiliar words, and was

Words that were connected to the plot, that were vivid, or that were associated with a familiar concept were easily learned.

read three times over a period of seven days. There was some discussion of the story, but no explanation of the unfamiliar vocabulary was provided. Nonetheless, classroom gains from pretest to post-test scores of vocabulary ranged from 13% to 21%, averaging about 15%. When the scores were analyzed by ability levels of the children, the top 75% averaged a 15% gain, while the lowest-ability children averaged about a 23% gain.

The study was repeated with eight-year-olds but with a twist. In this study, half of the students listened to a book read aloud three times. The other half also heard the story, but the teacher stopped to explain unfamiliar words. Students who participated in the indirect lesson, again averaged a 15% gain, but those who heard explanations of the unfamiliar words gained 40% on the post-test.

Frank May (1998) presents an interesting study done by Edward Maher that deals with vocabulary gain and various study methods such as reading aloud to older students (fifth graders). For each group, vocabulary words were listed on the board before a selection was read. The control group looked up the words in the dictionary and read the selection silently. The experimental group had the story read to them by the teacher. As the vocabulary words were encountered in reading, the teacher asked if any of the students knew the word. If they didn't, she simply told them the meaning, reread the sentence, and continued. Brief pretests and posttests were administered. The control group retained less than 50% of the words on the post-test, but the experimental group retained over 90%.

Many words are learned through guided reading and discussion although they are not formally taught. Very often the teacher just mentions a detail: The *fronds* are the leaves on a palm tree. Or, a student gives a vocabulary clue or a definition in a response, "The monster took so long to surface because he had to *depressurize*. If he came up too soon, he would have burst."

Choose only two or three words from the day's reading and teach those words in depth.

Choosing Words for Direct Teaching

There are several guidelines for choosing which vocabulary words to teach. May (1998) suggests choosing only two or three words from the day's reading and teaching those words in depth. He considers that a few words well taught is a far superior situation to teaching many words superficially, most of which will not be remembered anyway. Nagy

(1988), in synthesizing several studies, concluded that to make a difference in reading comprehension, vocabulary knowledge must be "encyclopedic," or thoroughly understood, and not merely rely on definitional knowledge of the words in the text. This implies that to acquire deep knowledge of words, sufficient time is needed. Therefore, fewer words should be taught. Other guidelines for choosing vocabulary follow.

Lack of Clues by the Author

If a word in the book being read by the class is critical, but the author gives few or no clues as to its meaning, teach the word. If the author has provided direct explanations, or if he has provided sufficient context clues, or if the words can be skipped without affecting the meaning of the story, then there is little reason for the teacher to provide instruction.

Words That Are Important in Their General Usage

Some words may not be critical to the story, but they are going to be encountered over and over again in general usage. These words are worthwhile choices for instruction.

Concept Words

Words that represent new concepts need to be taught, but make sure they are not taught as synonyms for already known concepts. *Accomplice* is not synonymous with *friend* or *helper.* It does not seem to have a single-word synonym. In the content areas, new concepts abound, such as *superconductor* or "changing to a *democratic* form of leadership." These words need considerable explanation and a whole background of connected ideas and examples, not just a definition.

Words Used Inappropriately

On the spot mini-lessons can be used to clear up confusion caused by words used inappropriately. For example: The *pheasants* lived on feudal lands under the rule of the lord of the *manner;* the *sail* was tied to the mast with oxhide *tongs;* it was *funner* to work in groups than to work alone.

Words Critical to the Story Line

Camille Blachowicz and Peter Fisher (1996) offer a useful suggestion for teaching vocabulary. For an upcoming story, map out the story line choos-

To make a difference in reading comprehension, vocabulary knowledge must be "encyclopedic" or thoroughly understood.

VOCABULARY STORY MAP: "THE NECKLACE"

Characters

Mathilde, who believes there is nothing more **humiliating** than to look poor among other women who are rich.
M. Loisel, who gives his wife 400 **francs** for a ball gown.
She suffered **ceaselessly** from the ugliness of her curtains.

Setting

The **vestibule** of the palace
The **ministerial** ball
A rented **garret**

Problem

Mathilde loses a borrowed diamond necklace and is sick with **chagrin** and **anguish**.
M. Loisel borrows money and accepts **ruinous obligations**.
They are **impoverished** by the debt.

Resolution

M. and Mme. pay the **accumulation** of debt and interest for ten years.
After the debt is paid, Mathilde sees the friend from whom she borrowed the necklace and finds out it was only **paste**.

Possible Big Ideas

Putting on airs, **humiliation**, egotism, arrogance, conceit, vanity, **disdain**, haughtiness, destitute, indigent, irony, false pride, image, deprivation, poverty, **calamity, compromised, luxuries**

Figure 8.1 Story map for "The Necklace" by Guy de Maupassant.

ing vocabulary words that are critical to the story elements. This vocabulary should be used multiple times in discussing, explaining, summarizing, and responding to the story. Figure 8.1 is an example of a vocabulary story map at the high school level. The Possible Big Ideas section includes words that may not be in the story but are needed for effective discussion.

These are exactly the kind of words that students often lack, such as words describing character traits or precise concepts and description (*haughtiness* and *destitute*). Without those words, the summary usually reads like this:

> Mathilde felt sad because she was sort of poor. To cheer her up, her husband got an invitation to a fancy dance, which made her happy. She bought a dress that cost a lot and borrowed a diamond necklace from a friend. She was sad when she lost it. They worked for ten years to pay for a new necklace. After they finished paying for it, she found out the necklace was fake, which made her mad.

The story map could be shared with the students prior to reading or used by the teacher to select vocabulary that is integral to understanding, discussing, and writing about the story. Certainly in "The Necklace," the teacher would not want to include the word *paste* in prereading vocabulary. The teacher could also give the students an altered form that would help them understand the story structure and identify vocabulary, yet not give away the story.

Prereading Activities for Directly Teaching Vocabulary

Nagy (1988) states there are three principles that contribute to deep understanding of vocabulary. They are: (1) integration, which is tying in new words with familiar concepts and experiences, (2) repetition, and (3) meaningful usage.

Integrating new vocabulary with a student's schema or prior experiences makes a new idea more accessible. Repetition usually occurs during extensive reading but can also be achieved as students use vocabulary in responses to reading. Meaningful usage can be provided through reading, discussion, and writing as students manipulate the words in context. Various activities for direct instruction of vocabulary use these principles in different combinations and degrees.

Using the Dictionary

The most common vocabulary exercise is to look up meanings in the dictionary and write a sentence for the targeted vocabulary words. The frustration that teachers feel with the amount of time this takes for such meager results is validated by researchers. G. A. Miller and P. M. Gildea (as cited in May, 1998, pp. 211-212) conclude, "The errors children made

Integrating new vocabulary with a student's schema or prior experiences makes a new idea more accessible.

[using dictionary definitions] were so serious and frequent as to make the task instructionally useless." Dictionary usage lacks integration, repetition, and meaningful usage.

The dictionaries themselves are usually less than helpful. Classroom dictionaries are constrained by space so definitions are compacted, technical, or impossible to understand unless the meaning of the word is already known. Every part of the entry is fraught with problems. Words are defined by their roots; for example, *glandular*—of or like a gland; having glands; made up of glands. Correct usage depends on the child knowing the parts of speech that are rather abstract and often not truly conquered until seventh or eighth grade. Every teacher has seen sentences similar to "He luminoused the room with the candle." Pronunciation keys are undecipherable. Who actually uses guide words when a writer could look at a single word, anywhere on the page, and tell if their vocabulary word comes before or after that single word? "Definitions alone can lead to only a superficial level of word knowledge. By itself, looking up words in a dictionary or memorizing definitions does not reliably improve reading comprehension" (Nagy, 1988, p. 5).

Nonetheless, dictionaries are occasionally needed, and at some time in their education students need to be taught how to use them. They need to know how to locate a word, how to identify and use the parts of the entry, and how to choose among multiple meanings. Electronic dictionaries and thesauruses are promising because they take less time to use. It is best to teach dictionary skills with words that are needed for a content lesson or a story, so that two goals are accomplished simultaneously—vocabulary growth and reading comprehension. It is also a more authentic and integrated task.

At some time in their education, students need to be taught how to use dictionaries.

Enhanced Dictionary Assignments

Dictionary usage can be made more successful by supplying additional clues, such as using the word in context. The context should be directly from the story being read by the class. Using actual story context will trigger greater recognition of the vocabulary word during reading than will using the word in an unrelated sentence. Guessing from context allows students to construct their own meanings, and having a preliminary general idea aids students in choosing the correct definition and understanding what the definition means. This works very well as a partner activity.

Another helpful cooperative activity is to assign a group of four or eight words in context to a team of four students. They must share the dictionary search, teach the words to each other, and develop sentences cooperatively. The discussion and self-correction that occurs makes this a surprisingly effective activity, and it actually takes less time than having students do it independently.

Presenting Vocabulary in Context

Learning vocabulary in context is more effective because additional cueing systems are used. Out of context, students can only use graphophonemic clues, roots, and affixes. Context provides syntactic and semantic clues. Imagine a student who is unfamiliar with *artichoke*. It could be anything, and *choke* is quite misleading. Add *hearts of* to artichoke. Although it sounds like the cardiovascular system of some beast, it can at least be identified as a noun by the syntactic clue. Add "Donna dipped the light green hearts of artichoke into butter and ate the delicacy with delight," and it gives far better clues although it may still be interpreted as rather barbaric. Semantically, light green hearts do not make sense so the student probably reconsiders the beast theory and considers a vegetable theory.

Context helps to develop a theory about the meaning of a word, but it is usually general. Context clues work better for identifying synonyms of known words than they do for figuring out words that represent new concepts. "Most contexts in normal text are relatively uninformative" (Nagy, 1988, p. 8); nevertheless, general knowledge from context is a starting place.

More activities for direct teaching of vocabulary follow. Some activities include formal use of context, but mostly the context and usage patterns develop from modeling and discussion within the activity. Most of these prereading activities aim to integrate the new vocabulary with students' schemas and backgrounds, but the principles of repetition and meaningful usage must be carried out through responses to reading.

Word Splash

Word splash is a versatile technique. A variety of words, usually five to ten, are splashed (written randomly) across a paper, a transparency, or the chalkboard. Most of the words are unknown vocabulary words, but a few might be more common words that will give clues about the content,

> Learning vocabulary in context is more effective because additional cueing systems are used.

characters, or setting of the story. A student chooses any word from the set and then offers a sentence or definition. The teacher expands with an example, steering the conversation to its usage in the story. The procedure continues with supportive conversation until all the words have been defined or used in context. Students are called upon to use one of the words in a sentence and then combine two of the words in a sentence. The teacher checks off words that have been used. Students tend to volunteer promptly so that they will be able to choose those with which they are most comfortable. The technique sounds very simple, and it is, but an amazing amount of connected information is shared in a relatively short amount of time. An example of word splash with content material is shown in Figure 9.2 in the next chapter.

The next step can be to predict the story based on the vocabulary words. These predictions stay close on target if the teacher has chosen words that apply to the setting, the plot, and the characters, although any predictions that can be justified are acceptable. Students cannot wait to read the selection to see whose predictions will come the closest.

Word splash sounds very simple, but an amazing amount of connected information is shared in a relatively short amount of time.

Predicted Sentences

With predicted sentences, students are presented with a list of words in the order that they appear in a story. The words are defined, illustrated, used in context, related to other stories, matched to other concepts, or elucidated upon in any other useful way. Students are then asked to predict sentences that might be in the story and eventually to tell a short story using the words in order. A single student can tell the entire story, or it can be a class effort in which each student builds from the previous student's sentence. It is great fun, and the words are used in meaningful and sometimes inventive context. Finally the real story is read, and the students not only have worked with the vocabulary, but they have predicted the story, both of which enrich comprehension.

Vocab-o-Gram

Vocab-o-Gram (Blachowicz and Fisher, 1996) is another activity that relates vocabulary and story prediction. This time, students are asked to predict how a list of vocabulary words might fit into a story structure. Working in teams allows students to share their knowledge and make better predictions. Figure 8.2 shows one set of a child's initial predictions for *The Greyling* by J. Yolen (1993). In this case, the predictions are inaccurate.

VOCAB-O-GRAM: THE GREYLING

Use vocabulary to make predictions about . . .

(May be used more than once)

The setting townsfolk roiling seas sandbar	What will the setting be like? little town by the sea
The characters fisherman greyling Baby wail townsfolk	Any ideas about the characters? There's a big wail. Maybe the fisherman is re-lated to baby. Greyling is a fish.
The problem or goal	What might it be? Somebody gets stranded on sandbar
The actions	What might happen? Fisherman saves baby. Fisherman is saved.
The resolution	How might it end? Joyously or sad (grief) both sad and happy; bittersweet
What question(s) do you have?	What happens to the baby?
Mystery words selchie, slough off	

Figure 8.2 Vocab-o-Gram for *The Greyling* by J. Yolen. From *Teaching Vocabulary in All Classrooms* by C. Blachowicz and P. Fisher, © 1996. Reprinted by permission of Prentice-Hall, Inc.

After reading the selection, students can reject or verify their predictions. In the example, the students moved *wail* from being a character to being a sound made by the wind. The mystery words (unknown words) were solved; a *selchie* is a seal child, and *slough off* is what the seal child did with his skin.

Possible Sentences

This activity is appealing to children, produces much discussion, and dictionaries are often voluntarily pulled out to settle disputes. With possible sentences, the teacher provides sentences that may or may not use all the words correctly. In other words, the sentences could possibly make sense, but may not. Figuring out the vocabulary is essential for finding out whether the sentence makes sense (Blachowicz and Fisher, 1996). Possible sentences can also be used for discriminating characteristics.

> The staunchly built house collapsed in a storm.
>
> The heat was oppressive in the closed up house.
>
> The canary breathed slowly through its gills.
>
> The borscht was blue and supported by steel rods.
>
> Could a philanthropist be a miser?
>
> Could a virtuoso be a rival?

Though the possible sentences themselves are not included in any book the class is reading, the vocabulary used in the sentences should be associated with a subject, story, or book under study.

Word Sorts

Word sorts can be used before reading to get general ideas about the categories in which words fit, or they can be used after reading to consolidate meanings. If the teacher chooses the categories, it is an open sort; if students determine the categories, it is a closed sort. Words can be sorted by story elements, by parts of speech, by sections of the story, by traits of specific characters, or in any other useful way. A sample word sort is provided in the next chapter.

Drawing and Labeling Pictures

When the vocabulary consists of mostly nouns, children enjoy drawing representations of the words and assembling them into a picture. Teams of students pool their knowledge and then divide the task of looking up

When the story is read, the students not only have worked with the vocabulary, but they have predicted the story, both of which enrich comprehension.

the remaining unfamiliar words. Pictures are completed by each student independently. Pictures are great memory cues to use on vocabulary note cards, in vocabulary books, or at any time words are learned because visual images have such staying power.

Extension Activities for Directly Teaching Vocabulary

The following activities, which range in scale and complexity, are useful for the direct teaching of vocabulary.

Character Trait Maps

Words for labeling character traits are often missing in students' vocabularies. Even if the words are known, students are unable to distinguish the subtle differences among *smart, witty, cunning, perceptive, wise*, and *clever*. Learning these vocabulary words and their connotations is easily done through discussion of characters in literature.

Some experts suggest teaching the words prior to reading, but students may not yet have examples in their schemas so the words do not "stay put." It works better to label character trait maps after reading. The students will be able to relate the incidents and verbalize the character trait in some general way. The students or the teacher can then provide the word that exactly describes the trait. Using these words in a written response after developing the map will cement the words in place more firmly. Figure 8.3 is an example of a character trait map for the character of Brian from *Hatchet* (Paulsen, 1987).

Semantic Gradient Scales

When working on the subtle differences in the character trait map, it may be useful to establish words differentiated by degrees in a semantic gradient scale (Blachowicz and Fisher, 1996). For example, in Figure 8.4, several words are arranged from hottest to coldest. This scale helps students to see how new words fit into a pattern of known words. The weather-related words offer a clear example to emulate. Developing words that fit between courageous and cowardly might coordinate with a literature lesson, for example, while the freedom list might fit either social studies or a science fiction story.

Pictures are great memory cues to use on vocabulary cards because visual images have such staying power.

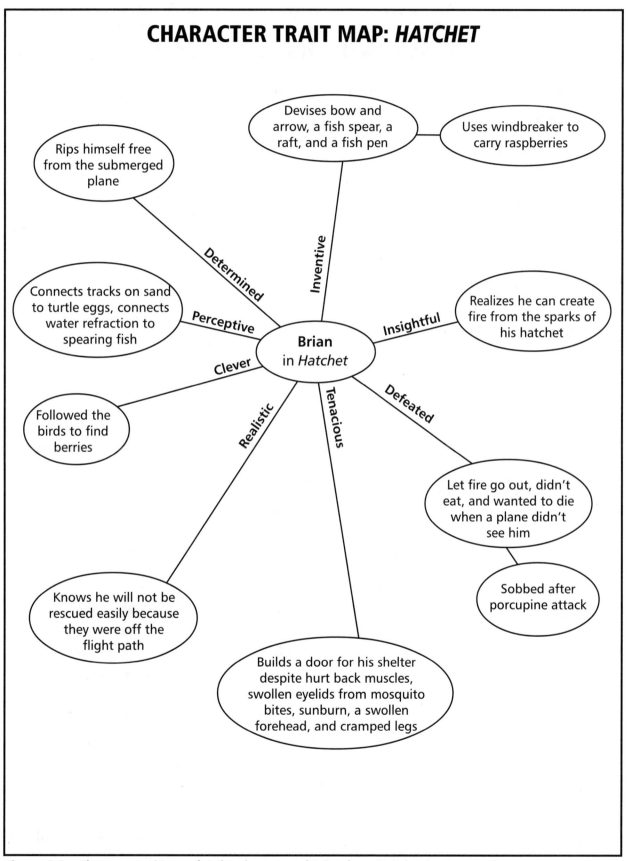

Figure 8.3   Character trait map for the character of Brian from *Hatchet* by Gary Paulsen.

THE SEMANTIC GRADIENT SCALE

Hottest	Courageous	Free to Do As You Please
scorching		
sultry		
steamy		
tropical		
balmy		
sunny		
cool		
nippy		
raw		
freezing		
frigid		
glacial		
Coldest	**Cowardly**	**Totally Controlled**

Figure 8.4   A semantic gradient scale helps students to see how new words fit into a pattern of known words.

Semantic Mapping

Semantic mapping or webbing is meant to extend the meaning of a concept word or to activate related concepts that would be useful for understanding a story, as illustrated in Figure 8.5. Semantic maps go far beyond just learning a definition and usage for a word. The targeted word is placed in the middle of the web, and related, categorized terms are contributed by the class for the spokes of the web. "Because semantic webbing helps students see relationships between ideas and connect known information with new information, it is a valuable tool for developing their vocabulary and conceptual understanding" (Irvin, 1990, p. 23).

Semantic webbing is most useful for either a complex idea that the students are not familiar with, such as *communism*, or for a simple word that the teacher can use to activate associated ideas for an upcoming story,

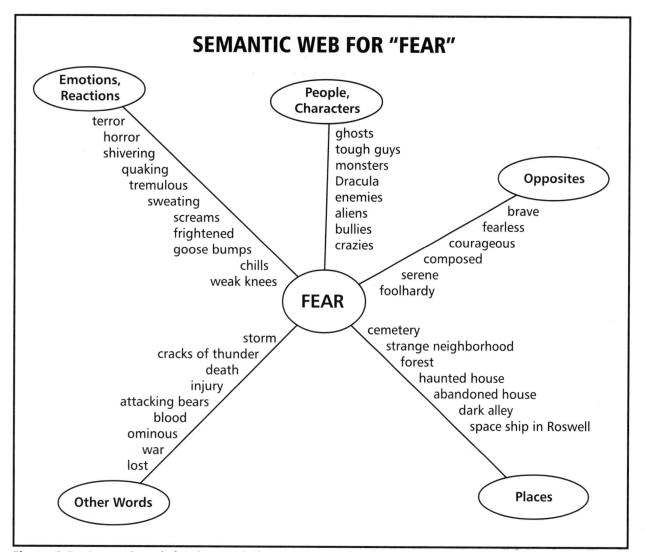

SEMANTIC WEB FOR "FEAR"

Emotions, Reactions
terror
horror
shivering
quaking
tremulous
sweating
screams
frightened
goose bumps
chills
weak knees

People, Characters
ghosts
tough guys
monsters
Dracula
enemies
aliens
bullies
crazies

FEAR

Opposites
brave
fearless
courageous
composed
serene
foolhardy

Other Words
storm
cracks of thunder
death
injury
attacking bears
blood
ominous
war
lost

Places
cemetery
strange neighborhood
forest
haunted house
abandoned house
dark alley
space ship in Roswell

Figure 8.5   Semantic web for the word "fear." Adapted from *Teaching Vocabulary to Improve Reading Comprehension* by W. Nagy.

such as *fear*. Figure 8.5 is based on Nagy's semantic map (1988). The teacher can add items to the web in terms of more precise vocabulary or nudge the discussion to be in line with the impending story. Semantic maps can also be used to review information after reading, or to gather information while reading if the categories are predetermined or the students know how to group by topics.

Semantic mapping can be done individually by students, with the results combined on the board or overhead projector, or it can be done as a class activity. The advantages of semantic mapping include being able to see the relationships visually and to determine the categories. Most importantly, the students can participate in the discussion that will accompany the construction of the map.

Word Wall

Word walls are usually displays of high-frequency words above or below an alphabet that are used in the primary grades, but the idea can be adapted for vocabulary words. It provides a growing list of vocabulary words that is visible throughout the year. This supports the repetition principle for the deep learning of vocabulary. My friend, Mary Conrad, an eighth grade teacher, gives extra credit points when her students use these words appropriately in their daily assignments.

Frayer Model

A strategy for deep vocabulary development is the Frayer Model, which is time consuming but suitable for developing very important concept words. The procedure has seven steps:

Frayer Model Example Defining "Guided Reading"

1. Define the new concept, discriminating the attributes relevant to all instances of the concept.

2. Discriminate the relevant from the irrelevant properties of instances of the concept.

3. Provide an example of the concept.

4. Provide a non-example of the concept.

5. Relate the concept to a subordinate concept.

6. Relate the concept to a superordinate concept.

7. Relate the concept to a coordinate term.

1. Guided reading: the teacher and students read the same text together and discuss it as they proceed.

2. It is irrelevant if the text is fiction or nonfiction or how many students are in the group.

3. The teacher and class discuss an inferred cause in a passage.

4. Silent reading beginning to end is a nonexample.

5. Reading for a purpose is a subordinate concept.

6. Reading instruction is a larger concept.

7. Transactional reading is similar.

The advantages of semantic mapping include being able to see the relationships visually and to determine the categories.

Word Play

Sometimes it is just fun to play with words, especially when there are five or ten minutes left before taking the class to music, or before dismissal. Several activities are suitable in these short segments of time.

Figurative language, such as idioms, provides obstacles for young students. Consider the following phrases: stealing his thunder, raining cats and dogs, head over heels, once in a blue moon, top drawer, dressed to kill, and middle of the road. They tend to interpret the words literally, leaving much confusion in their wakes. Since it is hard to find a story in which several examples of figurative language are used in meaningful context, teaching figurative language can be done out of context. Illustrations of the figurative and literal meanings can be quite inventive.

Analogy study develops precision in word relationships and increases vocabulary. *Daily Oral Analogies* (McDougal Littel, Evanston, IL) provides many interesting examples using a variety of relationships. Students can also develop their own analogies. The analogies in Figure 8.6 were devised by a sixth-grade class working on a science fiction unit. It was hard to tell which they enjoyed more—making them up or solving their classmates' analogies.

Acronyms, palindromes (words or phrases that read the same forward and backward, such as *kayak*, or *Madam, I'm Adam*), metaphors, mixed or otherwise, riddles, and games are all enjoyed by children. In the book *Teaching Vocabulary in All Classrooms* (1996, Merrill-Prentice Hall), Blachowicz and Fisher included several word-play activities that exploit these word games as well as thirteen commercially published vocabulary-word games.

> **Young students tend to interpret idioms literally, leaving much confusion in their wakes.**

Teaching Students Strategies for Learning New Words

Students need to be consciously aware of vocabulary strategies so they can use them on their own to determine the meaning of unknown words.

Scaffolding

Teachers can provide scaffolding for students who are struggling to learn new words. One of the best types of scaffolding is modeling during guided reading. The teacher demonstrates with the word as a blank, reads

ANALOGIES

_____ : Milky Way :: Planet : Earth	galaxy
Dark : _____ :: light : star	black hole
sphere: moon :: _____ : orbit	oval
space ship : escape pod :: _____ : parachute	airplane
Martian : Mars :: _____ : Earth	Earthling
Star Wars : movie :: *Deep Space Nine* : _____	TV show
Godzilla : Tokyo :: King Kong : _____	New York
20,000 Leagues Under the Sea : Jules Verne :: *Sphere* : _____	Crichton
Darth Vader : _____ :: Luke Skywalker : rebels	Empire
Spock : _____ :: Data : Cyborg	Vulcan

Figure 8.6   Analogies provide an example of word play.

to the end of the sentence, and makes guesses about what the unknown word must mean. She might use the root or affixes, the picture, or the structure of the sentence to speculate on what the word might mean. She reads on and finds clues to confirm or reject her guess. She might try them all, demonstrating that readers often have to try several strategies before finding one that provides the necessary information.

Teachers who model can ask their students to try the same procedures that she used. Since students have acually seen the procedure, they can replicate the steps and try out strategies for themselves.

Students can practice the fill-in the-blank procedure by doing cloze exercises, which provide practice in using both semantic and syntactic clues. A blank is substituted for every eighth word. See the previous chapter for a more detailed explanation.

Zip Cloze

Zip cloze can be used with young students who are just learning about vocabulary strategies. Blachowicz and Fisher (1996) suggest putting a story on an overhead transparency and blocking out words with masking tape. Choosing selected vocabulary words seems more useful in this exercise than deleting every eighth word. Students use all of the strategies they know to guess the missing words. When a word is guessed, the tape is "zipped" off and students can compare their choice with the author's. The increasing number of visible words provides additional context.

Context Clues

Teaching students how to identify and use context clues provides a strategy for independently determining unfamiliar word meanings, but it is quite difficult to estimate how useful context clues really are. Readers can tolerate a fairly high number of unknown words, 15%, without comprehension being impaired. "Replacing one content word in six with a difficult synonym did not reliably decrease sixth graders' comprehension of text" (Freebody and Anderson, as cited in Nagy, 1988, p. 29). Students can easily read a cloze passage in which every eighth word is left out by using semantic and syntactic context clues. Is it that readers are using the known text to get the gist of the story despite the hard words, or is it that they get the gist of the hard words through the remaining story? The answer is probably both.

Some texts provide direct clues, words within commas or dashes, to define words. Other texts provide very few context clues either at the sentence level or in the selection as a whole. Context clues are also more helpful for identifying synonyms of known words than for identifying new concepts. Nonetheless, I would rather have students be able to use context clues than not be able to even if the strategy is not always highly useful.

Context clues come in a variety of forms. Modeling and examples always seem to work better than explaining so here are several modeled formats. The varieties clearly overlap. Although some of these formats seem obvious, many students are unaware of how they work.

Print Clues: On her head the prom queen wore a *tiara,* a circlet of silver and rhinestones, which sparkled in the spotlight.

The snake's new scales were *glistening*—shining in the sunlight—after he peeled off his old skin like a glove.

Piranha (small fish that eat meat and have sharp teeth) are so dangerous that Mr. Schroeder would not sell them in his pet store.

> Readers can tolerate a fairly high number of unknown words, 15%, without comprehension being impaired.

Definitions: When you *quarter* troops for the night, you provide them with lodgings.

Category: The Gordon's *whippet* won first prize in the dog show.

Visualization: *Petite* Mrs. Wiley could not see over the heads of the crowd.

Opposites: The kitten got tangled in the yarn but was quickly *extricated*.

Summary: *Asters, bleeding hearts, irises,* and *lilies of the valley* are flowers that grow in my yard.

Mood: The people dressed in black were in a *sober* mood as they watched the coffin being carried down the steps.

Experience: Mrs. Winton could not get a taxi during the thunderstorm so when she reached home she was *drenched*.

Words Connected in a Series: Oaks, elms, *catalpas,* and maples lined the shady streets.

Story or Paragraph Level: The meanings of many words do not become clear until later in the paragraph or story. Good readers keep checking back to clarify the meaning.

Root and Affix Clues

Relating the root of a known word to an unknown word is often, but not always, useful. Relating words to their Greek and Latin ancestors is marginally useful except for scientific vocabulary. Endings can often identify the part of speech: *-ed* and *-ing* are usually verbs, and *-ist* and *-er* usually identify a person. The number prefixes, *uni-, bi, tri-,* are usually consistent, but I did have a student tell me that *bird* was two "rds"! It is worthwhile to draw children's attention to root word families and common affixes.

Testing Vocabulary

There must be something better than matching or multiple choice vocabulary tests. Being able to respond to a multiple choice test may or may not indicate deep knowledge. Here are a couple of quick ideas suitable for classroom testing that probe a little deeper. The teacher needs to choose

Although some formats seem obvious, many students are unaware of how they work.

certain response categories for certain words as one type will not fit all. Another alternative is asking students to choose between several response options, which will make them consider which option may be the most suitable and provide the best explanation.

1. Use the word in an original sentence that is explanatory.

2. Use the application of a word. For example, a radiologist is most likely to use: a) a pitchfork b) an x-ray machine c) marketing research d) a screwdriver.

3. Give a synonym or an antonym.

4. Give a larger classification category or an example.

5. Draw a picture.

6. Give a choice in context. Because the farmers were poor, Carver taught them how to use (organ, organic, synthetic) fertilizers, which were made from natural materials.

Probably the best way to assess vocabulary usage is through written responses to the text from which the vocabulary was drawn. A reader knows a word when it helps him understand a passage he has read and when he uses the word to add precision to his answers.

Vocabulary study doesn't need to be the dull, superficial exercise most of us remember as students. With careful selection of the words we teach, vocabulary study can improve reading comprehension and have long-lasting effects.

Vocabulary study doesn't need to be the dull, superficial exercise most of us remember as students.

CHAPTER

9

Reading and Writing Across the Curriculum

Not only is there an art in knowing a thing,
but also a certain art in teaching it.

—CICERO

Nearly twenty years ago, I gave a conference presentation called "What To Do While Waiting for Reading to be Taught in the Content Areas." Today, I don't have to wait quite as much. Attitudes about reading and writing across the curriculum are different now. Once, content teachers, who loved their subject areas, saw their sole goal as helping students learn the content—not teaching reading strategies. Even teachers who worked in self-contained classrooms did not always think about teaching reading strategies for content books. Some teachers assumed that once children had been taught to read and write in language arts classes, they could automatically understand the content and management of textbooks as well as write organized content papers.

Those assumptions are not true, then or now. Just because you can breeze through a John Grisham novel does not mean that you can read an aeronautical engineering journal with ease and comprehension. One reason that reading skills and strategies do not easily transfer to textbooks is because content books are written in different organizational patterns than novels. Other causes have to do with the heavy load of new concepts, specialized vocabulary, and the lack of prior knowledge. Even the sentence structure in textbooks tends to be different.

The notion of balance, in this context, is to establish greater equality between the teaching of literature and the teaching of expository text. Reading strategies can be taught through authentic texts, while all the language arts can be integrated with and used for learning content.

The Differences Between Reading a Textbook and a Novel

In order to learn in content areas, students need to know how to manage textbooks and the organizational patterns of expository material. However, aside from sharing the English language and being a means of communication between the author and reader, it seems that little else is shared between stories and textbooks. The purposes for reading are not the same, the formats vary, and textbooks have a much heavier concept and vocabulary load. Texts can be read in nonsequential segments, use more formal language, and have graphs, charts, diagrams, and other visuals not found in novels.

Since the purpose of a textbook is to teach something new and unknown, it can be expected that the reader will not have extensive previous knowl-

> Just because you can breeze through a John Grisham novel does not mean that you can read an aeronautical engineering journal with ease and comprehension.

edge about the topic, which will cause gaps in comprehension. Novels are likely to deal with the familiar. In addition to the text not matching the reader's schema, many textbooks are written above grade level.

Difficulty of Text

Many textbooks are not written at the appropriate grade level. W. Hill and Erwin (as cited in Richardson and Morgan, 1997) found that more than half of the textbooks they studied were written at least one level above their targeted grade. Social studies textbooks intended for a single grade were found to have a range of six grade levels (Kinder, Bursuck, and Epstein as cited in Richardson and Morgan, 1997). Even if a text is written at grade level, not all students are reading at grade level. A quick way to determine the level at which a text is written is to use the Fry Readability Graph, Figure 9.1. To find the grade level of a selection, determine the number of sentences and the number of syllables in a 100-word passage. The grade level is found at the intersection of the two lines.

> **Many textbooks are not written at the appropriate grade level.**

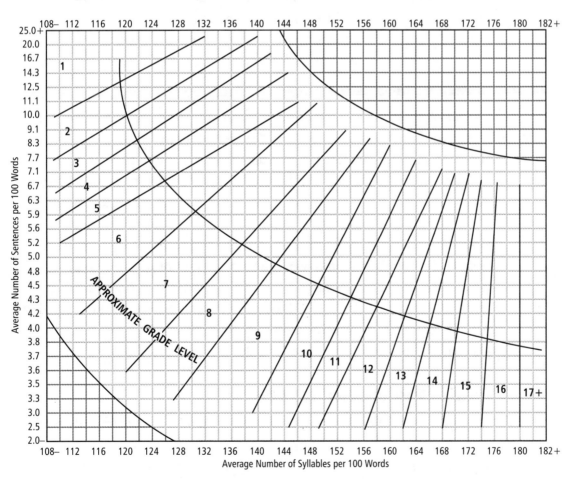

Figure 9.1 Edward B. Fry, 1968. Fry Readability Graph from "A readability formula that saves time." *Journal of Reading*, II (7), 513. Reprinted by permission.

SkyLight Training and Publishing Inc.

Even if texts have the "right" number of syllables and sentences per 100 words, many textbooks are still difficult to understand because they are not well written. The desire to fit in as much content as possible often makes the text disconnected and incoherent. Vocabulary words are not explained, and the relationships between ideas are not apparent.

The negative consequences of a poorly written textbook can be indirect—and sometimes surprising. I was working with fifth grade teachers, helping them use a social studies text to develop prompts for writing. We looked for topics that had at least four supporting details that could be used to write expository pieces. Because the book covered such a range of material—from prehistoric to current times on all seven continents—there were only about ten possibilities in the entire book that had four details connected to the same topic that contained sufficient information for writing a paper. The text consisted of 400 pages of sequential but unrelated facts. Good readers chunk and organize information so that recalling one main idea calls up all the correlated details. Poor readers try to memorize in a laundry list fashion. This poorly written text made it impossible for good readers to use their efficient strategies unless they already possessed enough prior knowledge to connect these lists of unrelated facts.

A series of studies on incoherent texts done by Margaret McKeown, Isabel Beck, and their colleagues was summarized by Frank May (1998, pp. 418–419). The researchers found children's prior knowledge of historical periods to be too "vague and inaccurate" to supply the missing connections in the text. If the text were rewritten to have explicit explanation of new concepts and vocabulary, and relationships of facts were clearly stipulated, the children had better comprehension of the text. In the final study of the series, students were given a preparatory lecture to provide background and clarify relationships of the historical period. Both students who read the incoherent texts and students who read the revised texts did better than students who only read the texts. Those students who had the preparatory lecture and the revised texts did the best.

Trade Books and Text Sets

To supplement poorly written texts, many teachers are using trade books, which are independently published content books for children. They are no longer the dull, meant for the library-style books they once were. Barbara Moss (1991) offers several compelling reasons to use trade books as an accompaniment to textbooks. Nonfiction trade books have both

Nonfiction trade books have both content and visual appeal. They provide current, in-depth information on a huge variety of topics textbooks cannot offer.

content and visual appeal. They provide current, in-depth information on a huge variety of specific topics that textbooks cannot offer. Because they treat narrower topics, trade books are often more logically arranged and coherent. Teachers can also better accommodate the range of reading abilities in their classes by using a text set, that is, a set of diverse books at varying levels on the same topic. Their smaller size also makes them less intimidating than textbooks.

Good resources for finding trade books are *Outstanding Science Trade Books for Children* and *Notable Children's Trade Books in the Field of Social Studies* compiled by the Children's Book Council in conjunction with the National Science Teachers Association, and the National Council for the Social Studies. These can be obtained by writing to Children's Book Council, 67 Irving Place, New York, NY 10003.

Removing Obstacles to Comprehension with Prereading Activities

When a selection of trade books is not available and rewriting the textbook is not a viable option, then preparing students by providing them with a broader background prior to reading is the best solution.

Wouldn't it be wonderful if background knowledge could be developed through direct experience! My first choice would be a unit on world cultures in which we started with a field trip to Mexico so students could see the shadows of Quetzalcoatl, the plumed serpent, slithering down the temple railings on the days of the equinoxes. They could experience a jungle without rivers, and they could walk upon the steps of a temple that demonstrates how calendars and astronomy were related. These students would never forget the sights, the concepts, or specific vocabulary and would read historical accounts of Mexico with much greater comprehension. I am afraid that choice is not possible this year. Movies, videos, museums, picture books, and guest speakers will make a good second choice.

Some concrete experiences are available, and if the teacher can show students how common experiences relate to the text, abstract text will suddenly have greater meaning. When studying atmosphere in a weather unit, ask children which bunk bed is warmer, the top or the bottom one. Have students hypothesize about where the water comes from on the outside of an icy drink on a hot day. Why does it look like steam is rising off a bald football player's head during a November game? Which direc-

> Nonfiction trade books have both content and visual appeal. They provide current, in-depth information on a huge variety of specific topics that textbooks cannot offer.

tion does the water swirl down the toilet? Students who can connect text to real experiences or revisualize a setting have an easier time learning material than those who can't.

Building enthusiasm or curiosity also provides a good start. The mysteries of ancient Egypt, such as the Giza pyramids without any interior decoration or written messages, the little bird-like *bas* with beards, the dismemberment and reassembling of Osiris, and the beautiful temple of Karnak, provide inspiration for students to enter a lost realm. After they become interested in the attention grabbers, the teacher can then introduce irrigation, centralized government, and public works projects. How does a teacher capture all this enthusiasm, interest, and prior knowledge? A KWL is an easy place to start.

KWL

The *K* stands for what do I *know*, the *W* for what I *want* to know, and the *L* for what I *learned*. Even young readers of nonfiction can use KWL to activate their prior knowledge, match their schemas to the text, and tickle their curiosity. To participate in this activity, students should set up a three column chart and brainstorm in small groups all the things they know about the topic. Next they list the things they want to know. With older students, it often works better to do a KTL, what I *know*, what I *think* I know for sure, and what I *learned,* because the answer to "What do you still want to know?" is occasionally "Nothing." I like KTL better for all ages because the first column can be speculative, and anything not listed in the T column automatically functions as a topic for inquiry.

KWL can be modeled with the whole class first, but deeper involvement happens in small-group work. The teacher can be very helpful, and a little manipulative, as she walks around from group to group asking them to be as specific as possible with their lists. If the topic were sea turtles, she might ask the groups to guess exactly how much the turtles weigh, or if the eggs are the size of ping pong balls or baseballs, or why mother turtles cry as they lay their eggs.

KWL, developed by Donna Ogle (1986), is an easy strategy for students to transfer to independent reading. Setting the purpose helps students ferret out information from difficult texts because they know what they are looking for. When students transfer a technique to independent reading, it becomes a reading strategy—a procedure students can use by themselves in various situations to construct meaning from text.

When students transfer a technique to independent reading, it becomes a reading strategy.

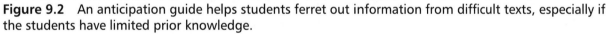

ANTICIPATION GUIDE

Before Reading

Agree Disagree

After Reading

Agree Disagree

____ ____   1. Earth's population has remained steady
                until about 500 years ago.   ____ ____

____ ____   2. The increased productivity of crops due to
                the use of pesticides outweighs the medical
                problems caused by pesticides.   ____ ____

____ ____   3. Carbon dioxide is one of the gasses that
                contributes to the greenhouse effect.   ____ ____

____ ____   4. Composting yard waste will reduce trash
                put into landfills by 40%.   ____ ____

Figure 9.2 An anticipation guide helps students ferret out information from difficult texts, especially if the students have limited prior knowledge.

KWL works with all age levels. I have known exhausted teachers who are attending graduate classes in the evening after a hard day's work exclaim, "Oh, you were right! I didn't think they were that big! I saw that on *National Geographic!*", when they found that turtles weigh up to 1,500 pounds, their eggs are the size of golf balls, and her tears keep her eyes free from loose sand.

Anticipation Guide

If students are likely to have sufficient prior knowledge that can be aroused, a KWL would be my choice because it requires active participation. If the students are being introduced to a topic about which they have limited prior knowledge, an anticipation guide, Figure 9.2, is preferable.

Anticipation guides supply more information than a KWL, but beneficial discussion and high involvement can still be generated during a prereading activity. The exercise can be extended by asking students to prove their answers during reading or by reanswering after reading.

Removing the Obstacles of Concept Vocabulary

Unfamiliar vocabulary and technical jargon can be real obstacles to comprehension. New vocabulary can be divided into three categories, which are elaborate words for known ideas (*aspic* for *Jell-o*), familiar words with new meanings (*plate* in *plate tectonics*), and new words for unfamiliar concepts (*magnetic alignment*). The third category provides the most challenge. Terms such as *magnetic alignment, Pangaea,* and *continental drift* represent whole concepts—and fairly abstract concepts at that.

These new concepts and terms will obstruct comprehension unless they become familiar to the student by the time the student meets the text. Techniques such as word splash and word sort will help students develop general familiarity and background.

Word Splash

To use word splash, a variety of words that are integral to the chapter is spread across a page or a transparency. Variety in the style of print seems to aid memory. The teacher elicits from the class what is already known about the terms, adding elaboration or clarifying definitions. Examples may be drawn from the class or provided by the teacher. Soon the teacher is asking students to develop sentences with the words.

The wider the discussion, the more likely that students will make a connection. Discussion of the vocabulary words in Figure 9.3 may elicit connections to the movie *The Tomb of the Mummy*, burn ointments, divinity fudge, an inscription on a friendship ring, characters in computer games, an account from a student who is reading a book about the Middle Ages that includes falconry, and Celestial Seasonings Tea. This activity may not produce precision with vocabulary, but when the words are encountered in the text, they will not be complete strangers.

Word Sort

When doing a word sort, randomly list important words from the chapter for groups of students who must sort them into categories of their own choice and label the categories. Children may use their texts, their experiences, and any other reference sources to find out if an *acropolis* is a

> New concepts and terms will obstruct comprehension unless they become familiar to the student by the time the student meets the text.

falcon   celestial   ancient

Osiris

tomb

deceased

DISMEMBERED

INSCRIPTION

ointments

divinities

dynasty

sarcophagi   *mumiform*

netherworld

Figure 9.3   Word Splash

person, place, tool, or geographical feature. After the sorting is finished, groups must justify the placement and provide a rationale for their decisions. Other groups may challenge the placement if they can justify their claim. This activity is an excellent strategy for generating interest, encouraging discussion, developing concepts, and practicing one of the patterns of expository writing—topic-subtopic. Figure 9.4 shows an example of a word sort for ancient Greece.

ANCIENT GREECE

acropolis	citizen	monarchy	colony	Mt. Olympus
oligarchy	democracy	Athens	Athenians	Homer
agora	city-state	Sparta	javelin	Odyssey
armor	Athena	Parthenon	Socrates	bronze
Plato				

CATEGORIES

People	Places	Government	Things	Related to Myth
citizen	acropolis	oligarchy	armor	Athena
Athenians	agora	democracy	javelin	Mt. Olympus
Plato	city-state	monarchy	Odyssey	
Socrates	Athens		bronze	
Homer	Sparta			
	Parthenon			
	colony			

Figure 9.4   Word Sort for Ancient Greece

Webs and Semantic Maps

These techniques share common features. They are visual representations of relationships, they can be used before, during, or after reading, and they are relatively easy to use or to have students develop. Webs and semantic maps remove some of the barriers to comprehension of texts by activating prior knowledge, discussing new vocabulary and concepts, and setting in place some of the relationships among ideas before students reach that incoherent text.

Like KWL, simple **webs** can be used for brainstorming in the prereading stage. The teacher places the key word, *volcano*, as in Figure 9.5, in the center of the web and asks students to contribute associated terms. In the

SkyLight Training and Publishing Inc.

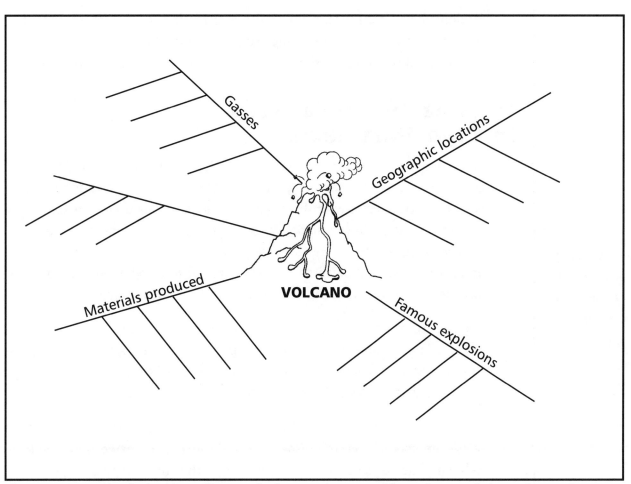

Figure 9.5 A web of related words around a key word extracted from the story helps activate prior knowledge before reading a new book.

earliest stages, the teacher decides on the relationships of the suggested words. If the children start the web with the teacher, this activity can carry through to the reading stage as students fill in missing information. The clever teacher makes sure the categories in the web match the sections in the textbook.

Semantic maps as developed by Camille Blachowicz and Peter Fisher (1996) are more thought provoking than simple webbing. In constructing a semantic map, the teacher first selects a key word and target words. The key word is written at the center of the map, and the target words are listed at the side. Students then generate words related to the key word and target words, and relationships between the words are discussed. The map can be constructed by the entire class, in small groups, or individually. Finally, the students add to the map as they read or work on the topic.

Students have more responsibility for determining the relationships and subtopics with semantic mapping. The more thought required about the organization of the topic, the greater the recall and understanding.

Organizational Patterns in Expository Texts

Prereading activities can remove some of the obstacles associated with new concepts, new vocabulary, and disconnected text, but students still need to learn to cope with the organizational patterns used in textbooks. Readers who only have a narrative schema read in a chronological pattern of "and then, and then, and then, and then." Without understanding other organizational patterns, students are reduced to trying to memorize long lists of information that is beyond the capacities of most people.

The structures used in expository text are listing, sequence, cause and effect, comparison and contrast, description, topic-subtopic, and problem-solution. Students need to learn to recognize these structures so that they can organize their thoughts and/or their notes in the same structures.

The samples of text organization in this section are in **list** format. Cue words are *another, several, also,* or *the following*. **Sequence** is crucial for following the steps of weather formation or the chronology of English royalty. This expository organizational pattern is one of the few that fits well with the "and then" strategy. Cue words are *before, after, following, first, next, then, finally, during, by,* and *last*.

> Then a year later, on November 14, 1854, the Crimean War Allied fleet found itself anchored off the Russian port of Balaklava....During the afternoon, violent rainstorms began to lash Balaklava, and by nightfall a full-scale hurricane was blowing. By morning the entire fleet had been sunk (Burke, 1996, p. 136).

Cause and effect is a critical organizational pattern in both science and social studies. Cue words are *so, because if . . . then, as a result,* and *therefore*. Understanding cause and effect seems to influence personalities as well as reading comprehension. Think of the adults or children you know who believe that things just happen to them out of the blue for no apparent reason. Nothing is ever their fault. Then think of others who seek to understand why things happen and attempt to manage their lives by changing the cause of the effect.

Without understanding organizational patterns, students are reduced to trying to memorize long lists of information.

In lower grades "there was a significant negative relationship be-tween the amount of homework assigned and student attitudes," Cooper says, reflecting the not-surprising fact that kids resent the stuff. But in grades six and up, the more homework students com-pleted, the higher their achievement. It is not clear, however, what is cause and what is effect: are already good students finishing more assignments because they are motivated and good at academics, or is completing assignments causing students to do better? (Begley, 1998, p. 51).

For **comparison and contrast**, cue words are *in comparison, on the other hand, in contrast, alike, same as, however,* and *but.*

> The wonderful Maya mural art has its roots in the Chicanel wall paintings of Tikal, but by Tzakol times it had reached a very high degree of elaboration (Coe, 1993, p. 84).

Although narrative contains a great deal of **description**, it tends to be interwoven with the plot and enhances characterization or setting. Ex-pository description is an end in itself. Cue words are *for example, characteristics are,* and *looks like.* The following passage is from a fifth grade selection about mallard ducks.

> Females are mixed brown, with whitish tail and white borders on each side of bright purplish-blue wing patches. During the summer, the males shed their bright feathers (Peterson, 1986, p. 73).

While researching this chapter, I found few experts listed **topic-detail (topic-subtopic)** as an expository pattern. Perhaps they just thought of this pattern as lists of paragraphs or a type of description. When I started examining students' texts, especially social studies texts, an overwhelm-ing amount of material was organized in this way. While the authors may have understood how the topics were interrelated, it was seldom made apparent to the student.

> The history of Prussia is in large measure the history of the Hohenzollern family. This aggressive and prolific dynasty was first heard of in the tenth century. At that time the Hohenzollerns were obscure counts ruling over the castle of Zollern and a tiny bit of surrounding territory in southwest Germany, just north of the Swiss border (Harrison and Sullivan, 1963, p. 409).

Problem and solution is a common pattern, but it is often confusing to students because the problem or solution may be inferred rather than stated, or solutions are described before the problem. Cue words are *questions, answer, solved,* and *purpose.* To make things even more tricky

> **Cause and effect is a critical organizational pattern in both science and social studies.**

for the student, the problem may be in one paragraph, and the solution several pages away.

> Meanwhile, it soon became clear to even the dullest government minister that one way to cut down on the massive bullion drain was to establish one's own colonies. Their only purpose in life would be to provide raw materials for the mother country's domestic industry and thereby also boost her re-export business (Burke, 1996, p. 166).

Teaching Text Structure

Young children, if they have been lucky, have heard many stories. They have heard nursery rhymes, bedtime stories, stories from Grandma, and stories from their teachers. They see stories on television and soon have an excellent story schema, or familiarity with the pattern of a story. They know that the story will unfold in a linear fashion, with a beginning, middle, and end, and there will be a problem that will be solved.

Without having many texts or nonfiction books read aloud to them, it is not surprising that few children have an expository schema.

Without having many texts or nonfiction books read aloud to them, it is not surprising that few children have an expository schema and are thus bewildered by these patterns. A preliminary strategy is to read informational trade books aloud in the primary grades so children begin to develop that expository schema. Several good choices for beginning readers include *Castles* (Jeunesse, Delafosse, and Millet, 1990), which has terrific transparent overlays; *Great Snakes* (Robinson, 1996); *Homes Around the World* (Kalman, 1994); and *Spiders* (Gibbons, 1993).

May (1998) recommends that teachers choose passages of a particular pattern, teach students the organizational pattern, and then apply that knowledge to other passages with the same format in textbooks being used in their classes. He also recommends that students be shown how to produce the structure within their own writing. So much more thought, sorting, categorization, and manipulation of language are required for producing text that students truly understand how information can be organized.

Other Characteristics of Expositional Text

Textbooks have other characteristics that are significantly different than narrative text. The sentence patterns are more complex, and texts contain visual aids such as graphs and summary statements.

Sentence Patterns

The sentence structure in expository texts is much more formal and complex than in speech or in narrative prose. Without prior experience in complex sentence patterns, many will find reading textbooks like translating a foreign language. Two methods to help students understand complex sentences are pattern clubs and sentence combining. Not only will texts be less foreign, students' newfound competence will transfer to their writing.

Pattern clubs (Odegaard and May, 1972) help students to identify sentence patterns and to produce similar sentences of their own. May (1998) cites the following sentences from a social studies book.

> Unless Franklin got to the French on time, the money wouldn't be available.
>
> Unless the money became available, the soldiers would receive no supplies.
>
> Unless the supplies came soon, the soldiers would starve.

The teacher first models a similar sentence, "Unless my husband does the laundry tonight, the children will have no clean socks tomorrow." Students then suggest sentences with the same pattern until everyone is in the pattern club. Without getting entangled in formal patterns of grammatical explanation, students intuitively grasp the pattern.

Sentence Combining

In sentence combining activities, two separate sentences are combined into one sentence. The exercise should provide a sample for the students that will show how the sentences can be combined.

> Jimmy was throwing paper airplanes. Jimmy was redirected by the teacher.
>
> Jimmy, who was throwing paper airplanes, was redirected by the teacher.

Students combine several sets of sentences by following the pattern. This seems to work best when students work in partners so they can talk out the patterns and check with each other to see if their sentences have retained the original meaning. "Jimmy, who was throwing the teacher, was redirected to paper airplanes," will not be counted as correct. As a follow up, students compose original sentences in the same pattern.

Without prior experience in complex sentence patterns, many will find reading textbooks like translating a foreign language.

The research on sentence combining is overwhelmingly positive. George Hillocks (1986) found that 60% of studies done on sentence combining from 1973 to 1986 reported significant gains in syntactic maturity. Other researchers, all cited in Hillocks, reported that sentence combining worked well with students of all levels, especially disadvantaged or remedial students, and that sentence combining instruction helped to build confidence because of its positive approach. These studies were all interested in improvement in writing, but if students can produce complex sentences by themselves, they are also more likely to be able to understand such structures when reading.

Special Features in Textbooks

Special features include charts, graphs, diagrams, pictures, headings, tables of contents, glossaries, indexes, end-of-chapter summaries, and preview and review questions. The most common reaction of students to these features is unremitting joy because they take up space in the book, which means there is less to read. They just skip over them. Students need to be taught the usefulness of these features as well as how to use them.

Most students learn how to interpret charts, graphs, and diagrams by making their own. When I taught eighth grade, I saved the graph and chart unit until late May and June. The students found that making their own charts and graphs from provided and original information was much more challenging and intriguing than simply answering questions about prepared graphics. After constructing their own, it was a snap to read any others. The same is true of maps, time lines, and other graphics. When creating their own graphics, students discover the need for scale, titles, symbols, and labels.

Standard Techniques That Do Not Work Well

A standard technique that students use, or are asked to use, to set a purpose for reading is to turn titles and headings into questions that they can answer while reading the text. This works fairly well with modeling from the teacher, but it is not very interesting. And, often, using titles and headings to make an outline does not work well because many texts contain irrelevant or superfluous information that does not match the topic heading. Students are left wondering what to do with these off-topic bits of information or create headings so general that they do not function well enough to categorize information.

Most children learn how to interpret charts, graphs, and diagrams by making their own.

Asking students to find the main ideas of text paragraphs does not work well either. The problem with texts is that main ideas occur in only one of every eight paragraphs (Donian, as cited in May, 1998), and the problem with readers is that constructing main-idea statements develops later than summarization skills (Brown and Day, as cited in Richardson and Morgan, 1997).

Guiding Student Comprehension During the Reading Process

To help students during reading, the teacher can use guided reading or some form of study guide that acts as a vicarious teacher, pointing out ideas, relationships, and applications that are important. The goal is for students to eventually use all of these strategies independently. Toward this end, students should be taught a variety of techniques for untangling the complexities of textbooks so they have multiple methods from which to choose.

It is not only young readers who need guidance. As students progress through middle school, high school, and then into college, the complexity of the content materials increases. At every grade level, students need to learn organizational patterns and methods of incorporating new ideas so that education entails more than just another long list of boring items to be memorized until the test.

One of the pieces of advice I recently read on how to help students conquer textbooks was to ask them to focus on the big ideas or key concepts, not just memorize the small details. It is sound advice, but the problem is that students have absolutely no clue which pieces are the key concepts. I found myself in the same situation when I recently attended a marvelous lecture about the history of the Silk Road. Much of the history centered around Turkmenistan, Uzbekistan, Azerbaijan, and great civilizations that sprung from those regions, and I was awash with unfamiliar geography, unpronounceable names, and unknown events. Marco Polo was the only name I could remember by the end of the evening. I had no idea which pieces of information were more central than others to the history of the Silk Road.

Students often feel the same way. They have a hard time identifying key themes until they have gathered enough comprehensible information to be able to sort the relevant from the irrelevant. One way to help students is through a study guide.

The problem with texts is that main ideas occur in only one of every eight paragraphs.

Study Guides

Study guides are prepared by teachers to accompany textbook reading and help students determine the main ideas and the relevant details. The best times to use them are when the students are thoroughly unfamiliar with the topic, or when establishing a pattern of what types of information are likely to be the most important, so that students can independently structure their own notes later.

One team of teachers organized a year long world history class around the theme that ideas are transferred through trade, travel, and warfare. In their study guides, the teachers highlighted the parts of the text that told about how ideas spread through time and distance. They asked the students to work mostly with those sections. On a more concrete level, another teacher had students note that each culture consisted of similar characteristics—government, daily living (food, clothing, housing, and child-rearing), the arts, religion, and economics. The students began to see the major themes as opposed to a collection of facts.

Study guides can take many forms. Some are partially filled-in outlines, some look like semantic maps, some are folded to fit over a page and match up exactly with the text, and some are in chart form. Teachers who are emphasizing cause and effect create study guides that look like flow charts so students can see how a particular effect may be the cause of another occurrence. If the text has a coherent organizational pattern, the study guide can emphasize the pattern. If connections are lacking, the study guide can provide them. Study guides encourage students to group information into a framework. This grouping takes advantage of how people learn, which is in clusters or families.

Graphic Organizers as Study Guides

Graphic organizers can be started as prereading activities and finished during independent reading. A good graphic organizer requires that the relationships be labeled as well as the topics. Figure 9.6 shows a graphic organizer for a textbook segment about the Middle Ages.

With instruction, students can develop their own graphic organizers. Joseph Boyle and Mary Weishaar (1997) conducted a study comparing learning-disabled high school students who used teacher-generated graphic organizers, students who created their own organizers, and a control group. All used the same text materials. Those students who

Study guides help students identify key themes.

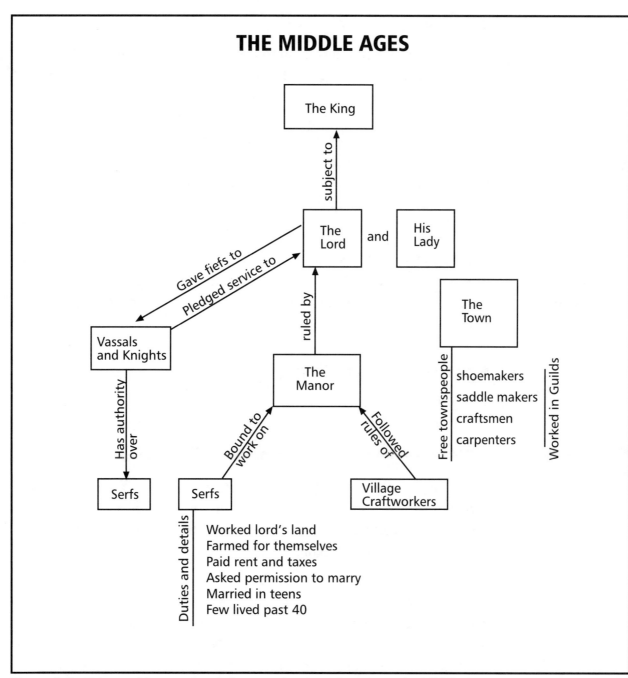

Figure 9.6 This graphic organizer is for a textbook section about the Middle Ages.

created their own graphic organizers outperformed the other groups on both literal and inferential comprehension. Those using teacher-generated organizers did better than the control group. Boyle and Weishaar concluded, "Using cognitive organizers during reading can help [students] to become more actively involved in the reading process, particularly if students construct their own organizers" (1997, p. 234).

T Notes

Teachers can help students learn to take T notes in an organizational pattern, but even unorganized T notes have a big advantage. This form of note taking received its name because a big T is written on the page. The topic name is written on top of the T, main ideas are written to the left of the T, and supporting details are written to the right of the T. The main advantage is that the paper can be folded down the middle, along the stem of the T, and the notes can be used for self-testing. No other form of note taking is as amenable as T notes for independent study, and it can be used at many grade levels, including college.

Students who learn how to group information in the expository patterns, especially cause and effect, comparison and contrast, topic-subtopic, and problem-solution, have developed a life-long strategy for reading and for writing.

No other form of note taking is as amenable as T notes for independent study.

Responding to Texts

When students are reading and thinking, they are in the process stage, in which all the real work of comprehension goes on. But, as teachers, we cannot see or assess what is happening. In order to make thinking visible, students are often asked to produce a product after reading. It gives the teacher a glimpse into the process, and it gives students an opportunity to revisit the text and once more interact with the material. I always think of Roger Farr's statement, "Children can read without thinking, but they cannot write without thinking."

Learning Logs

After reading a selection, students can respond in learning logs. The formats vary depending on the age of the students or the familiarity with the material. Logs can feature five minutes of free writing, summaries, personal reactions, implications, or observations during a science lab. Writing in words about how a mathematical operation functions is very effective for clarifying thinking. A log can be a one-time response or a daily occurrence to summarize lessons, elucidate thinking, or extend learning. Logs can be adapted to college-level students as a way to offer creative projects in lieu of standard term papers.

Entrance or exit slips are short and effective response formats that help to focus students' attention. An entrance slip can ask for a connected piece of prior information, a prediction, a recollection of a fact from the previous night's reading assignment, or an "I wonder" question. It must be completed before the child is admitted to the day's activities. An exit slip is completed in the last few minutes of the class. The purposes are similar. It can ask for a fact recalled from the text or class discussion, an everyday example or application of the lesson, a point unclear to the student, or a personal reaction. When students know a daily exit slip is required, they make sure to fix in their memories at least one segment of the lesson so they will have something to write.

Formal Writing

Formal writing can take the form of expository essays, all-about books, alphabet books, or reports. These are usually assigned at the end of a chapter to consolidate aspects of the unit. In the middle grades, a class collaborative report not only reviews the information but models the process of putting a report together: deciding on the topics, choosing relevant information, deciding on an organizational pattern, writing introductions and conclusions, citing sources, revising, editing, and producing copies of the finished product.

Formal writing can take the form of expository essays, all-about books, alphabet books, or reports.

Creative Drama, Newspaper Articles, Diaries, and Letters

These formats turn plain facts into real and vivid events. Human motivations and frailties become causes of historical events. The effects of sweeping changes are translated into the repercussion on a single life. Dramatic vignettes can provide a stage for ethical concerns in science. A letter may be sent from Benjamin Franklin in France or sent from a scientist surveying the Yucca Mountain area in Nevada who is deciding if it is a safe place for nuclear waste storage. A diary may be kept by a child on the Mayflower. A drama may portray decision-making in the control room of NASA. A newspaper article may recount the devastating effects of the 1906 earthquake in San Francisco. Not only are important facts sequenced and summarized, but empathy is developed.

Predicting Test Questions

Another way to respond to the text is to predict test questions. Students think that it is fun to write questions instead of answers. It can also be enlightening for the teacher to find out how students perceive her tests, or if children were paying attention only to the trivial details. Asking for and modeling certain types of questions, such as cause and effect, discus-

An expository paragraph frame (Figure 9.7) helps students determine meaning from textbooks.

EXPOSITORY PARAGRAPH FRAME

I learned many interesting things about how plants grow.

First, I learned that _____.

Next, I learned that _____.

Third, I learned that _____.

Finally, I learned that _____.

It was interesting to learn how plants grow.

Figure 9.7

sion questions, or application questions, can direct the students to a broader range of questioning.

Strategies Most Useful for Primary Grades

Primary textbooks suffer from all the same problems as texts at higher grade levels, and primary students also struggle with texts to determine meaning. Mary W. Olson and Thomas C. Gee (1991) surveyed primary teachers to determine which strategies were most effective in the primary grades. The teachers responded that previewing vocabulary and concepts, using manipulatives such as maps, films, models, and pictures, retelling or summarizing content, and visualizing information provided outstanding help for their students.

Olson and Gee also recommended semantic mapping, KWL, group summarizing, and expository paragraph frames. To develop a paragraph frame, Figure 9.7, the teacher determines the expository pattern used in the text and sets up a fill-in-the-blank paragraph based on the same pattern. Students first pair-share information that they learned while reading and then complete the paragraph frame. Class discussion can follow to cement the new learning.

Techniques that teachers thought provided little or no help for primary students were providing partial outlines, using a study guide, turning chapter titles and headings into questions, and providing a graphic overview prior to reading. Although these are terrific techniques, they will have to wait for students to mature to be able to use them effectively.

Writing in Math

Just in case this chapter is getting too long and your eyes are glazing over, here is a puzzle to arouse the mind.

Suppose a three-inch cube is painted blue. Assume the cube is cut into 27 one-inch cubes. How many of the smaller cubes will have blue paint on one face only? On two faces only? On three faces only? On no face? Show your work and explain in words how you arrived at your answer. (Illinois State Board of Education, 1995, Grade 10 sample assessment item.)

You could probably solve the problem, but did you attempt to write it out in words? The National Council of Teachers of Mathematics has called for mathematics instruction to be based on the process of problem-solving, which means math textbooks now have more written text. Learning how to communicate verbally in math is a new skill for students and for many teachers.

Margaret McIntosh and Roni Joe Draper (1985, p. 121) found, "As students now encounter mathematics books with extensive text, they find they lack the necessary skills and attitudes for dealing effectively with the text." To combat this problem, McIntosh and Draper taught their students question-answer-relationship strategy, as a method for reading and interpreting their math books. Literacy strategies that once applied mainly to language arts are now being used with math texts. By the way, the answer is: Six cubes have paint on one face only, twelve cubes have paint on two faces only, eight cubes have paint on three faces only, and one cube has no paint.

> Literacy strategies that once applied mainly to language arts are now being used with math texts.

Classroom Discussion

Classroom discussion following the reading of a textbook section is such a time-honored procedure because it is rich with possibilities. Although the activities in the previous sections require a great deal of interaction between reader and text, interaction is limited to the reader and the text. In a classroom discussion, there are all the other students, their perceptions, their experiences, their questions, and there is the teacher. Because a significant part of learning is social, much interaction is needed. Students can hear the answers to questions they were too timid to ask and can consider possibilities that never previously crossed their minds. They can also be enveloped and propelled by the enthusiasm of their teacher.

During discussion, do not forget to ask students to visualize. Do it verbally and let them draw and sketch too. What did Kubla Khan's palace look like when Marco Polo arrived? How high was the tidal wave? What was left crumpled on the ground? Is the wind blowing hard as you walk along the Great Wall of China, and what do you see? How anxious was Christopher Columbus' crew after not sighting land for so long? These scenes, these emotions are what make learning memorable.

Students need instruction in reading expository text and writing expository papers. Organizational patterns, concept loads, vocabulary, lack of prior knowledge, and sentence structure make them significantly different than narrative patterns.

Because a significant part of learning is social, much interaction among students is needed.

Balanced Writing

Of all those arts in which the wise excel,
Nature's chief masterpiece is writing well.

—JOHN SHEFFIELD

Balance in writing instruction emphasizes student and teacher leadership above the other principles of balanced instruction. Balance in writing instruction is the balance between student-directed writing and structured writing, and it includes modeled writing, children's personal writing, shared responses to writing, and experiences in learning how to structure and judge writing. The teacher who has a wide repertoire of strategies can coordinate and intermingle modes of instruction to teach students to enjoy being authors and produce coherent pieces of writing.

The different approaches to writing instruction have different effects, each important at different times. The most familiar philosophies can be broadly categorized as student-directed writing (the writers' workshop approach) and teacher-directed writing (structured writing). The main advantages of student-directed writing are motivation and ownership due to self-choice of topics and rich detail and elaboration because the content comes from the students' personal experiences. The optimum outcomes of student-directed writing are increased flexibility and fluency. The main advantages of teacher-directed writing are the abilities to concentrate on and refine one part of the writing process at a time, more structured teacher guidance, the development of criteria for good writing, and the ability to compare and contrast similar pieces of writing. The primary outcome of teacher-directed writing is craftsmanship.

Both approaches make use of peer discussion and revision groups, and both approaches are far superior to prior practices of assigning without instruction and grading primarily for correct English conventions. You probably remember the venerable "What I Did During Summer Vacation," which was assigned without direction (so as not to inhibit creativity) and graded by some process shrouded in mystery (believed to have something to do with the throwing of darts). Students have no problem shifting from student-directed to teacher-directed writing assignments, and the skills and strategies transfer from one to the other as both share the same elements of the writing process.

Elements of the Writing Process

The writing process can be thought of as having five stages: prewriting, drafting, revising, editing, and publishing. It would be wonderful if the entire process actually progressed in a fixed, stable order, but no writer, eight or thirty-eight-years-old, can keep the entire process from being messy. The process gets messier as the writer matures and is able to

Balance in writing instruction is the balance between student-directed writing and structured writing.

mentally switch back and forth among the steps, anticipating how changes in one step will affect the others. However, for the sake of explanation, let's assume that it were an orderly process.

Prewriting

Prewriting is the planning stage, and it includes deciding on a topic and planning the general development of the piece. Prewriting can be a solitary or a group activity. Modeling prewriting with the whole class is called brainstorming. If the class is doing student-directed writing, in which each student is writing about a topic of her choice, the brainstorming will include all the possible topics that might interest a student. An idea will spark in the imagination of the writer, or a topic might be tucked away for development at a later time. If the writing is teacher-directed, in which a specific assignment is given by the teacher, the brainstorming session will be narrower. It will consist of various ways to approach the topic or components that need to be included within the assignment. During the brainstorming process, not only are ideas generated, but explicit language to express the ideas and supporting details comes to the foreground.

> An outcome of brainstorming is that students learn not to simply take the first topic that pops into their heads.

The point of brainstorming is not only to find a topic but also to consider the possibilities of different topics and their relative merits. An outcome of brainstorming is that students learn not to simply take the first topic that pops into their heads but to choose a topic that will work out well, is better suited to the purpose, or is more pleasing. Better writers take longer to plan. Stallard (as cited in Hillocks, 1986) found that good writers take 4.18 minutes to plan, but average writers take only 1.2 minutes to plan.

All but the youngest writers can work from an outline of a few key words and phrases. First and second graders are more concrete and may need to actually write out whole sentences as they do not yet have the executive function that allows more mature writers to internally manipulate, accept and reject ideas, and make changes without putting the first word on paper. The youngest writers, and sometimes the older ones, often plan by drawing or by talking it out.

Drafting, Revising, and Editing

For the youngest writers, there is only one draft. Done is done! The process of physically forming letters, spelling, and composing is a joyful but monumental task. They approach writing in a straightforward manner, producing text just for the pleasure in it, not for the product. There is no going back; they just go forward to the next thought and the next piece of primary writing paper. In second grade, students begin to make "sloppy copies" and then final drafts.

Revising means changing ideas, organization, and content whereas editing refers to the mechanical aspects of spelling, punctuating, grammar, and paragraphing. Specific strategies for planning, revising, and editing will be found in more detail in the structured writing section.

Publishing

Publishing means polishing a draft and sharing it with a wider audience. The youngest writers love sitting in the Author's Chair. The designated writer sits in a specially reserved chair to read her piece to the class. Positive comments and suggestions are given, and questions for the author may be asked. Young writers experience the pride of having composed a piece and then reading it to an appreciative audience. The process alerts writers to missing details when the audience responds with questions.

Another publishing technique is making bound classroom books of illustrated stories written by the young authors. Class anthologies can be compiled and shared with students in other classes, shared through a school publication, or can be sent home as a class project. Other teachers elect simply to post pieces on the bulletin board.

Writers' Workshop

Writers' workshop was popularized by Donald Graves (1983), Nancie Atwell (1987), Lucy Calkins (1994), and Carol Avery (1993). Because each child writes about topics of his own choice, the hallmark of writers' workshop is personal ownership. Thus, in a single classroom, children are writing about a multiplicity of topics, and each may be in a different point in the writing process.

During workshop time, some children may be drafting independently while others may be working with a partner trying out new ideas, developing details, or determining organization. Other students may be looking for a peer to whom they will read their papers aloud and ask for a response. Students working in the drafting area, however, may not be disturbed by others or asked to peer edit. Peer partners may be found

> **Because each child writes about topics of his own choice, the hallmark of writers' workshop is personal ownership.**

through a sign-up sheet or by waiting in a specified corner of the room where two chairs and a workspace have been set aside just for peer editing. Other children may have finished the revision process and found peers who are helping them edit for spelling, sentence structure, punctuation, or paragraphing. Others may be preparing the final copy for publication. Students are free to move around but must stay quiet and on task.

Underlying Structure of Writers' Workshop

A strong organizational structure underlies writers' workshop. Early sessions begin with the whole class brainstorming to choose an idea to cultivate immediately or to store for later use. For accountability purposes, at the start of each session, the teacher asks for the status of the class, quickly inquiring of each student what her agenda is for the day and recording the information on a chart. Although students generally move at their own pace, children occasionally need to be spurred along or are sometimes told what must be accomplished by the end of the session. Some classes may start with a ten minute mini-lesson if the teacher notices that several students are stuck at the same stage. The lessons may focus on leads, introducing different genres, or how punctuation is used in dialogue. Drafting centers with a large supply of papers, pens, markers, scissors, portfolios, glue, and staplers need to be prepared. On some days, the last seven to eight minutes are set aside for sharing. Some students will have final pieces to read aloud. Others may disclose a problem and ask for possible endings, motivations, or details to make the piece more descriptive. The procedures for writers' workshop need to be taught, and many of the initial mini-lessons are used for procedural issues.

> The procedures for writers' workshop need to be taught, and many of the initial mini-lessons are used for procedural issues.

Barry Lane (1993) suggests a simple form for students to follow during peer revision to make conferences more productive. A piece of paper is divided into columns with one of the following sets of headings:

1. Questions the reader wants to know more about
2. Comments
3. Concerns

1. I like
2. I wonder
3. Questions
4. Plan for Action (to be completed by author)

The students may use the form to evaluate specific areas of revision or they may respond to the piece as a whole. A teacher-student conference can use this format, a student-student conference can use this format, and eventually the student will self-revise with these questions in mind.

Writers' workshop allows for abundant social interaction. Children enjoy sharing ideas, working with a partner, and listening to and telling stories. This sharing is not only allowed but is encouraged and very necessary. For writers to improve their writing, they must practice and listen to readers' responses (Kruzich, 1995).

The Teacher's Role in Writers' Workshop

In writers' workshop, the teacher circulates among the class asking if help is needed or asking a student to share the most exciting, pleasing, or difficult part of his piece. On some days, just a minute or two is spent with each child. On other days, the teacher is available for longer conferences with writers. Because not all writers are at the same stage of the writing process, it becomes possible for the teacher to confer individually with students instead of grading papers at night and writing long copious notes to the students which may or may not be read. Students can request conferences with the teacher at the beginning of the class when the teacher asks for the status of each student.

During a teacher conference, the teacher responds reactively, asking open-ended questions, as in Figure 10.1 (Zaragoza and Vaughn, 1995). When the teacher takes a nondirective role, then the writer must make the decisions, which is the first step to becoming a self-evaluating writer. Teacher-nudging is occasionally allowed.

A predictable block of time for uninterrupted writing is one of the requirements for writers' workshop. Atwell recommends a minimum of three hours or three class periods each week. Children will be on the look out for some intriguing topic because they know writing time is coming up.

The underlying beliefs of writers' workshop are that "pupils will learn or invent forms as they develop their own meanings" and that "knowledge is best provided through audience response from peers while the writing is in progress or after its completion" (Hillocks, 1986, p. 121). Children's personal writing is an important element of balanced writing because of the fluency, flexibility, and ownership that students develop. Through responses of other writers, they begin to determine when their writing has been effective.

Children's personal writing is an important element of balanced writing because of the fluency, flexibility, and ownership that students develop.

OPEN-ENDED QUESTIONS FOR WRITERS' WORKSHOP

1. Tell me about your story.

2. Where did you get the idea?

3. What is the main idea? What is the beginning, the middle, the end?

4. What was the problem and how was the problem solved?

5. Who is your favorite character?

6. What is your setting?

7. What part do you think needs more work?

8. What are you going to do next?

9. What is your favorite part of the story?

10. Are you going to publish this?

11. Were you trying to write this the way a certain author writes?

12. Is your story fiction or nonfiction?

Figure 10.1   Adapted from N. Zaragoza and S. Vaughn, 1995.

Structured Writing

While many teachers are pleased with the fluency and flexibility that is developed with student-sponsored writing, they find that specific instruction and clear criteria also help students become better writers. Hillocks found this to be true in a meta-analysis conducted for the United States Department of Education's Educational Resources Information Center (ERIC) in 1986 in which he analyzed sixty-three research studies that included experimental groups totaling 6,313 students and control groups of 5,492 students.

The greatest gains in writing were with what Hillocks (1986) called the environmental mode of writing instruction, which consisted of clear and specific objectives, a set of materials and problems selected to practice specific aspects of writing, and high levels of peer interaction. The average effect size for the environmental mode of writing was .75 as compared to .26 for the writers' workshop-style of instruction, which Hillocks termed natural process writing. Scales to judge writing and to develop criteria are often used in environmental writing.

Scales to Judge the Quality of Writing

Children sometimes use different criteria than adults do to judge the quality or effectiveness of writing. This mismatch of criteria occasionally produces pieces that are neat and spelled correctly but also long and devoid of coherent content. Writing scales can provide common criteria so students no longer have to guess how the writing will be evaluated or what are the desired ends for a particular format or genre of writing.

Each aspect of writing may have a separate scale called an analytical scale. The individual scales may provide evaluation criteria for focus, support, organization, and English conventions. Focus means sticking to one topic and not digressing throughout the entire piece. Support refers to the richness of elaboration, details, and examples. Organization describes an orderly and cohesive development, and English conventions cover all the aspects of spelling, punctuation, and grammar. In nonfiction pieces, accuracy may also be considered on a separate scale. Sometimes scales are developed for vocabulary, sentence structure, or voice in writing. Put all the scales together, and it is called a rubric. Checklists of writing features have long been used in the classroom, but a rubric is more specific because each performance level is specifically described.

Scales or rubrics have many advantages. They can help children develop a set of standards for good writing, they can be used for an assignment to provide clarification of the expectations, they can be used as students self-revise or participate in revision groups, and they can be used for grading. Rubrics may be as complex as the one in Figure 10.2 for a persuasive essay with a six point scale, or they may be simplified to a three point or four point scale for everyday classroom use. While it may take some effort to prepare a rubric, it is well worth it because of its multiple uses.

Prewriting

Although rubrics may be used in all stages of writing, they are especially helpful to clarify expectations. If children know the requirements, they will be better able to construct a plan for the entire piece and shape the

SIX-POINT RUBRIC: "ALL SUMMER IN A DAY"

Performance / Criteria	1	2	3	4	5	6
FOCUS	• No focus • Wanders	• Focus unclear • Conflicting focus • Changes position • Retelling • Not cause and effect	• Focus clear but must be inferred • Introduction or conclusion may not match body	• Focus stated • Has introduction and conclusion • Introduction or conclusion may be unclear	• Focus stated • Has introduction and conclusion • Body matches	• Focus and reasons announced in introduction • Body matches in order • Conclusion matches
DETAIL	• Almost no detail	• Little detail • List of reasons with no detail	• Few details • Invalid argument • Inaccurate details • Cause of unhappiness unclear	• Major and some minor detail • At least one reason well explained • More general than specific	• Major and lots of minor detail • Two reasons well explained • Gives examples	• All reasons well explained with second order details
ORGANIZATION	• Rambling	• Lacks cohesion • Major digression	• Beginning clear, may drop off at end • More than one topic in a paragraph • Minor digression	• Has introduction, body, and conclusion • One topic/paragraph	• Argument carries throughout introduction, body, and end • Has main idea sentences	• Argument carries throughout • Clearly shows cause and effect • Paragraphed appropriately • Uses more than one transition
CONVENTIONS	• Cannot be understood because of grammar, structure, or inappropriate vocabulary	• Several sentences do not make sense • Inappropriate vocabulary • Many common spelling errors	• Many errors • Several sentence run-ons or fragments • Appropriate vocabulary	• Some errors • Appropriate vocabulary • Awkward sentences	• Minor errors • Appropriate vocabulary	• 1–2 errors at the most • Appropriate vocabulary

Figure 10.2   Rubric for "All Summer in a Day" by Ray Bradbury.

SkyLight Training and Publishing Inc.

purpose and organization of the final product. Clarifying expectations with a rubric can come before or after brainstorming.

Brainstorming and planning are the first stages of the writing process and thus are common to both student-directed writing and structured writing. Imagine a classroom in which reading and writing are integrated and that the students are going to read a story about a child who is lost, such as *Julie of the Wolves* (George, 1972). The teacher wants the class to empathize with the character's feelings of distress and fear. Children might activate their prior knowledge and develop empathy for the character by writing about a time when they were lost. Personal writing can also be a part of structured writing. The difference between writer's workshop and this assignment is that all students are working on the same assignment for the same purpose.

As the class brainstorms about their own experiences of being lost, the teacher acts as scribe, writing on chart paper or on the chalkboard so ideas are not forgotten. Various students relate their own stories as the teacher helps them bring to the forefront emotions and solutions to the problems. As students relate being lost in the woods on a hike, being lost in a department store as a toddler, being ditched by their cohorts, being turned around in a strange city on a vacation, or being in a big, new school on the first day, images and stories begin to percolate, even in the minds of those students who usually protest that they have no stories to tell. All the aspects—character, plot, setting, sequence, emotion, and climax—begin to be set into motion. Brainstorming not only helps students come up with a topic, it encourages them to consider several stories before settling on the final choice. It also brings details and vocabulary to the surface for immediate use.

Planning with Graphic Organizers

Graphic organizers are the visual equivalents of outlines and are used in planning. They come in all shapes and organizational patterns. They are easy to devise and much less intimidating than the traditional outline. Depending on the type of writing desired, there is a graphic organizer to support it. Since persuasive and expository writing are organized on a topic-subtopic basis, while narrative and story writing are organized along sequential lines, the graphic organizers are different for each. Figure 10.3 is a graphic organizer for expository or persuasive pieces to develop the introduction, body, and conclusion. Figure 10.4 is a primary

Brainstorming brings detail and vocabulary to the surface for immediate use.

expository organizer in which the teacher has modeled the opening and closing and the students need only to write the body after studying an undersea unit. For a narrative, Figure 10.5 helps to develop the sequence of the story, and Figure 10.6 is a Venn diagram used to plan comparison and contrast writing.

Once they are taught how to use a few key words to develop a plan, few children will want to write out whole sentences. When the plan is written down on a graphic organizer, there is a strong likelihood that the writer will follow the plan and produce a coherent piece of writing. This works extremely well with children in third grade or older. Second grade students often write the sequel to the plan instead of following the plan. It is just a matter of maturity until that internal executive function allows them to intermingle the stages of writing (Calkins, 1994).

Planning discourages children from writing in the "what next?" mode. In this mode the child writes the first sentence and asks himself, "What next?" The second sentence has a connection to the first, and the third has a connection to the second, but by the end of the piece, the final sentence has absolutely no relation to the beginning (Bereiter and Scardamalia, as cited in Hillocks, 1986). You probably know an adult who still carries on a conversation in this manner.

Using Models for Prewriting

Using models of exemplary writing seems to have a limited effect on the quality of students' writing (Hillocks, 1986) so its value should not be overestimated. Exposure to high quality literature has a cumulative and long-term impact, but it is too far removed from the task of composing a shorter essay or story to have immediate effect. The use of exemplar pieces, however, facilitates transfer.

Teachers who have a stable curriculum often keep outstanding pieces, exemplars, from previous classes. The reading of two or three exemplars will give students a global idea of expectations—perhaps the desired length or general organizational pattern that they are expected to incorporate into their own writing. The prewriting stage may be too early to identify and to study specific qualities or features of the exemplars, but students need to know what a good paper sounds like.

Exposure to high-quality literature has a cumulative and long-term impact, but it is too far removed from the task of composing a short essay to have immediate effect.

Figure 10.3   This graphic organizer for persuasive or expository writing is used to help develop the introduction, body, and conclusion.

PRIMARY EXPOSITORY ORGANIZER

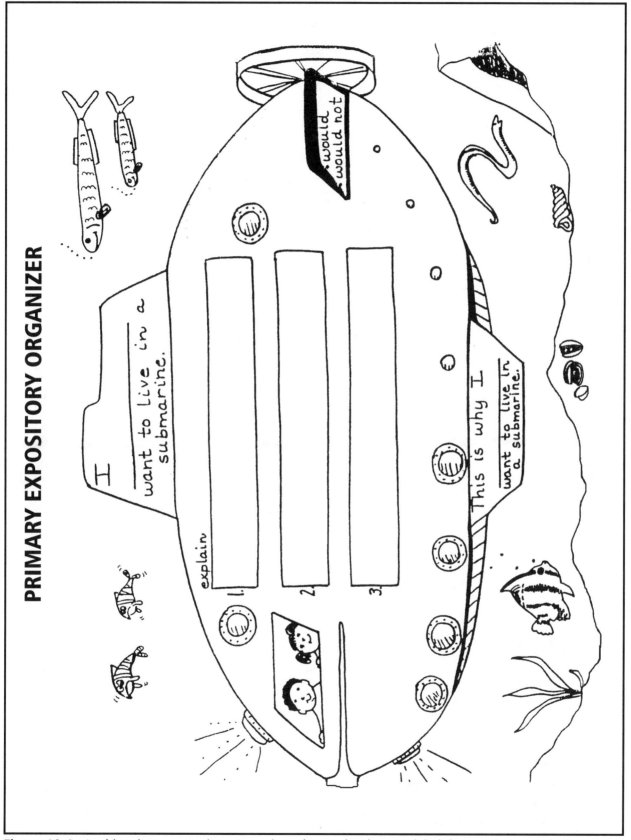

Figure 10.4 In this primary expository organizer, the teacher has modeled the opening and closing. (Developed by Deborah Behm.)

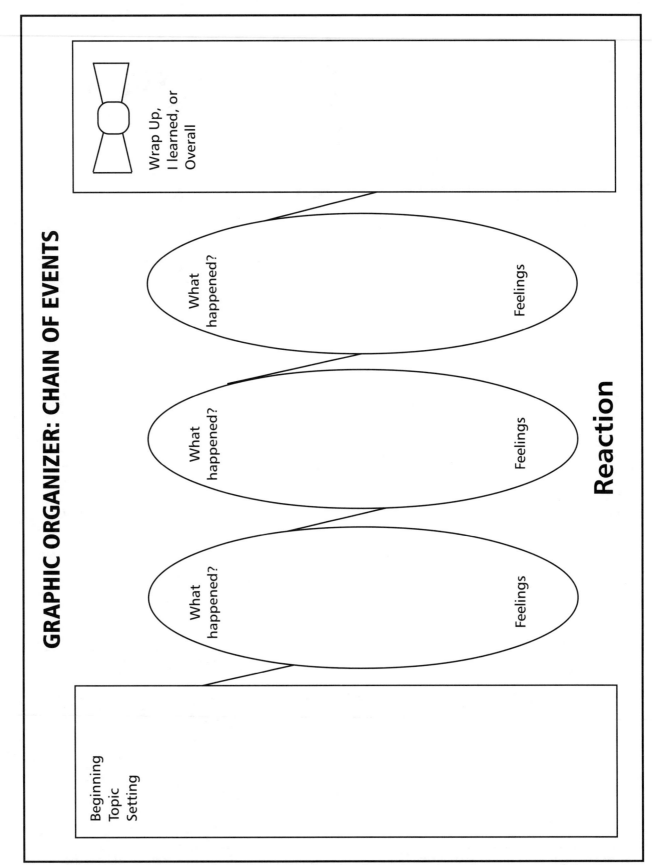

Figure 10.5 This graphic organizer helps to develop the chain of events, or the sequence, of the story. (Developed by Sue Schulte.)

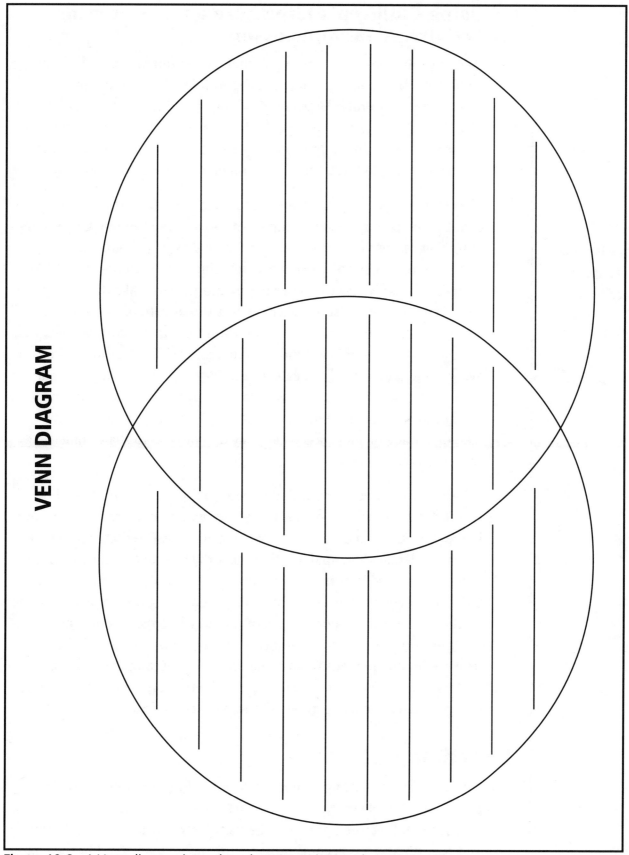

VENN DIAGRAM

Figure 10.6   A Venn diagram is used to plan comparison and contrast writing.

Using Children's Literature as a Prewriting Activity: A Sample Lesson

Using picture books as a writing prompt can be fun for writers of any age. Many have beautiful illustrations, delightful language, and universal themes. *Wilfrid Gordon McDonald Partridge* (1985), a picture book by Mem Fox, describes a little boy who helps elderly Miss Nancy recover her memories. This activity, developed by Patricia Braun, can also help students in any grade level retrieve their memories for a writing assignment.

The teacher should read the book aloud and elicit from the class the qualities of memories: something warm, something from long ago, something that makes you cry, something that makes you laugh, and something as precious as gold. Using artifacts similar to the ones that Wilfrid brought to Miss Nancy to restore her memories can make the experience more vivid. With the list of the characteristics of memories on the board, ask each student to write down a key word for a memory of his own that fits each category. Whip around the room and ask for a short answer from every student in each of the categories. The teacher should participate in each round, but she should answer last. Hearing the possibilities may prompt some of the students to change their minds or to add a new memory. Students may pass when they do not wish to share something that is too personal.

Ask students to freewrite for five minutes on one or two of their choices and then to pair share. There is always something more that will surface in the discussion, and perhaps questions will be asked that will rouse a few more details. The final decision must then be made, and students can write. Undoubtedly, everyone will have a favorite story to tell, and the whole class will be engrossed for some time writing their memoirs. If the teacher writes her memory on the overhead while the students are drafting, this provides additional modeling. Later, the students will share, revise, edit, and perhaps publish the final piece accompanied by an artifact or an illustration that represents the treasured memory. Expect a deluge of teddy bears, pictures, and family keepsakes.

Drafting

Following the prewriting activity, children draft their pieces. Drafting is actually the simple part. The real growth in writing comes between the first draft and the final product. That is the place where rubrics, scales, and peer discussions become most useful and when the children are most interested in improvement.

> Using picture books as a writing prompt can be fun for writers of any age.

Revision

Very significant gains occur when students work with standards or criteria and apply them to their own writing or to the writing of others (Hillocks, 1986). When revising with criteria scales, the teacher should introduce one scale at a time so students can learn which features score what rating. Too many aspects at one time just yield a diffused focus and little is mastered. After students have determined how to apply the criteria of one scale, others can be introduced, leading up to the use of an entire rubric. As an example, let's start with a single scale for elaboration. Criteria sheets can be elaborate and technical, or simple and student-designed. In Figure 10.7, there are two scales, one from the Illinois State Board of Education (1995) and the other student generated.

An easy way to introduce criteria rating to the whole class is to have a short section read orally or prepared on an overhead transparency. The

CRITERIA SCALES

Technical Criteria for Support and Elaboration

1. Little or no support
   Very confusing
   Insufficient

2. Support and elaboration attempted
   Confusing
   Unrelated list

3. General
   Related list
   Sufficiency

4. Some 2nd order elaboration
   Mix of general and specific
   Sufficient

5. Most elaboration is 2nd order
   Most developed by specific detail

6. Almost all elaboration is 2nd order
   Elaboration for each key point shows
     evenness or balance

Simple Criteria for Support

1. Nothing there
   No details
   Can't imagine the scene

2. Some details
   Doesn't match topic
   Partially wrong details

3. Lots of details
   Related to topic
   Lots on some points, little on
     others

4. Tons of details
   Makes sense
   Can really "see" it

Figure 10.7 First column adapted from *Effective Scoring Rubrics,* Illinois State Board of Education, 1995.

rating scale must be visible on the board or a poster. After listening to or reading the piece, children hold up their fingers to give a number rating. Hands should be held in front of the chest rather than overhead so everyone has to decide independently. The teacher then calls on several students to justify their ratings. The teacher also needs to tell her rating and reasoning so the criteria of everyone begins to build along the same lines. It is a high-participation activity, and soon everyone is on the same page. To make the activity even more worthwhile, students can suggest revisions so that the sample will meet the highest standard. Several studies have shown that revising the work of others is as effective in improving the quality of writing as revising one's own work.

When working with criteria, there are both short-term and long-term gains. For the short-term, students are able to evaluate their own papers and make changes before handing in the paper to the teacher for grading. After the grade has been given, postmortems hold little interest for students. The long-range gains are more important. What students learn with modeling, discussion, and criteria sheets today transfers to an independently written piece tomorrow.

Peer Editing Groups

It is during the revision process that peers can provide the most help. The discussion among children in peer revision appears to be a factor in promoting growth in writing. Revision groups using criteria show more improvement than students who revise and edit independently, even with a set of scales. Revision groups have a greater impact than teacher comment (Hillocks, 1986).

Peer editing groups are used both in writer's workshop and in structured writing, but in structured writing instruction, it is more likely that the peer groups will be using specific criteria. In order for peer editing/revising to work successfully, students need to be taught both evaluation criteria and how to interact with other students in the group. Without criteria for evaluation, the judgment will be made in terms of whether the editor personally liked the author rather than if the editor liked the piece.

The procedure for teaching revision techniques progresses from whole class to small group. First, the teacher explains the rating scale and asks students to make judgments about a sample piece. The piece used for modeling revision should have all the grammatical and spelling errors removed, so the students' attention is not diverted with editing correc-

Several studies have shown that revising the work of others is as effective in improving the quality writing as revising one's own work.

tions. After ratings are made and discussed, revisions are suggested, with the teacher questioning students about the placement of the revisions. Demonstrating where to place the changes is very helpful. Writers can place changes between the lines, use a caret, use a letter to make an insert mark and then list the changes on another sheet, or use arrows and cross-outs. Students then repeat the process with their own papers and a partner, looking primarily for the same kind of revisions that were modeled. Students work long and hard with partners following modeling because they have a specific purpose. The process is also more objective because it is criteria based.

Do not be afraid to spend significant time revising a single aspect of writing. A whole class period working just on introductory paragraphs will yield a whole class that knows how to write an introduction. During a revision session, it is vital that each child has his draft in front of him and is actively applying the strategy being taught.

Social skills also need to be taught for revision groups to succeed. These include learning not to complain when partners are assigned and listening without interruption to what the editor has to say. The author always has the option of making the suggested revision or not. Role playing appropriate and inappropriate reactions can be helpful for learning desired behaviors.

Revising with Comparison

Some children may have criteria endlessly explained to them without apparent effect. What they need to see is an example, what a "good one" looks like. Exemplars and modeling revision with pieces on the overhead help students understand the criteria through comparison of the various pieces to the student's own work.

Another choice is to allow students to read each other's work. Seeing how other writers developed the topic, crafted details, or supported reasons to persuade is especially useful to the writer who is lacking ideas or who is unfamiliar with a particular format.

Comparison also demonstrates what can be expected when students are introduced to new or higher standards. What was acceptable in eighth grade is no longer the norm in high school. Upon seeing the more complex work of classmates, most students are willing to work toward the higher expectations, and now they have an example with which to work.

> Social skills also need to be taught for revision groups to succeed.

Editing

Editing should be done after revising, although almost all writers start penciling in corrections as they go along. Editing partners can work with a checklist that can be moderately helpful, although partners are more effective if looking for just one or two types of editing problems, such as incomplete sentences or inappropriate punctuation. Between drafts is the best place to teach mechanics. When students have their own pieces in front of them and have just finished struggling with how to punctuate dialogue, they are ready to learn how to make their content more accessible to the reader. They can apply what they have just been taught to their own work, which is always more meaningful than applying it to ten sentences from the English book.

Occasionally, have students do an exercise in which they list the first word of every sentence and then count the number of words in those sentences. Write the results on a page with two columns, one column for the first words and one with the word totals. If every sentence begins with *I* or *Then*, it is easy so see that some variety is needed in sentence structure. For those sentences with 52 words, there is a good chance that some run-on sentences might exist within the big one.

Editing partners are most effective if they are looking for just one or two types of editing problems.

Writing in Response to Reading

Personal writing in the form of stories, narratives, journals, and diaries is probably the most common genre of writing, especially in the lower grades. But what about those children who are private in nature and do not wish to share? Writing in response to reading—in response to literature and in response to text materials—allows all children to respond and can employ the entire range of formats. When reading and writing are taught together, research shows that "writing can have a positive affect on children's reading comprehension and on their critical thinking abilities (Qian, as cited in May, 1998, p. 307). Writing clarifies reading and thinking.

Unlimited Genres and Formats

There are many possibilities for writing in response to reading, including narratives, persuasive essays, expository essays, newspaper articles, interviews, diaries, journals, poems, commercials, revised endings or sequels, advice columns, critiques, editorials, notes, reviews, plays, articles, and letters. For writing assignments suitable for working with a content text, see the strategies in chapter 9. While some of these genres are great fun, the teacher needs to consider what aspect(s) of writing will be taught through the assignment. Producing a newspaper article is not really the objective. It may look like an editorial on the outside, but the inside structure has to do with strong reasoning, relevant details, and coherent organization. This is another place in the writing process in which rubrics can be used to clarify the objectives to students. Short activities such as writing bumper stickers, greeting cards, and slogans may be motivational but are not rich enough in content or process to be useful for improving writing skills.

Roll of Thunder, Hear My Cry (1977) provides a rich example of the variety of writing assignments that can be derived from a single source. This novel by Mildred Taylor follows the life of the Logan family in Mississippi in the 1930s. All of the assignments listed below not only provide opportunity for the development of writing skills but they also require that the student revisit the text. If students listen and discuss the assignments in revision groups, then all the aspects of literacy are integrated.

> **Writing in response to reading allows all children to respond and can employ the entire range of formats.**

1. Expository essay: Explain why Cassie's day in Strawberry was the worst day of her life.

2. Interview: Interview Mr. Logan about the night of the fire.

3. Narrative retelling: Retell how Cassie finally got even with Lillian Jean.

4. Newspaper articles: Jefferson Davis School Bus Disabled. Unknown Assailants Responsible for Death of John Henry Berry.

5. Editorial: Accounts with the Company Store Leave Residents Without Choice and in Greater Debt.

6. Advice Column: There is this girl who has been mean to me and got me in trouble for something I didn't do....

7. Expository: Explain why the Logans are a strong family.

8. Diary: Mrs. Logan contemplates if her stance about the school books and her decision not to shop at the local store are worth losing her job.

9. Persuasive: T. J. (should/ shouldn't) be held responsible for his decisions. T. J.'s "friends" (have/ have not) excessively influenced him.

10. Journal: Of what unfair circumstances does this book remind you?

11. Poem: The Night Men are Riding.

12: Commercial: Mr. Barnett's General Store.

13. Persuasive: Racial prejudice is (as prevalent now/ less now) than in Mississippi in the 1930s.

14. Play: Change the scene of shopping at the Barnett store into a scene from a play.

15: Letter: Mrs. Logan writes to Uncle Hammer telling him that the mortgage has come due but begs him not to come.

It is the diagnostic teacher who decides which aspects of writing her children need to practice. Based on those needs, she chooses the appropriate writing assignment. Cassie's worst day will provide practice in sequence and elaboration. Writing a poem about the night men will surely be a fine platform for visualization, description, vivid vocabulary, and metaphor. Explaining why the Logans are a strong family will require that children examine their own beliefs about how families support each other. Once the objectives have been decided upon, children always appreciate a choice of assignments. It is not very difficult to devise a similar assignment in the same genre so that options are available.

Children always appreciate a choice of assignments.

Help for Retellings and Summaries

A standard written response to reading is the retelling or summary. Just think of the involvement in rereading for sequence, the determination of major and minor events, visualization, relevant details, and required manipulation of the text to turn it into the student-writer's own words. Students make the text meaningful as they paraphrase, reinterpret, and set the events clearly into their memories.

A terrific technique to help students learn to summarize is the tic-tac-toe picture summary. Older students as well as younger ones love to respond to a story through drawing. The tic-tac-toe nine-square is a simple format to prepare and has a beginning row, a middle row, and an ending row for events from the beginning, middle, and end of the story. Scenes can be drawn with stick figures or with complex drawings that can be labeled or not. Once the events have been decided upon and drawn in sequence, each picture idea is turned into a written sentence. The sentences can be written in paragraph form by a third grader, or they can be connected, elaborated upon, and smoothed out by a high school freshman for a summary.

W. Dorsey Hammond (1992) has suggested several categories of written responses to literature or texts that students have read and studied. In

personal responses to story events and themes, children use the story as a springboard to remember and interpret their own experiences. A response often starts, "That happened to me one time when . . . ."

Another written response to writing involves students **interpreting characters or events**. Interpretation requires that students use their own experiences and the text to infer motivations in the story. In Rudyard Kipling's *The Jungle Book*, students may be asked to write a persuasive piece indicating if they think Mowgli belonged with the men or with the animals. High school students might write why Odysseus was a tainted hero. The shared inquiry approach of Junior Great Books uses this method extensively for discussion groups. Many of the discussion questions can be turned into high interest writing assignments.

Metacognitive responses are open-ended responses about the thoughts and reading processes of the child as she reads the story, passage, or chapter. This kind of response is often recorded in a reading journal. Modeling and instruction are required for this response or it will turn into a summary of the chapter. Children can respond to literature "beyond the lines" by noticing the **style and techniques used by an author**. Even very young students can identify the style of their favorite authors after reading several books. It can be much easier for students to **debate moral dilemmas** in literature than to reveal dilemmas in their own lives. Learning to consider consequences and multiple viewpoints may not only make an interesting composition, but they could have important effects in the lives of the writers.

Hammond's last suggestion for writing in response to literature is to make **comparisons**. Comparisons can be used to make connections between themes, plots, characters, settings, or any element of literature. Be sure to teach children how to set up comparison and contrast pieces or they may read, "He was tall, but she was Norwegian." The Venn diagram, as in Figure 10.6, is useful for planning this type of writing.

> It can be much easier for students to debate moral dilemmas in literature than to reveal dilemmas in their own lives.

The Content and Purposes of Writing

Students need to write for a variety of purposes and audiences. Most writing assignments are done for the teacher, but a different audience might provide an additional incentive. Mem Fox, author of *Wilfrid Gordon McDonald Partridge*, wrote about her college students who had to prepare an annual presentation, consisting of poems, passages from read-aloud picture books, and excerpts from children's novels, for their peers. It was "merely satisfactory," according to Fox, until she asked her students to present their projects to groups of school children. "Dreading the imminent and real audience galvanized them into quite a different sort of action: they ached with caring about the response and rehearsed for hours outside class times" (Fox, 1988, pp. 114–115).

Letters to real people, articles for newspapers, stories to be read to younger children in the school, movie reviews for the school newspaper, thank you notes, or even the promise that every paper will be stapled to the bulletin board may alter the level of engagement when students are writing.

The teacher is still an important audience and many students will put forth their best for the teacher. E. S. Metviner (as cited in Hillocks, 1986) found that ninth-grade papers written for the teacher for a grade were more effective than papers on the same subject written for possible publication in the school newspaper. Since all students are not motivated by the same incentives, as in all aspects of teaching, it is good to offer to students a variety of assignments and audiences.

Looking Back at Objectives and Balanced Writing

When a classroom teacher decides to balance the writing program, she needs to know a wide variety of strategies and techniques as well as which benefits will accrue from which techniques. She also needs to analyze the current level of writing abilities of the students in her class in order to make the right matches.

What should be the ultimate objective in teaching writing? The final outcome is that each student can self-evaluate his own performance accurately because he has developed internal criteria of what a "good one" is. The goal must be for students to no longer be dependent on the grade of a teacher to tell if they have produced writing suited to the purpose and accessible to the reader. Students will have learned to write well independently.

> The goal must be for students to no longer be dependent on the grade of a teacher to tell if they have produced solid writing.

CHAPTER

Assessment

*And still they gazed, and still the
wonder grew,
That one small head should carry
all it knew.*

—OLIVER GOLDSMITH

Testing happens occasionally, but assessment goes on continually. Teachers make assessments every time they listen to a response from a student and each time they read a line written by a student. Experienced teachers use those assessments to make beneficial instructional choices, not just to assign grades on a report card.

Literacy teachers need several types of assessment. Teachers of emergent readers need to know how well students can manipulate the decoding system, and reading teachers at every level need to know how well children comprehend and apply what they are reading and which strategies they are using to construct meaning. Teachers need to know how children go about learning and what attitudes influence their motivations. Literacy assessment also involves evaluation of writing, listening, and speaking.

Students benefit from assessment when they receive feedback on their work and then use that knowledge to develop criteria for future work. However, students seldom view tests as diagnostic and helpful unless their teachers show them how to assess their progress on a developmental scale and set future goals. From a very early age, children think that tests are exceedingly important. They develop ideas about what is significant in school by the kinds of tests they are given. If teachers only ask for informational tidbits, then students will believe that collecting tidbits is the ultimate goal of an education. If teachers could develop tests to show progress, then students might view schooling differently. The kinds of tests teachers give and the information that is gathered for the test influence the attitudes and actions of both teachers and students.

Teachers can provide balance in the minds of their students and gather the information they need by using a broad repertoire of assessments, including formal and informal as well as product and process assessments. Formal tests provide fast, reliable, and comparative data. Informal tests provide more comprehensive information and are usually authentic, that is, accomplished within the curriculum and with classroom materials. Product assessments are samples of completed work, such as writing pieces, portfolios, logs and journals, or drawn summaries. Each type of work is judged according to specific criteria. Process information is often obtained through observation and documentation of work at various stages.

Experienced teachers use assessments to make beneficial instructional choices, not just to assign grades on a report card.

Assessment Through Observation, Checklists, and Anecdotal Records

An extraordinary amount of information can be gathered informally and unobtrusively as teachers watch their students participating in daily activities. Merely observing a class of students for a year is probably more instructive than any three undergraduate classes! Teachers learn about the achievement and learning styles of individual students, and at the same time they also build a mental framework about seventh-grade students in general and what seventh-grade students are capable of doing. They learn what lessons have made an impact, and they decide what goals are worthwhile.

Individual observations and general observations are important. The first yields diagnostic information, and the second provides a framework for interpreting the observations. A scope and sequence chart from a basal reading series or a state-wide list of language arts standards can help teachers to broaden and to refine which expectations are developmentally appropriate.

To remember and document how twenty-five to thirty students are progressing and who needs help with what, most teachers use checklists or write anecdotal notes during observations. Checklists lend themselves to those questions that can be answered yes or no. For example, during classroom activities, a teacher might observe whether a student demonstrates phonemic awarenesss, or if they know sound-symbol relationships. She might also check off whether a student can identify a word-family word by analogy, if a student stops at punctuation, or if he can add common endings to known words. Letter formation or editing concerns in writing make for good checklist items, too. Evaluating reading comprehension, on the other hand, does not lend itself to a checklist format.

Anecdotal records are appropriate for recording student behaviors that cannot be checked off in a yes or no fashion. Teachers use anecdotal notes to record examples of strategies and cueing systems that students are using, to record book selections, or to note cooperative group behaviors. Teachers may jot down revealing comments during story discussion or comments that divulge students' attitudes toward literacy. Some teachers carry sticky-note pads or index cards on a clipboard so that nothing has to be recopied, and the note can be dated and placed in the teacher's file or

> An extraordinary amount of information can be gathered informally and unobtrusively as teachers watch their students participating in daily activities.

a child's folder. A good time to take notes is when the students are working harder than you are, and you are doing more listening than talking.

In order to find observation time, a teacher might divide the class into groups of three children. She specifically observes one set of students during the morning on Monday, another on Monday afternoon, and the remaining sets on the remaining days. This method will yield more than thirty-five individual observations per child in a year's time.

When Efficiency Is More Important Than Natural Learning Situations

While taking notes and checking lists in authentic contexts are natural and fluid, sometimes it is easier and faster to test even when the tests are given individually. Figure 11.1, for example, consists of the BAF Test for phonics (May, 1998), which will quickly yield diagnostic information about all the graphophonic relationships. It is out of context and nonauthentic, but that is the point. There are no semantic, syntactic, or sight cues. The children have to know the sounds. The teacher can check off fifty-nine different consonant sounds and combinations in less than three minutes. If a child misses one of the nonsense words but can read other similar words in connected text, then the teacher knows he is using a cueing system other than phonics. This brief test is systematic and efficient, and it could be given more than once during the year to determine growth with comparable test data.

Parts A and B are more suitable for first grade than parts C and D, which are more suitable for second. Yet, this test could be used at any grade level when the teacher needs to know if the student has learned all of the sound-symbol relationships. The teacher needs one copy for marking, and the child needs an enlarged copy to read.

Determining Appropriate Reading Levels

To determine a child's reading level, divide the number of words read correctly by the total number of words in the passage. If 95% or more of the words were read correctly, the material is at the student's independent level. The instructional level is equal to 90-94%, and the frustration level is below 90% (Tompkins, 1997). Interest level and the level of predictability within sentences will make a big difference, but this system gives a good indication of the match between the reader and the book.

THE BAF TEST FOR PHONICS

Read these directions to the child: "These words are nonsense words. They are not real words. I'd like you to think about what sound the letters stand for; then read each word out loud without my help. Don't try to go fast; read the list slowly. If you have trouble with a word, I'll just circle it and you can go on to the next one. The first word is /baf/. Now you say it. All right, now go on to the rest of the words in row 1."

Part A: Consonant Letters
1. baf   caf   daf   faf   gaf   haf   jaf
2. kaf   laf   maf   naf   paf   raf   saf
3. taf   vaf   waf   yaf   zaf   baf   bax

Part B: Consonant Digraphs
4. chaf   phaf   shaf   thaf   whaf   fack   fang   fank

Part C: Consonant Clusters
5. blaf   braf   claf   craf   draf   dwaf   flaf   fraf
6. glaf   graf   fanf   plaf   praf   quaf   scaf   scraf
7. skaf   slaf   smaf   snaf   spaf   splaf   spraf   squaf
8. staf   straf   swaf   thaf   traf   twaf

Part D: Vowel Letters, Vowel Digraphs, and Vowel Clusters
1. baf   bafe   barp   baif   bawf
2. bef   befe   berf   beaf
3. bof   bofe   borf   boaf   bouf   boif   boof
4. bif   bife   birf
5. buf   bufe   burf

Figure 11.1 From *Reading as Communications,* Fifth Edition, by Frank May, © 1998. Reprinted by permission of Prentice Hall, Inc.

A quick rule of thumb, or in this case a rule of hand, is to have a student read a full page of text, putting down one finger for every word she does not know. If all five fingers go down, the book is not at her independent reading level and may not be a suitable choice. Since the number of words per page differs greatly from book to book, this is not a highly technical method, but it is a technique that youngsters can quickly learn to use.

Reading Assessment

Several methods exist for the evaluation of reading comprehension, including assessment by miscue, by retelling, by writing, by drawing, and even by end-of-the-book tests.

Assessment By Miscue Analysis

Miscue analysis is a type of reading strategy assessment developed by Kenneth Goodman. Miscues are deviations from the text or unexpected responses that are made by the student. Comparisons between the original text and the child's reading reveal the reader's knowledge, experience, and reading strategies. Miscue analysis is considered authentic assessment because a previously unread portion of whatever book the student is reading becomes the test material. Passages may be several paragraphs or several pages in length. During this type of assessment, a student reads the unfamiliar text aloud while the teacher records a transcript. Meaning is actually being constructed as the oral response is generated so it is as close as a teacher can get to seeing the process of comprehension occur. Miscue analysis can be done one-on-one, or when the child is reading aloud in a small group, or with the whole class. It is much easier when the teacher has duplicated the page or pages and can mark directly on the duplicated sheet.

The material needs to be "long and challenging enough to produce sufficient numbers of miscues for patterns to appear. In addition, readers receive no help and are not interrupted" (Goodman and Goodman, 1998, p. 103).

As the child reads, the teacher notes words that were omitted, repeated, or substituted, words that were supplied by the teacher after an extended waiting period, and words that the child attempted (for example, *wa-wash-watching*). Self-corrections are also noted. Goodman recommends that the teacher should wait a full thirty seconds before supplying a word.

> Miscues are deviations from the text or unexpected responses that are made by the student.

Although there is a formal system of marking miscues, most teachers develop their own shorthand for omitted, repeated, and supplied words and then write in substitutions and attempts. The recording goes much faster if no marks are made for all the words that were correct. After the transcript is completed, the teacher asks the child to retell the story in his own words.

The following paragraphs offer brief examples of how to determine what strategies the readers are using by revealing their miscues. Author: "Paddy came down the stairs as fast as his short legs would carry him, paddity pat, paddity pat." Meg responds, "Paddy came downstairs as fast as his little legs would carry him, piddy pat, piddy pat." Although Meg didn't exactly reproduce the text, she did not lose any of the meaning. Since the brain can process and store information faster than the reader can read aloud, good readers know what is coming and sometimes substitute synonyms or patterns that sound more comfortable to their ears. Proficient readers often make semantically acceptable miscues. Meg's reading has been meaningful and fluent, and she has preserved syntactic sentence patterns. These types of "errors" are hardly errors at all, and the teacher need not correct them or insist on an exact reproduction.

Author: "When the digging is over, the female gathers leaves and grasses." David reads, "When the doggy is over, the... the family gaheres leave and grows." It is clear that David has no understanding of what he is reading, nor does he understand that reading is supposed to be meaningful. He substituted *gaheres*, a nonword, for *gathers*. His choices retain graphophonemic similarities as he uses initial sounds and some medial and ending consonants. Probably his strategy is to proceed one word at a time until he gets to the end and then assumes his part is done.

He is possibly using some syntactic clues. *Doggy* could follow *when the,* and the verb *is* might make him confirm his idea that this is the beginning of a workable sentence, but everything falls apart after that. He is not watching for semantic cues, and he is not monitoring his comprehension at all. This passage is clearly above his reading level. David needs to be working at an easier level, learning through guided reading with his teacher as they explore the idea of reading as communication. "The errors that interfere with meaning and the errors that are syntactically unacceptable are the most serious because the student doesn't realize that reading should make sense" (Tompkins, 1997, p. 447).

"The errors that interfere with meaning and the errors that are syntactically unacceptable are the most serious because the student doesn't realize that reading should make sense." (Tompkins, 1997).

Miscues give teachers greater insight into the strategies a reader is using than a perfect reproduction of the text does.

Author: "Roy saw a little boat pull a big boat." Tommy repeats, "Roy was a little boat pulled by a big boat." This example is taken from Frank May's *Reading as Communication* (1998, p. 381) because it is such a perfect illustration of a child who has miscued at the beginning of the sentence and then makes adjustments so that the remainder of the sentence makes sense. After changing *saw* to *was*, Tommy probably decided *Roy* was the name of the little boat, and it was more logical that a big boat would pull a little one. Tommy's choices are syntactically acceptable and he uses sound-symbol relationships or sight words. He just needs to pay attention to some of the subtle details.

Author: "The cow bumped into the churn, knocking it over." Betsy reads, "The cow jumped . . . it bumped into the cream, knocking it over." Betsy's class had seen sweet cream poured in a jar, closed up, and shaken until butter and buttermilk appeared so she knew something about making butter. She was unfamiliar with the word churn, but she had followed the previous part of the story and made a substitution based on her schema. She knew what she was reading about so she kept going. This example was adapted from Goodman and Goodman (1998, p. 109).

Author: "I'll light a fire in the fireplace and the porridge will be ready in a few minutes." Betsy responds, "I'll light a fire in the fireplace and I'll . . . and the porridge will be ready in a few minutes." Miscues also occur at pivotal points in a sentence. Betsy had predicted a parallel structure, but when the second *I'll* didn't fit with the following words, she self-corrected (Goodman and Goodman, 1998, p. 106).

Author: "And what do you think Father pulled out of his pocket? A little grey kitten with two white paws." Adam reads, "And what do you think Father pulled out of his pocket? A little grey kitten with two white paws." What can you tell about Adam? He is able to reproduce the author's text. Maybe he is using sight words, maybe sound-symbol relationships, and maybe both semantic and syntactic clues. Miscues give teachers greater insight into the strategies a reader is using than a perfect reproduction of the text does. Does Adam have any idea about what Father pulled from his pocket? The teacher will need to ask that question to ascertain if Adam is word calling or if he understands that there is meaning in the text.

Using miscue analysis, the teacher can assess many aspects of reading in a relatively short period of time. Is the child reading the text for meaning or just decoding word by word? Are syntactic clues being used to predict what type of word should come next? Do the words being read match the general context of the story? When a word does not match the context, does the reader backtrack and correct the word or phrase that mislead him? Do the substitutions make sense? Which strategies does the student rely on most often?

Assessment by Retelling

Whether children are reading the author's text aloud accurately or they are reading silently, retelling is a good choice for further assessment of reading comprehension. The directions are simply to ask the child to retell the story in his own words, remembering as much as he can. Young students may retell an entire picture book, but older ones are more likely to retell a chapter or a significant event in the plot. L. B. Gambrell, W. Pfeiffer, and R. Wilson (as cited in May, 1998, p. 388) found that children who had practice in retelling improved in both comprehension and recall. "They also gain in the ability to organize and retain text information." As young readers retell the story orally, the teacher checks off significant events from a prepared summary of the story. The teacher can question the student about any events that were missed during the retelling. "Guided questioning forces them to rethink the passage, and their retellings often improve substantially. Poor readers, who lack confidence, benefit greatly from the teacher's probing" (Routman, 1991, p. 323). Primary teachers have flannel board figures, cut-outs, or manipulatives available for the child to use to aid in the storytelling. The summary sheet makes a good portfolio artifact or entry for an assessment folder.

> **Children who had practice in retelling improved in both comprehension and recall.**

Beyond first and early second grade, students usually write the retelling. Although a teacher can learn a great deal about students' comprehension in oral discussion during shared reading, a question is usually answered by no more than a few students. When answers are written, everyone has an opportunity to respond.

An especially positive aspect of retelling is that every student will be able to respond at some level of specificity. The student receives credit for all the things she does know. Retellings can reveal a great deal about the breadth and depth of students' comprehension. Four questions that aid in assessment through retelling are: (1) Is it just a list of facts, or are there relationships between the facts? (2) Does the child understand the character's motivation, or do events just happen? (3) Is he accurately retelling the author's story? (4) Does he miss or misinterpret something that caused his understanding to be different from the author's? Greater depth of comprehension is usually demonstrated through retelling than with a set of quiz questions, and students learn that they have to read the whole section to be able to tell how it fits together. There is a different sense of accountability than merely skimming to find the answers to the questions. Some children like to be succinct, some have difficulty with the physical process of handwriting, and some think a few lines about the main events are sufficient. The teacher should model a response of the expected depth so students understand how much they need to retell to demonstrate comprehension. Comparing several papers containing different levels of elaboration or developing a class rubric will also work. Unclear expectations of depth are often more of a problem than lack of student knowledge and comprehension.

When students' understanding does not match the author's intentions, sometimes mismatched schema is the culprit. A class was reading Langston Hughes' "Thank You M'am," about a woman living in a boarding house who was mugged by a young boy. Instead of turning him in to the police, she took him home, fed him, and gave him money for his fondest desire, which was a pair of suede shoes. Several students thought it was no big deal for a rich woman to give a boy some money. Upon closer questioning, they revealed their reasoning. She lived in a three-story house with many bedrooms and had dinner in the dining room every night with several other people. Their schemas did not include *boarding house*, other boarders, and *hot plate* so they paid attention only to the clues they could interpret. When the confusion was straightened out—so that their schemas matched to the schema of the author—the students understood the compassion and personal sacrifice of Mrs. Jones. The teacher also learned that this particular story needed some preteaching. Quizzes with specific questions would not have revealed the students' mismatched schemas.

Assessment by Writing

Retelling is not the only way to respond to reading. There are abundant possibilities involving writing. The caveat is that writing as a reading assessment must demonstrate comprehension of the material. It cannot be merely related to the reading. Writing assignments on the same topic, creative responses, and stories of the same genre make good extension activities, but they are not good assessments. The teacher's expectations need to be clarified when assigning an assessment project, especially if previous writing experiences have been creative responses to the material rather than assessment-based responses.

> **When students' understanding does not match the author's intentions, sometimes mismatched schema is the culprit.**

Assignments that are assessment-based include: a diary or letter from a character (which are variations of retelling); a post card from a character (a five-minute evaluation of plot and sequence and perhaps character); a newspaper article (evaluates plot, sequence, setting, and character); an advice column (assesses if the student understands the conflict and can generate evaluative solutions); or, an interview with a character (reveals understanding of motivation and characterization).

Another great assignment is for the students to write an epilogue to the story. Only a few stories leave enough of an opening to allow for different but realistic epilogues. The student's epilogue cannot change any facts from the story and must logically follow the events and characterization of the story. A book that begs for an epilogue is *Julie of the Wolves* by Jean Craighead George. Ms. George finally wrote the epilogue herself, *Julie*, published nearly twenty-five years after the first book. There is a rubric, Figure 11.4, later in this chapter for assessing the epilogue.

A persuasive essay is an excellent way to judge critical reading because the student evaluates options and makes a decision. Only certain stories are suitable for persuasive writing. There must be enough viable options in the story to evaluate. Most novels do lend themselves to persuasive writing at some point. Journal responses can be assessment tools if students have been taught to keep this type of journal. Students without instruction and direction tend to write global, wandering entries that are not much good for assessing anything.

A persuasive essay is an excellent way to judge critical reading because the student evaluates options and makes a decision.

Grading of these assessment-based assignments is done with rubrics. One or two of the analytical features must relate to content from the story. It cannot be graded only in terms of the quality of writing.

Two other tried-and-true assessment-based assignments include book reviews and comprehension questions. Book reviews assess critical reading skills because the student makes an evaluation and recommendation. A set of comprehension questions should include two factual and one inferential. When students know they will have to respond to what they read, they are more likely to concentrate. If this sounds old fashioned or coercive, just think about your actions when you know you are going to be held accountable for something and when it does not make any difference. A few questions give the teacher an indication that the students are on track. A more complex assignment at a later time will give greater depth of assessment.

Assessment by Drawing

Drawing is an appropriate response for every grade level. Most students find drawing a welcome and creative break from written responses. Students can draw the book or chapter by using a nine-square grid (like a tic-tac-toe board) to draw events from the beginning, middle and end, a story map, or a chart that categorizes.

More complex endeavors include constructing a flip book. Use three pages of blank paper. Fold each piece with a horizontal fold but at a different point on the page, so that when the three pages are tucked together at the fold, each edge sticks out farther than the previous edge. You should be able to see the bottom edge of each of the six pages. See the top half of Figure 11.2. An eight-page fold book is a similar idea, but the pages are very tiny, making it more suitable for the upper grades. Fold one page of paper along the lines indicated in the bottom half of Figure 11.2. Cut where indicated.

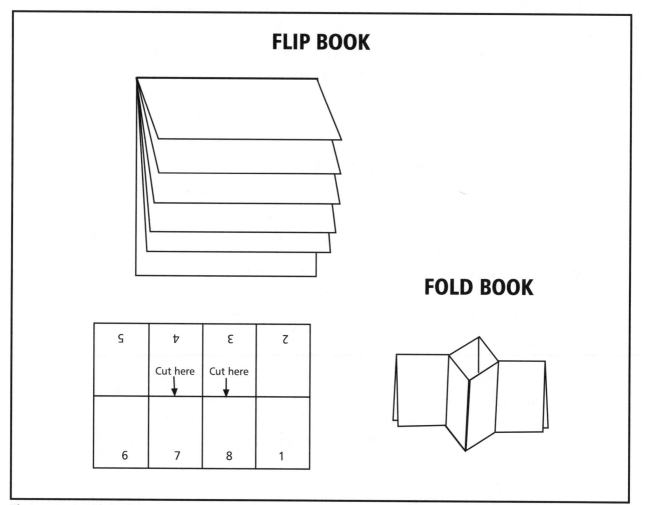

Figure 11.2 These instructions for a flip book and a fold book are simple and easy to follow.

Assessment by End-of-the-Book Tests

It is worthwhile to have an end-of-the-book test as long as the teacher knows what is being tested is a combination of reading comprehension and listening comprehension. If there has been guided reading and discussion as the reading progressed, there is no way to tell how the child learned the information for the final test. For an assessment of reading comprehension only, assess immediately after silent reading. For a broader assessment of comprehension, one that includes the ability to change one's mind after hearing conflicting evidence, test after discussion.

Standardized Assessment

Formal standardized testing, commercial or state-wide, also gives information to the teacher if she knows how to interpret the results. Standardized assessment has been severely criticized in the last few years. It is characterized as being a group administered, timed, snapshot picture that samples only knowledge. The tests are not diagnostic and do not reveal the processes used by students to think. This is all true, but then again most standardized testing was only meant to be quick, inexpensive, indicative, and comparative. It is unrealistic to expect more of standardized testing than it was designed to deliver.

Also, no other assessment methods can do what standardized testing can do, which is to give an indication of where children stand in relation to their classmates, to other students in the district, and to students across the country. Sometimes growth indicators are needed, but sometimes comparative indicators are needed. Every teacher wants to know how successfully her class is progressing, and every parent wants to know if his child is making average progress. Standardized testing is akin to asking a knowledgeable, unbiased outsider to take a quick peek into the classroom and give an indication about how well the kids are doing.

Teachers need to know how to interpret norm-referenced standardized test scores. Using a tricky example, decide what you think about the following statement. "There is little disagreement over the seriousness of the nation's literacy problem. About 40% of 10-year-olds can't read at grade level" (*USA Today*, 1997, 12A). Are you shocked? Teachers who understand the constraints and development of norm referenced standardized tests are whooping with elation—10% less than expected are reading below grade level.

> Standardized testing gives an indication of where children stand in relation to their classmates, to other students in the district, and to students across the country.

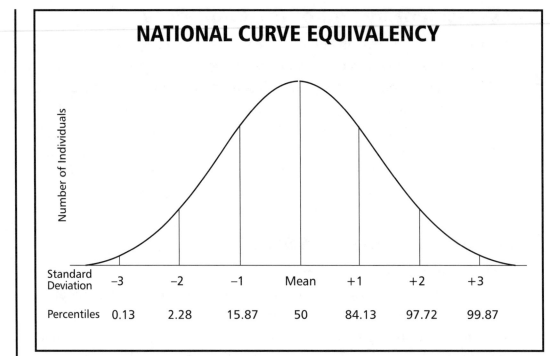

NATIONAL CURVE EQUIVALENCY

Number of Individuals

Standard Deviation	−3	−2	−1	Mean	+1	+2	+3
Percentiles	0.13	2.28	15.87	50	84.13	97.72	99.87

Figure 11.3   From *Educational Research: An Introduction* 5/E. V. Borg, J. Gall, and M. Gall, © 1989. Reprinted by permission of Addison-Wesley Educational Publishers.

The average score of a group is designated to be at grade level so 50% have to score at or below grade level.

Testing norms that are normal distributions of scores are developed through initial testing of large sample groups of children. The average score of the group is designated to be at grade level so 50% have to score at or below grade level (May, 1998). Thus it is unrealistic to expect every child to score at or above grade level. Figure 11.3 (Borg, Gall, and Gall, 1993, p. 149) shows a national curve distribution and how percentile scores and standard deviations match the curve.

Take standardized testing with a grain of salt, and understand the constraints. The ranking on the tests will most likely match the teacher's classroom ranking because the tests are indicative. Use standardized testing as only one of the instruments in the assessment repertoire.

Standards, Criteria, Benchmarks, and Exemplars

The idea of standards is critical to the discussion of assessment. Benchmarks or anchor points are other terms used to indicate standards. Assessment that uses standards—criteria-referenced testing—does not have to be comparative or competitive. It just means that there are criteria against which to measure growth or performance. Using standards for assessment is the difference between *what* the child is doing (uninterpreted observation and collection) and *how well* the child is doing (evaluation).

Making judgments about the quality of work or the rate of growth implies that the work is being compared to a standard or criteria, although there is intense debate over whether the standard should be uniform for all students or a personal-best standard. Many educational leaders (Wiggins, 1992; Sizer, 1993; O'Neil, 1992) believe that attainable, uniform standards should be used, because both teachers and students know the target for which they are aiming. Grading becomes objective, goal setting is easier, and teachers can develop instructional activities with a clear objective in mind.

Teachers who provide their students with clear expectations, exemplars (quality examples), and criteria will help students feel secure because they know what is expected. Teachers who develop standards and expectations with their classes build a spirit of collaboration in evaluation.

Performance Assessment

Performance assessment is so important to literacy evaluation because it is the most logical way to evaluate speaking and writing. Performance assessments require students to produce a product or to demonstrate a process. The assessments often have more than one right answer or more than one way to complete the process. Essays, writing, oral discourse, exhibits, experiments, portfolios, and constructed response items (fill in the blank or write an answer) are examples of performance tasks. "The key to effective performances is setting the standards and criteria in advance" (Burke, 1993, p. 59). These types of assessments are graded with a rubric. Grant Wiggins (1993) believes that performance assessment is such a strong assessment technique that it causes students to reconsider the meaning of knowing a concept or skill. Performance assessment asks students to perform at the application level rather than the knowledge level, or the can-do rather than the know-how stage.

Performance tasks are often classroom assignments that are integral to the curriculum so they fit more fluidly into classroom activities than forced-choice testing. They require more than simple recall, and they help students apply what they have learned. My favorite performance assessment was an assignment called Court of the Gods. Pairs of students were asked to research a story in Greek mythology in which a punishment occurred (usually some poor mortal entrapped by a capricious god). Students acted as opposing advocates for the mythical characters and had to be ready to tell the story orally to an adult judge, although only one

Performance assessment is the most logical way to evaluate speaking and writing.

actually did so during the trial. Students had to submit a written brief that told the facts of the case (which each pair wrote cooperatively), and a statement of argument for or against the original penalty (which each student wrote individually). The briefs ended with a request for the appeal to be denied or for damages and retribution. A decision was made by the judge based on the arguments presented. Students had to find and read the myths, interpret them carefully, work cooperatively, evaluate the actions of the characters, find reasons to support or condemn those actions, reflect on ethical issues, apply the information in written briefs, use word processing, and present their recommendation in a mock trial.

It sure beat fill in the blank!

Rubrics

Rubrics, which are relatively new in education, are undoubtedly one of the most efficient and objective ways to grade written compositions and other performance assessments. And, writing is the subject most commonly tested by performance assessment (Feuer and Fulton, 1993). A writing rubric can be found in chapter 10. In addition to their usefulness for grading, rubrics can be used by students for revision and editing in writing, when preparing for a speech, or as a checklist before a final project is presented. Teachers also use rubrics to clarify expectations when explaining a new assignment.

A rubric is a grading grid that can be written in a general manner, such as a rubric for expository essays; or it can be written for a specific purpose, such as a rubric for a newspaper article for *Number the Stars* (Lowry, 1990). Customarily, when making up a rubric, the levels of development that the assignment uses are written across the top of the page, and the analytical features or subcategories are listed down the side. The lowest developmental level usually represents the performance of the least knowledgeable student, and the highest level represents an outstanding performance. The levels or stages of development should have an even number, four or six, so that the student or teacher must decide if the assignment is basically on track or not there yet.

The analytical elements are the subfeatures of the assignment. In a writing rubric, the elements may be focus, support and elaboration, organization, accuracy, and English conventions. For a speech, they may be volume and pace, lack of distracting movements, organization, clarity of

> Rubrics can be used by students for revision and editing in writing, when preparing for a speech, or as a checklist.

speech, eye contact, and content. Each trait is consistently applied across the developmental levels.

Merely listing the objective and several numbers to designate the quality of the assignment does not constitute a rubric. That would be a grading scale. While grading scales are helpful to illuminate the objectives, the characteristics are not defined nor is the degree of quality assigned to each number specified.

In a rubric, within each box of the grid, the characteristics are described as accurately and succinctly as possible so that two people, grading independently, would render the same score. This is called inter-rater reliability. Using 40 to 50% rather than comparative descriptors such as *seldom* insures that everyone has the same criteria in mind. The language in a rubric should be written so that the terms can be understood by students and parents as well as by teachers. Figure 11.4 demonstrates specificity in several categories and is the previously mentioned rubric for the epilogue to *Julie of the Wolves*.

Merely listing the objective and several numbers to designate the quality of the assignment does not constitute a rubric.

Rubrics can also be used to help students learn to appraise their own work and set new goals. Ask students to grade themselves on the rubric after the performance is finished or when the written assignment is completed. When students turn in work that they have graded low, it is the perfect time to confer and find out if the student did not understand or just did not put enough time and effort into the project to meet a higher standard. The teacher can grade on the same sheet and the two evaluations can be compared. Because the scores are analytic (separate scores for different categories) rather than holistic (your grade is a B) both student and teacher can use the rubric as a diagnostic tool. The more often students are asked to self-evaluate, the more they will internalize the criteria and understand their application. Rubrics can also help students develop goals. Because of the developmental nature of a rubric, a student can easily see what is needed for the next level of achievement.

Analytical grades can be added up, weighted, or reviewed diagnostically. If standard ABC grades or a holistic grade are to be given, it works better to assign grades, 24=B, rather than to calculate percentages 24/30 = 80% = C. Rubrics just do not convert to percentages very well.

Although it takes time to develop a rubric, it is time well spent because the teacher clarifies in her own mind the desired qualities of the product.

RUBRIC FOR *JULIE OF THE WOLVES* EPILOGUE

	1	2	3	4
Plausibility	Has nothing to do with *Julie*	Implausible Unclear how and why	Plausible Most parts clear Picks up where story ends	Plausible extension of the story Clear how and why Picks up where story ends and relates epilogue to past
Supporting Details	1–2 details	3–5 details	6–10 details Includes feelings of characters	More than 10 details Includes feelings of characters
Focus	Can't stay on topic No introduction or conclusion	Some straying off topic Introduction or conclusion missing or don't match body	Mostly stays on topic Introduction and conclusion match body	Stays on topic Introduction and conclusion match body
Organization	No paragraphing Everything lumped together	Illogical paragraphing	Correct paragraphing	Correct paragraphing One topic per paragraph Details match topic sentences
Conventions	Difficult to understand	More than eight errors in grammar	3–8 errors in spelling and punctuation	Fewer than three errors in spelling and punctuation No incomplete or run-on sentences
Drafts	Only rough draft submitted	Only final draft submitted	Final draft and rough draft submitted	Final draft, rough draft and revisions submitted

Score = /24

Figure 11.4 (Developed by Debra Davidson.)

Rubrics also help to delineate expectations and clarify grading standards for the students. "This paper just felt like a C" is not likely to be a big hit when explaining grades to a parent, nor is it helpful to the student who cannot figure out what she is doing wrong.

Portfolios

A portfolio is a collection of a student's work. Each piece by itself may not mean much, but in conjunction, they can provide an accurate and holistic portrait of the student (Burke, 1993). Portfolios can be anything from an assorted collection of material to a highly delineated collection of examples showing growth and accomplishments in specific areas. Because all pieces reflect actual classroom work, a portfolio is authentic assessment (Henrickson, 1992). Although portfolios can be used for many purposes, self-assessment may be the most advantageous.

What kind of artifacts can be collected in a portfolio? Anything that a child produces could be collected. For tasks that do not leave a paper trail, such as a speech, a graded rubric could be included, or a photo of an oversized project could be added. It is also appropriate to include checklists and anecdotal notes especially for primary students. What distinguishes a portfolio from any other type of assessment is that process can be made visible. The plan, the drafts, the revisions, and the final copy of a report can all be there. Story maps, Venn diagrams, completed questions, summary sheets, reading-response journals, and retellings offer a more comprehensive picture than an end-of-the-book test. However, it is best to determine the purpose of a portfolio before making choices of artifacts.

> **It is best to determine the purpose of a portfolio before making choices of artifacts.**

Keep in mind that assessment portfolios differ from working portfolios. A working portfolio is a temporary folder for works in progress, lists of ideas for writers' workshop, interest inventories, instruction sheets, editing checklists, lists of "Skills I Now Know," records of books read, and other references to be kept.

Portfolios and Multiple Intelligences

A noteworthy attribute of portfolios is that they can present a multi-dimensional view of the student. Portfolios might contain videotapes of presentations, musical performances, or choral readings. They could contain mention of services performed by the student both in and out of school or contain projects done in cooperative settings. Art projects or visual displays might be included. This is certainly the place for demonstrating multiple intelligences. For the student who is not academically strong, a portfolio such as this can show off the strengths and talents he does possess. The problem is that oversize pieces and videotapes are really bulky and storage becomes a serious problem. A graded rubric does not provide nearly the imagery, but it is easier to store. Balance is a serious problem when trying to show multi-faceted aspects of a child's growth.

Portfolios and Self-Evaluation

Students learn to self-assess when they choose and critique a limited number of pieces for inclusion in their portfolios and complete a reflection or analysis sheet explaining why they made that choice. Students who do not know how to evaluate the quality of their own work finish their assignments and turn them in without a second thought. They depend on the teacher's grade to determine the quality. Thus, they are handicapped when faced with future assignments and are always dependent on the teacher's directions. Self-assessment helps to build internal criteria about what makes a "good one."

Reflection sheets that accompany portfolio items often use stem starters, such as the following: This is an example of my best work because . . . .; I chose this piece because . . . .; In order to do this well, I had to know . . . .; Two things I liked about my selection are . . . .; What was hard for me to do on this piece was . . . .; My special strengths are . . . .; One thing I would like to work on in the next quarter is . . . .

Until children become familiar with metacognition or self-evaluation, they may be tempted to choose the pieces with the highest grades. Much discussion is needed about how to select a piece that shows growth, took effort, showed insight, or represents a high standard of work. It is helpful for students to hear reflections of other students so they can hear the reasoning behind someone else's choices and the wording that can be used for their own reflection sheets.

What about the students' less successful pieces? They actually have a place in the portfolio, too. Finding a piece that could have been improved if the student had more time or a second chance leads to self-assessment. Children sometimes discover that work that was rushed through or done without thought is more likely to have a lower grade. Sometimes they find, much to their delight, they can now solve a problem that was so puzzling before.

> Students who do not know how to evaluate their own work finish their assignments and turn them in without a second thought.

Assessing portfolios once per quarter seems sufficient for formal reflection. The chosen pieces with an attached reflection sheet can be kept in a permanent portfolio while the remainder of the students' work is sent home. At the year's end, the pieces are culled even further. This procedure has two qualities: The child becomes self-reflective, and the mass of what is to be kept at school is reduced.

Portfolio Conferences, or What to Do with All Those Collected Artifacts

The student-parent portfolio conference is another good reason for developing a portfolio. This conference is usually conducted in the spring of the year and can take the place of a parent-teacher conference. It requires another round of culling and self-evaluation to winnow down the pile again. Usually papers from all of the subjects are included in this portfolio.

A very workable conference format is to have parents ask questions that were developed by the child. A sample is shown in Figure 11.5. This procedure eliminates many potential problems, because parents often do not know what to ask. They have forgotten what is studied in fourth-grade science, and they are not sure what degree of competence should be shown by a fourth-grade writer. Parents tend to focus on things like spelling errors, not realizing that their child's writing assignment also consists of an introduction, a clear development of an idea, good organization, and a convincing conclusion. Developing questions also eliminates the need for students to memorize a half-hour presentation about their work as the parents will prompt them with the next question.

Another benefit of student-directed conferences is that parents actually spend considerable time talking with their child about learning, instead of asking the cliched, "What did you do in school today?" To which the response is always, "Nothing." Because a formal student-directed conference asks for specific time and is conducted in the school setting, it is more effective than sending work home and asking the parents to return a response sheet. Six student-directed conferences can go on simultaneously in the same room without any difficulty. The teacher pauses at each conference and spends more time listening than talking. When parents are unable to attend the conference, some schools arrange for a teacher or other adult in the building to participate in the conference with the student. After the conference, the portfolio goes home with the family, and files are cleared out once again. If permanent portfolios are kept in

> Assessing portfolios once per quarter seems sufficient for formal reflection.

the school, some pieces need to be held back from the student-parent portfolio conference.

Portfolios for Grading, or High-Stakes Assessment

Using portfolios for grading or high-stakes assessment has several inherent problems. Using them for reflection and discussion of literacy is probably a better idea. Developing good judgment for self-evaluation, after all, is the desired end. However, if portfolios are going to be used for high-stakes assessment, then pre-established criteria are absolutely necessary.

There are several serious problems in using portfolios to give grades. If you choose to give quarter grades on the basis of a few samples submitted for the portfolio, it can be problematic if the pieces were unwisely selected by the students. Also, if writing pieces have been worked and reworked by the student and the teacher, is the final draft really representative of the student's ability? (Farr, 1990).

If you assess portfolios at the end of a term, then remember that almost everyone who has waited until the end has been sorry as he carted home boxes of portfolios for grading. Even if the whole portfolio receives a single grade, all the individual pieces still need to be evaluated according to criteria to fairly justify the single grade. Waiting until the end may work if only a few pieces from the portfolio are to be evaluated, but then that is grading by samples that may or may not be representative. Waiting until the end is also unfair unless the teacher has provided feedback on the quality of the work as the pieces were entered in the portfolio.

Grading pieces as they are placed in the portfolio evens out the workload and provides students with current feedback. The combined pieces still provide a holistic picture, if not a holistic grade. When Vermont tried state-wide portfolio evaluation in writing and math in the early 1990s, preliminary results of reliability were .33 to .43. That is, two raters would only give the same score about four out of ten times (O'Neil, 1993). High-stakes portfolio assessment has failed "to obtain evidence of validity by correlating portfolio scores with other more standard writing assessments" (Bracey, 1995, p. 647). Vermont's rubrics caused confusion when trying to differentiate between "distinctive" and "effective" tone in writing (Berger, 1998), and reviewers described the categorization of writing genres as unconventional and ambiguous (Bracey, 1995, p. 647).

> **Grading pieces as they are placed in the portfolio evens out the workload and provides students with current feedback.**

A Portfolio of My 6th Grade Work

Dear Mom and Dad,

This conference provides a chance for me to show you the kind of work that I do in school. It's also a chance for me to explain my work and tell you how I feel.
Here are some questions I would like you to ask me.

Language Arts

_____

_____

Math

_____

_____

Science

_____

_____

Social Studies

_____

_____

Exploratories and P.E.

_____

_____

My social skills, teamwork, and good manners

_____

_____

Some of the goals I would like to work on in 4th quarter are

_____

_____

Figure 11.5   Student-directed portfolio conference questions are a way for parents to spend time talking with their child.

SkyLight Training and Publishing Inc.

Grading by portfolio requires careful thought and criteria. Self-reflection, building internal criteria, discussion of literacy, and documentation of personal progress seem to be the most justifiable purposes for portfolios.

Assessing Assessment

Assessment is a complex issue that intimidates many teachers. It is complex because it serves so many masters—individual diagnosis, class progress, informed teaching decisions, grades and progress reports for parents, criteria to be internalized, application of standards, and data provided for goal setting. In addition to multiple purposes, it is intertwined with emotional issues concerning competition and self-esteem, compounded by an overlay of statistics and technical terms. Yet, it doesn't have to be intimidating if the teacher decides what she is looking for and is methodical and cumulative. There is a broad repertoire of assessment techniques that teachers can learn and successfully use in every classroom.

Self-reflection, building internal criteria, discussion of literacy, and documentation of personal progress seem to be the most justifiable purposes for portfolios.

References

Adams, M. J. 1990. *Beginning to read: Thinking and learning about print: A summary.* Prepared by S. Stahl, J. Osborn, & F. Lehr. Urbana-Champaign, Ill.: Center for the Study of Reading.

Adams, M. J. 1991. *Beginning to read: Thinking and learning about print* (4th ed.). Cambridge, Mass.: MIT Press.

Adams, M. J., B. R. Foorman, I. Lundberg, and T. Beeler. 1998. *Phonemic awareness in young children.* Baltimore: Brooks Publishing.

Almasi, J. 1995. The nature of fourth graders' sociocognitive conflicts in peer-led and teacher-led discussions of literature. *Reading Research Quarterly* 30, 314–351.

Anderson, R. C., E. H. Hiebert, J. A. Scott, and I. A. G. Wilkinson. 1985. *Becoming a nation of readers: The report of the commission on reading.* Urbana, Ill.: Center for the Study of Reading.

Anderson, R. C., P. T. Wilson, and Fielding, L. G. 1988. Growth in reading and how children spend their time outside of school. *Reading Research Quarterly* 23, 285–303.

Atwell, N. 1987. *In the middle: Writing, reading, and learning with adolescents.* Portsmouth, N.H.: Heinemann.

Avery, Carol. 1993. *...And with a light touch.* Portsmouth, N.H.: Heinemann.

Ball, E. W., and B. A. Blachman. 1991. Does phoneme awareness training in kindergarten make a difference in early word recognition and developmental spelling? *Reading Research Quarterly* 26 (1), 49–66.

Baumann, J. F., J. V. Hoffman, J. Moon, and A. M. Duffy-Hester. 1998. Where are teachers' voices in the phonics/whole language debate? Results from a survey of U.S. elementary classroom teachers. *The Reading Teacher* 51 (8), 636–650.

Baumann, J., H. Hooten, and P. White. 1996. *Teaching skills and strategies with literature.* In J. Baltas, and S. Shafer (Eds.), *Scholastic guide to balanced reading 3–6:* 60–70. New York: Scholastic.

Begley, Sharon. 1998, March 30. Homework doesn't help. *Newsweek*, 50–51.

Berger, P. 1998, January 14. Portfolio folly. *Education Week*, p. 75.

Blachowicz, C., and P. Fisher. 1996. *Teaching vocabulary in all classrooms.* Englewood Cliffs, N.J.: Merrill-Prentice Hall.

Borg, W., J. Gall, and M. Gall. 1993. *Applying educational research: A practical guide* (3rd ed.). White Plaines, N.Y.: Longman.

Boyle, J., and M. Weishaar 1997. The effects of expert-generated versus student-generated cognitive organizers on the reading comprehension of students with learning disabilities. *Learning Disabilities Research and Practice* 12 (4), 228–235.

Brown, A. 1997. Changes for effective schools. Unpublished manuscript.

Brown, K., G. Sinatra, and J. Wagstaff. 1996. Exploring the potential of analogy instruction to support students' spelling development. *The Elementary School Journal* 97 (1), 81–99.

Brown, R., P. B. El-Dinary, and M. Pressley. 1996. Balanced comprehension instruction: Transactional strategies instruction. In E. McIntyre and M. Pressley (Eds.), *Balanced instruction: Strategies and skills in whole language,* 177–192. Norwood, Mass.: Christopher-Gordon Publishers, Inc.

Bruck, M., and R. Treiman. 1992. Learning to pronounce words: The limitations of analogies. *Reading Research Quarterly* 27 (4), 375–388.

Burke, J. 1996. *The pinball effect: How renaissance water gardens made the carburetor possible and other journeys through knowledge.* Boston: Little, Brown and Company.

Burke, K. 1993. *How to assess authentic learning.* Palatine, Ill.: IRI/Skylight Publishing.

Burke, K., R. Fogarty, & S. Belgrad. 1994. *The portfolio connection.* Palatine, Ill.: IRI/Skylight Publishing.

Burns, Bonnie. 1998. Changing the classroom climate with literature circles. *Journal of Adolescent and Adult Literacy* 42 (2), 124–129.

Burroughs, R. 1993. The uses of literature. *Executive Educator* 15 (7), 27–29.

Button, K., M. J. Johnson, and P. Furgerson. 1996. Interactive writing in a primary classroom. *The Reading Teacher* 49 (6), 446–454.

Byrne, B., & R. Fielding-Barnsley. 1993. Evaluation of a program to teach phonemic awareness to young children: A 1-year follow-up. *Journal of Educational Psychology* 85 (1), 104–111.

Calkins, L. M. 1986, rev. 1994. *The art of teaching writing.* Portsmouth, N.H.: Heinemann.

Castle, J., J. Riach, and T. Nicholson. 1994. Getting off to a better start in reading and spelling: The effects of phonemic awareness instruction within a whole language program. *Journal of Educational Psychology* 86 (3), 350–359.

Chall, J. S. 1967. *Learning to read: The great debate.* New York: McGraw-Hill.

Coe, M. 1993. *The Maya.* London: Thames and Hudson.

Cole, A. D. 1998. Beginner-oriented texts in literature-based classrooms: The segue for a few struggling readers. *The Reading Teacher* 51 (6), 488–501.

Cunningham, P. M., and D. Hall. 1994. *Making words: Multilevel, hands-on, developmentally appropriate spelling and phonics activities.* Torrence, Calif.: Good Apple.

Cunningham, P. M., D. P. Hall, and M. Defee. (1998). Nonability-grouped, multilevel instruction: Eight years later. *The Reading Teacher* 51 (8), 652–664.

Cunningham, P., and D. Hall. (undated). *Practical phonics activities that build skills and teach strategies.* Torrence, Calif.: Staff Development Resources.

Davey, B. 1983. Think aloud: Modeling the cognitive processes of reading comprehension. *Journal of Reading* 27 (1), 44–47.

Diamond, L. and S. Mandel. 1998. Building a powerful reading program: From research to practice. <http//www.csus.edu/ier/reading.html>. Emeryville, Calif: Report prepared for the Consortium on Reading Excellence.

Donelson, K. L., and A. P. Nilsen. 1989. *Literature for today's young adults* (3rd ed.). Glenview, Ill.: Scott, Foresman and Company.

Duke, N., and B. Stewart. 1997. Standards in action in a first-grade classroom: The purpose dimension. *The Reading Teacher 51* (3), 228–237.

Ehri, L. C., and C. Robbins. 1992. Beginners need some decoding skill to read words by analogy. *Reading Research Quarterly* 27 (1), 13–27.

Ehri, L. C. and L. S. Wilce. 1985. Movement into reading: Is the first stage of printed word learning visual or phonetic? *Reading Research Quarterly* 20 (2), 163–178.

Elbaum, B., J. Schumm, and S. Vaughn. 1997. Urban middle-elementary students' perceptions of grouping formats for reading instruction. *The Elementary School Journal* 97 (5), 475–499.

Elley, W. B. 1996. The benefits of reading stories aloud. In D. Berliner and U. Casanova (Eds.), *Putting research to work in your school,* 77–82. Arlington Heights, Ill.: IRI/SkyLight Training and Publishing.

Farr, R. 1990. Setting directions for language arts portfolios. *Educational Leadership* 48 (3), 103.

Feuer, M., and K. Fulton. 1993. The many faces of performance assessment. *Phi Delta Kappan* 74 (6), 478.

Fink, R. P. 1998. Successful dyslexics: A constructivist study of passionate interest reading. In C. Weaver (Ed.), *Reconsidering a balanced approach to reading*, 387–408. Urbana, Ill.: National Council of Teachers of English.

Flippo, R. F. 1997. Sensationalism, politics, and literacy: What's going on? *Phi Delta Kappan* 79 (4), 301–304.

Foorman, B. R., D. J. Francis, J. M. Fletcher, C. Schatschneider, and P. Mehta. 1998. The role of instruction in learning to read: Preventing reading failure in at-risk children. *Journal of Educational Psychology* 90 (1), 37–55.

Forsyth, S., and C. Roller. 1998. Helping children become independent readers. *The Reading Teacher* 51 (4), 346–348.

Fox, M. 1988. Notes from the battlefield: Towards a theory of why people write. *Language Arts* 65 (2), 112–125.

Fresch, M. J., and A. Wheaton. 1997. Sort, search, and discover: Spelling in the child-centered classroom. *The Reading Teacher* 51 (1), 20–31.

Fry, E. B. 1968. A readability formula that saves time. *Journal of Reading* 11 (7), 513.

Gaskins, I. W., L. C. Ehri, C. Cress, C. O'Hara, and K. Donnelly. 1996–1997. Procedures for word learning: Making discoveries about words. *The Reading Teacher* 50 (4), 312–327.

Gambrell, L. 1996. Creating classroom cultures that foster reading motivation. *The Reading Teacher* 50 (1), 14–25.

Gaskins, I. W., L. C. Ehri, C. Cress, C. O'Hara, and K. Donnelly. 1996–1997. Procedures for word learning: Making discoveries about words. *The Reading Teacher*. 50 (4), 312–327.

Gaskins, I. W., L. C. Ehri, C. Cress, C. O'Hara, and K. Donnelly. 1997. Analyzing words and making discoveries about the alphabetic system: Activities for beginning readers. *Language Arts* 74, 172–184.

Gentry, J. R., and J. W. Gillet. 1993. *Teaching kids to spell*. Portsmouth, N.H.: Heinemann.

Glasser, W. 1986. *Control theory in the classroom*. New York: Harper & Row.

Goodman, Y., and K. S. Goodman. 1998. To err is human: Learning about language processes by analyzing miscues. In C. Weaver (Ed.), *Reconsidering a balanced approached to reading*, 101–126. Urbana, Ill.: National Council of Teachers of English.

Graves, D. H. 1983. *Writing: Teachers and children at work*. Portsmouth, N.H.: Heinemann.

Graves, M. F., B. B. Graves, and S. Braaten. 1996. Scaffolded reading experiences for inclusive classes. *Educational Leadership* 53 (5), 14–16.

Hammond, W. D. 1992. Writing as a response to literature. Workshop presented at River Forest, Ill. Public Schools.

Harding, C. 1998. Intervention strategies. Unpublished manuscript.

Harrison, J., and R. Sullivan. 1963. *A short history of western civilization*. New York: Knopf.

Henrickson, D. 1992. Student assessment. *Teacher today*. Glen Ellyn, Ill.: Institute for Educational Research.

Hicks, L. 1997. How do academic motivation and peer relationships mix in an adolescent's world? *Middle School Journal* 28 (4), 18–22.

Hillocks, G. 1986. *Research on written composition: New directions for teaching*. Urbana, Ill.: ERIC Clearinghouse on Reading and Communications Skills and the National Conference on Research in English.

Honig, B. 1997. Research-based reading instruction: The right way. *Education Digest* 63 (4), 16–22.

Hughes, R. 1940. With a First Reader. In K. L. Roberts (Ed.), *Hoyt's new cyclopedia of practical quotations* (p. 78). New York: Grosset & Dunlap.

Humphrey, J., J. Lipsitz, J. T. McGovern, and J. D. Wasser. 1997. Reading matters: Supporting the development of young adolescent readers. *Phi Delta Kappan* 79, 305–311.

Hunt, L. 1996–1997. The effect of self-selection, interest, and motivation upon independent, instructional, and frustrational levels. *The Reading Teacher* 50 (4), 278–282.

Illinois State Board of Education. 1995. *Effective scoring rubrics.* Springfield, Ill.: Department of School Improvement Services.

Illinois State Board of Education. 1995. *Performance assessment in mathematics: Approaches of open-ended problems.* Springfield, Ill.: Department of School Improvement Services.

Irvin, J. 1990. *Vocabulary knowledge: Guidelines for instruction.* Washington, D.C.: National Education Association.

Johnston, F. R. 1998. The reader, the text, and the task: Learning words in first grade. *The Reading Teacher* 51 (8), 666–675.

Joyce, B., and B. Showers. 1995. *Student achievement through staff development.* White Plains, N.Y.: Longman.

Juel, C. 1988. Learning to read and write: A longitudinal study of 54 children from first through fourth grades. *Journal of Educational Psychology* 80 (4), 437–447.

Kismaric, C., and M. Heiferman. 1996. *Growing up with Dick and Jane.* New York: Collins Publishers.

Kruzich, K. 1995. Classroom writing strategy analysis. Paper presented to the Skylight/St. Xavier Field-Based Masters Program, Orland Park, Ill.

Kucan, L., and I. Beck. 1997. Thinking aloud and reading comprehension research: Inquiry, instruction, and social interaction. *Review of Educational Research* 67, 271–299.

Laflamme, J. G. 1997. The effect of the multiple exposure vocabulary method and the target reading/writing strategy on test scores. *Journal of Adolescent and Adult Literacy* 40 (5), 372–381.

Lane, B. 1993. *After the end: Teaching and learning creative revision.* Portsmouth, N.H.: Heinemann.

Lapp, D., and J. Flood. 1997. Where's the phonics? Making the case (again) for integrated code instruction. *The Reading Teacher* 50 (8), 696–700.

Linderman, L. 1998. In.dict.ment. *Modern Maturity* 41 (1), 50–53.

Lundberg, I., J. Frost, and O. P. Petersen. 1988. Effects of an extensive program for stimulating phonological awareness in preschool children. *Reading Research Quarterly* 23 (3), 263–284.

Lyon, G. R. 1998, March. Why reading is not a natural process. *Educational Leadership,* 14–18.

MacWarehouse Catalog. 1998. Lakewood, N.J.: MacWarehouse.

Matz, K. 1994. 10 things they never taught us about teaching spelling. *The Education Digest* 59 (7), 70–72.

May, F. 1998. *Reading as communication: To help children write and read* (5th ed.). Upper Saddle River, New Jersey: Merrill-Prentice Hall.

McCormick, S., and E. Z. Becker. 1996. Word recognition and word identification: A review of research on effective instructional practices with learning disabled students. *Reading Research and Instruction* 35 (1) 5–17.

McGuffey, W. H. 1866. *McGuffey's new fifth eclectic reader: Selected and original exercises for schools.* Cincinnati, Ohio: Wilson, Hinkle & Co.

McIntosh, M. E., and R. J. Draper. 1985. Applying the question-answer relationship strategy in mathematics. *Journal of Adolescent and Adult Literacy* 39 (2), 120–131.

McIntyre, E. 1996. Strategies and skills in whole language: An introduction to balanced teaching. In E. McIntyre & M. Pressley (Eds.), *Balanced instruction: Strategies and skills in whole language* (pp. 12–20). Norwood, Mass.: Christopher-Gordon.

Mooney, M. 1995. Guided reading beyond the primary grades. *Teaching Pre K-8* (1), 75–77.

Morris, D. 1992. What constitutes at-risk: Screening children for first grade reading intervention. *Best Practices in Speech-Language Pathology* 2, 43–51.

Morrow, L. M., and D. H. Tracey. 1997. Strategies used for phonics instruction in early childhood classrooms. *The Reading Teacher* 50 (8), 644–651.

Moss, B. 1991. Children's nonfiction trade books: A complement to content area texts. *The Reading Teacher* 15 (1), 26–32.

Moustafa, M. 1998. Reconceptualizing phonics instruction. In C. Weaver (Ed.), *Reconsidering a balanced approach to reading,*135–157. Urbana, Ill.: National Council of Teachers of English.

Murphy, N. 1997. A multisensory vs. conventional approach to teaching spelling. ERIC Document Reproduction Service No. (ED 405 564).

Nagy, W. 1988. *Teaching vocabulary to improve reading comprehension.* Urbana, Ill.: National Council of Teachers of English.

Nessel, D. 1989. Do your students think when they read? *Learning* 17 (8), 54–58.

Odegaard, J. M., and F. B. May. 1972. Creative grammar and the writing of third graders. *Elementary School Journal* 73, 156–161.

Ogle, D. 1986. K-W-L: A teaching model that develops active reading of expository text. *The Reading Teacher* 39, 564–571.

Olson, M. W. and T. Gee. 1991. Content reading instruction in the primacy grades: Perceptions and strategies. *The Reading Teacher* 45, 298–307.

O'Neil, J. 1992. Putting performance assessment to the test. *Educational Leadership* 49 (8), 14–19.

O'Neil, J. 1993. The promise of portfolios: Vermont effort reveals benefits, shortcomings. *Association for Supervision and Curriculum Development Update* 35 (7), 1, 5.

Perkins, D. and G. Salomon. 1992. The science and art of transfer. In A. Costa, J. Bellanca, and R. Fogarty (Eds.), *If minds matter: A foreword to the future*, Vol. 1, 201–210. Arlington Heights, Ill.: Skylight Publishing.

Peterson, R. T. 1986. *Mallards*. Celebrations. Boston: Houghton Mifflin.

Podl, J. B. 1995. Introducing teens to the pleasures of reading. *Educational Leadership* 53 (1), 56–57.

Pressley, M. 1996. Concluding reflections. In E. McIntyre and M. Pressley (Eds.). *Balanced instruction: Strategies and skills in whole language*, 277–286. Norwood, Mass.: Christopher-Gordon.

Raphael, T. E. 1986. Teaching questions answer relationships revisited. *The Reading Teacher* 39, 516–522.

The Reading and Writing Wars. 1996, November 22. *The Wall Street Journal*.

Richardson, J., and R. Morgan. 1997. *Reading to learn in the content areas*. Belmont, Calif.: Wadsworth Publishing.

Robinson, H. 1960. The unity of the reading act. In H. Robinson (Ed.), *Sequential development of reading abilities* (pp. 237–244). Chicago: University of Chicago Press.

Routman, R. 1991. *Invitations: Changing as teachers and learners K-12.* Portsmouth, N.H.: Heinemann Irwin.

Samuels, J. 1997. The methods of repeated reading. *The Reading Teacher* 50 (5), 376–381. Originally published in January 1979.

Samway, K., and G. Whang. 1991. Reading the skeleton, the heart and the brain of a book: Students' perspectives on literature study circles. *The Reading Teacher* 45 (3), 196–205.

Schwartz, R. M. 1997. Self-monitoring in beginning reading. *The Reading Teacher* 51 (1), 40–48.

Shanahan, T. 1997a. Character perspective charting: Helping children to develop a more complete conception of story. *The Reading Teacher* 50 (8), 668–677.

Shanahan, T. 1997b. Reading-writing relationships, thematic units, inquiry learning . . . In pursuit of effective integrated literacy instruction. *The Reading Teacher* 51 (1), 12–19.

Shanahan, T. 1998. Twelve studies that have influenced K–12 reading instruction. *Illlinois Reading Council Journal* 26 (1), 50–58.

Sizer, T. R., and B. Rogers. 1993. Designing standards: Achieving the delicate balance. *Educational Leadership*, 24–26.

Snow, C. E., M. S. Burns, and P. Griffin. 1998. *Preventing reading difficulties in young children*. Washington, D.C.: National Academy Press.

Spiegel, D. L. 1992. Blending whole language and systematic direct instruction. *The Reading Teacher* 46 (1), 38–44.

Stahl, S. A. 1992. Saying the "p" word: Nine guidelines for exemplary phonics instruction. *The Reading Teacher* 45 (8), 618–625.

Stahl, S. A. 1997. Words, words, words. *Illinois Reading Council Journal* 25 (1), 58–62.

Stanovich, K. E. 1986. Matthew effects in reading: Some consequences of individual differences in the acquisition of literacy. *Reading Research Quarterly* 21 (4), 360–406.

Stauffer, R. 1969. *Teaching reading as a thinking process*. New York: Harper & Row.

Strech, L. 1995. Ability grouping for elementary reading instruction and its relationship to balanced reading. Unpublished master's thesis, California State University, Long Beach.

Strommen, L. T., and B. F. Mates. 1997. What readers do: Young children's ideas about the nature of reading. *The Reading Teacher* 51 (2), 98–107.

Toch, G. 1997. The reading wars continue. *U.S. News & World Report*. October 1997, 77.

Tompkins, G. E. 1997. *Literacy for the 21st century: A balanced approach*. Upper Saddle River, N. J.: Merrill-Prentice Hall.

Torgesen, J. K. 1998, January. Phonological Awareness. Presentation in Oak Park, Ill.

Tunnell, M., and J. Jacobs. 1989. Using 'real' books: Research findings on literature based reading instruction. *The Reading Teacher* 42 (7), 470–477.

Vandervelden, M. C., and L. S. Siegel. 1995. Phonological recoding and phoneme awareness in early literacy: A developmental approach. *Reading Research Quarterly* 30 (4), 854–875.

Wagstaff, J. M. 1997. Building practical knowledge of letter-sound correspondences: A beginner's word wall and beyond. *The Reading Teacher* 51 (4), 298–304.

Weaver, C. 1998. Toward a balanced approach to read. In C. Weaver (Ed.), *Reconsidering a balanced approach to reading*, 11–76. Urbana, Ill.: National Council of Teachers of English.

Why use volunteers when pros are available? (1997, November 10). *USA Today*, p. 12A.

Wigfield, A., and J. Guthrie. 1997. Relations of children's motivation for reading to the amount and breadth of their reading. *Journal of Educational Psychology* 89 (3), 420–432.

Wiggins, G. 1992. Creating tests worth taking. *Phi Delta Kappan* 49 (8), 26–33.

Wiggins, G. 1993. Assessment: Authenticity, context, and validity. *Phi Delta Kappan* 75 (3), 200–214.

Wilde, S. 1992. *You kan red this!* Portsmouth, N.H.: Heinemann.

Willis, S. 1995. Whole language: Finding the surest way to literacy. *ASCD Curriculum Update*. Alexandria, VA: Association for Supervision and Curriculum Development.

Worthy, J., and J. Hoffman. (Eds.). 1997. Critical questions. *The Reading Teacher* 51 (4), 338–340.

Yopp, H. K. 1992. Developing phonemic awareness in young children. *The Reading Teacher* 45 (9), 696–703.

Yopp, H. K. 1995. Read-aloud books for developing phonemic awareness. An annotated bibliography. *The Reading Teacher* 48 (6), 538–543.

Yopp, H. K. 1995. A test for assessing phonemic awareness in young children. *The Reading Teacher* 49 (1), 20–29.

Zaragoza, N., and S. Vaughn. 1995. Children teach us to teach writing. *The Reading Teacher* 49 (1), 42–47.

Zhang, Z. 1993. Literature review on reading strategy research. Office of Educational Research and Improvement, U. S. Department of Education. (ERIC Document No. ED 366 908).

Zutell, J. 1996. The directed spelling thinking activity (DSTA): Providing an effective balance in word study instruction. *The Reading Teacher* 50 (2), 98–108.

Zutell, J. 1998. *A student-active learning approach to spelling instruction*. (pamphlet) Columbus, Ohio: Zaner Bloser.

Literature Cited

Barrett, J. (1986). *Pickles have pimples and other silly statements*. New York: Atheneum.

Bradbury, R. (1984) All summer in a day. *Junior Great Books*. Series 6, Vol. 2, Chicago: The Great Books Foundation.

Bradbury, R. (1984). The Veldt. *Junior Great Books*. Series 6, Vol. 2, Chicago: The Great Books Foundation.

Brown, M.W. (1947). *Good night mom*. New York: Harper.

Burnett, F. H. (1987). *The secret garden*. New York: Holt & Co.

Carlstrom, N.W. *Jesse Bear, what will you wear?* (1986). New York: Aladdin Simon & Schuster.

Cushman, K. (1995). *The midwife's apprentice*. New York: Harper Trophy.

Duvoisin, R. (1950). *Petunia*. New York: Knopf.

Evslin, B. (1969). *The adventures of Ulysses*. New York: Scholastic.

Fox, M. (1985). *Wilfrid Gordon Mcdonald Partridge*. New York: Kane Miller.

George, J. C. (1972). *Julie of the wolves*. New York: Harper & Row.

George, J. C. *Julie*. (1994). New York: Harper Collins.

Gibbons, G. (1993). *Spiders*. New York: Holiday House.

Henry. M. (1951). *King of the wind*. Chicago: Rand McNally.

Homer. (1989). *The Odyssey*. (R. Fitzgerald, Trans.). New York: Vintage Classics.

Hughes, L. (1975). Thank you m'am. *Junior Great Books*. Series 5, Vol. 1, 130–134.

Jeunesse, G., C. Delafosse, & Millet. (1990). *Castles*. New York: Scholastic First Discovery Books.

Kalman, B. (1994). Homes around the world. New York: Crabtree Publishing.

Keats, E. J. (1972). *The pet show*. New York: Macmillan.

Kipling, R. (1955). The jungle book. In M. Martignoni (Ed.), *The illustrated treasury of children's literature*, 257–264. New York: Grosset and Dunlap.

Lessing, D. (1984). Through the tunnel. In *Junior Great Books*. Series 6, Vol. 1, Chicago: The Great Books Foundation.

Lowry, L. (1990). *Number the stars*. New York: Houghton Mifflin.

Martin, B. (1967). *Brown bear, brown bear, what do you see?* New York: Holt.

Martin, B. (1996). *Fire! Fire! Said Mrs. McGuire*. New York: Harcourt.

Maupassant, G. de (1978). The necklace. In R. V. Cassil (Ed.), *The Norton anthology of short fiction* (pp. 928–935). New York: W. W. Norton & Co.

McGraw, E. J. (1961). *The golden goblet*. London: Puffin.

Morley, D. (1984). *Marms in the marmalade*. Minneapolis, Minn.: Carolrhoda Books.

O'Dell, S. (1983). *Island of the blue dolphins*. New York: Dell.

O'Dell, S. (1980). *Sarah Bishop*. New York: Scholastic.

Paulsen, G. (1987). *Hatchet*. New York: Puffin.

Payne, E. (1972). *Katy No-Pockets*. Boston: Houghton Mifflin.

Pinkwater, D. (1977). *The big orange splot*. New York: Scholastic.

Potter, B. (1903). *The tale of Peter Rabbit*. New York: Scholastic.

Richter, C. (1980). *The light in the forest*. Toronto: Bantam.

Robinson, F. (1996). *Great snakes*. New York: Scholastic.

Saroyan, W. (1984). The Parsley Garden. In *Junior Great Books*. Series 6, Vol. 1, Chicago: The Great Books Foundation.

Sendak, M. (1964). *Where the wild things are*. New York: Harper & Row.

Showers, P. (1961). *The listening walk*. New York: Harper Collins.

Speare, E. G. (1983). *The sign of the beaver*. New York: Yearling.

Taylor, M. (1977). *Roll of thunder, hear my cry*. New York: Dial.

Taylor, T. (1969). *The cay*. New York: Avon Camelot.

Van Allsburg, C. (1987). *The Z was zapped*. Boston: Houghton Mifflin.

Williams, S. (1997). *I went walking*. New York: Macmillan/McGraw-Hill.

Wilson, S. (1995). *Good zap, little grog*. Bergenfield, N.J.: Candlewick.

Index

There are
one-story intellects,
two-story intellects, and
three-story intellects with skylights.

All fact collectors, who have no aim beyond their facts, are

one-story minds.

Two-story minds
compare, reason, generalize,
using the labors of the fact collectors
as well as their own.

Three-story minds
idealize, imagine, predict—their best illumination
comes from above,

through the **skylight**.

—Oliver Wendell Holmes

PEARSON
SkyLight